WHO'S YOUR FOUNDING FATHER?

Also by David Fleming

Breaker Boys: The NFL's Greatest Team and the Stolen 1925 Championship

Noah's Rainbow: A Father's Emotional Journey from the Death of His Son to the Birth of His Daughter

★ ★ ★

WHO'S YOUR FOUNDING FATHER?

★ ★ ★

One Man's Epic Quest
to Uncover the First,
True Declaration
of Independence

★ ★ ★

David Fleming

hachette
BOOKS
New York

Hachette Books
Hachette Book Group
1290 Avenue of the Americas
New York, NY 10104
HachetteBooks.com
Twitter.com/HachetteBooks
Instagram.com/HachetteBooks

First Edition: May 2023

Published by Hachette Books, an imprint of Perseus Books, LLC, a subsidiary of
Hachette Book Group, Inc. The Hachette Books name and logo is a trademark of the
Hachette Book Group.

The Hachette Speakers Bureau provides a wide range of authors for speaking events.

To find out more, go to hachettespeakersbureau.com or email HachetteSpeakers@hbgusa.com.

Books by Hachette Books may be purchased in bulk for business, educational, or
promotional use. For information, please contact your local bookseller or Hachette Book
Group Special Markets Department at special.markets@hbgusa.com.

The publisher is not responsible for websites (or their content) that are not owned by the
publisher.

Print book interior design by Amy Quinn.

Library of Congress Cataloging-in-Publication Data
Names: Fleming, David, 1967- author.
Title: Who's your Founding Father? : one man's epic quest to uncover the first, true
    Declaration of Independence / David Fleming. Other titles: One man's epic quest to
    uncover the first, true Declaration of Independence
Description: First edition. | New York : Hachette Books, 2023. | Includes bibliographical
    references and index. |
Identifiers: LCCN 2022061374 | ISBN 9780306828775 (hardcover) | ISBN
    9780306828799 (ebook)
Subjects: LCSH: Mecklenburg Declaration of Independence. | Mecklenburg Declaration of
    Independence—Historiography. | North Carolina—Politics and government—To 1775.
Classification: LCC E215.9 .F54 2023 | DDC 973.3/13—dc23/eng/20221223
LC record available at https://lccn.loc.gov/2022061374

ISBNs: 978-0-306-82877-5 (hardcover), 978-0-306-82879-9 (ebook)

Printed in the United States of America

LSC-C

Printing 1, 2023

For Kim, always
and
To our Queenies, Ally and Kate

CONTENTS

ONE

DUNKIN' ON THOMAS JEFFERSON

MY QUEST BEGINS HERE IN JOHN ADAMS'S QUAINT HOMETOWN OF Quincy, Massachusetts, where I'm on the trail of one of the craziest untold stories in American history, a mystery that could unravel the origin story of America and reveal the intellectual crime of the millennia.

But first: donuts.

It's a clear sign, at least to me, that the only logical entrance point for my epic journey down this historic rabbit hole also happens to be the original home of Dunkin' Donuts. As a lifelong connoisseur of both bizarre, unexplored tales *and* sugary, highly processed breakfast treats, this simply cannot be a coincidence. So with an hour to kill before my guided tour of Adams's birthplace and historic home estate, known as Peace field, I make my first pilgrimage of the day to the shore of Quincy Bay, but only after double- and triple-checking Google Maps since there are—no lie—eight Dunkin' Donuts within a two-mile radius of Adams's tomb. (Also known for its speckled granite, Quincy's other famous landmark is a giant 9.5-ton ball of polished stone once designated by *Ripley's Believe It or Not* as "The Most Nearly Perfect Sphere in the World.") Just down the road from what I can now confirm is a breathtakingly round piece of large rock stands the original Dunkin'. In 1950, Bill Rosenberg, an eighth-grade dropout and army veteran, was in his basement workshop halfway through the process of rebranding his Open Kettle diner when he realized he didn't have the materials or the roof space to spell out "Doughnuts" (or "Dunking," for that matter).

Thus, the artfully abbreviated Dunkin' Donuts was born. Nowadays, DD is a $10 billion behemoth with franchises all over the world, including one near the Burj Khalifa in Dubai, which, yes, I have also frequented. But it all started here at this narrow little corner spot where, this morning, a guy sporting neck tats, New England Patriots camo cargo shorts, and impeccable manners holds the door open for me as I breathlessly pass into my Munchkin mecca. And as soon as I hear "Mawnin', honey. Welcome to Dunks. Whatcha havin', love?" I know this wicked-awesome adventure is officially underway.

Admittedly, after my first stop I was a little worried about being dangerously over-caffeinated for my initial research on the solemn grounds of the Adams National Historic Park. Until, that is, I knocked on the screen door of Adams's classic New England–style country home and was greeted by our quirky, enthusiastic, and encyclopedic tour guide. (Is there any other kind?) Decked out in the full ill-fitting, army-green National Park Service ranger uniform complete with the iconic broad-brimmed Stetson-style straw hat, every time our guide spoke of John and Abigail Adams—one of the "greatest love stories in American history"—she would clasp her hands under her chin out of sheer excitement and reverence and rise up on her tippy-toes, which has to be a dangerous habit working inside historic homes with such impossibly low ceilings.

As we duck into the Old House at Peace field, one of the first things our ranger informs us of is that, in her mind, John Adams was actually a big old softie, "an absolute marshmallow who loved life and was very well-liked by everyone," which is very much the opposite of the fierce, irascible, and curmudgeonly character made famous by Paul Giamatti in the HBO miniseries based on the Pulitzer prize–winning book by David McCullough. Adams was a revered political theorist, negotiator, and orator, but he was also a fairly well-known grumpy pants who could be irritable, brash, and insecure, oftentimes all at once. So the idea of John Adams as a tender-hearted, *Notebook*-loving kind of guy is always going to be a tough sell, but especially here, in the family's formal dining room, with the final portrait of Adams skeptically looming over all of us. In the painting, the architect of American independence and the second president of the United States is seated on the red velvet camelback sofa that's still on display in the room just across the hall from the front door. And while signs of his age are apparent in his frail fingers and slightly disheveled silver hair, that piercing, pedagogical glare, and the iron-willed intellect that fueled it, are still very much ablaze in Adams's intense blue eyes—the same ones that, I swear, are tracking me as I bring up the rear of our tour group.

There are a lot of memorable things to discover in Quincy. For starters, the town is actually pronounced "Quin-zee." (Go figure.) When the Park Service Trolley went on the fritz, I also got to learn just how many lovely octogenarian tourists from Minnesota rocking Hoka sneakers you can fit in a mid-sized rental car full of empty Dunkin' Donuts containers (seven). Other highlights for me included the mold Abigail Adams used to make ammunition for the Continental Army after melting down her family's pewter spoons; the stone cairn that marks the spot where Abigail and a seven-year-old John Quincy Adams watched Charlestown burn during the Battle of Bunker Hill; the Bible gifted by the Mende people of Africa after John Quincy Adams successfully defended the kidnapped Africans who revolted on the slave ship *Amistad*; and the world's greatest honey-do note from Abigail (the family's true badass), who casually reminded John and his fellow delegates in Philadelphia to "remember the ladies" while crafting the Declaration of Independence.

During my time in Quincy, though, my mind always wanders back to that haunting dining room portrait of an elderly but still cantankerous Adams. Probably because when Adams reluctantly sat for the painting—I mean, the grouchiness just jumps off the canvas—he would have been in his eighties, which, I know, is right around the time when he picked up the Saturday, June 5, 1819, edition of the *Essex Register* and nearly keeled over from shock.

And learning more about what he uncovered in that paper is the reason I'm here.

Well, that and the donuts, of course.

That June morning in 1819, right there on the front page of Adams's favorite local newspaper next to the legal notices and ads for crockery and straw bonnets, was an explosive article reprinted from the *Raleigh Register* in

North Carolina containing a complete account of something called . . . the Mecklenburg Declaration of Independence.

The essence of the story was that a full fourteen months before Thomas Jefferson crafted his own, slightly more famous Declaration, a misfit band of fearless, feisty patriots in a remote corner of the North Carolina frontier had become the first Americans to formally declare themselves "free and independent" from England—thus, technically, making *them* our true Founding Fathers and Charlotte our country's actual cradle of liberty. As he continued reading through wire-rimmed spectacles teetering on the tip of his nose, a gobsmacked Adams learned that the Mecklenburg Declaration of Independence—the MecDec, for short—had been created in the Carolina backcountry by a perfect storm of zealous, hotheaded Scots-Irish patriots and other men who had already crossed three countries and an ocean to get away from the Crown's tyranny, along with a handful of whiskey-loving Princeton intellectuals and a firebrand preacher who was either the foremost American of his day in advocating for independence or, quite possibly, insane. Composed during a clandestine all-night session inside the county courthouse in Charlotte, the MecDec was signed on May 20, 1775—a date that's still featured prominently on the official state flag of North Carolina. A local tavern owner named Captain James Jack then volunteered to secretly race the MecDec 550 treacherous miles on horseback up to the Continental Congress in Philadelphia, where, a year later, in 1776, Thomas Jefferson is believed to have plagiarized the Mecklenburg Declaration of Independence and then, as he was wont to do, covered the whole damn thing up.

After reading about the MecDec, Adams was convinced that nothing had ever captured the genuine sense of America at that very moment, before, or since. And he was right. The document was majestic: bold, robust, and brave yet succinct and scalpel-like, it proved to be a soaring, stirring, and critical call to arms, especially in the all-important Southern Campaign of the American Revolution. This wasn't just some little Charlotte story, either. This was an important, unknown piece of world history that just happened to be set in Charlotte. To Adams, thinking of the MecDec as *just* a Charlotte story would be the same as believing only people in Yorktown would be interested in the Revolutionary War.

And deep down, Adams had always sensed what took the rest of us two hundred years to realize: that Thomas Jefferson was more than capable of a dastardly deed like this (or worse). For the sake of the new nation, despite their vast personal and political differences, Adams, the brash Massachusetts farmer, and Jefferson, the dandy southern aristocrat, had managed to play nice for decades. In 1800, however, Adams's bid for a second presidential term ended after a bitter battle with Jefferson. Convinced that he had been robbed of his legacy by the conniving Jefferson, a scorned Adams refused to attend Jefferson's inauguration. And in one of his distinctly less-marshmallowy moments, Adams publicly labeled Jefferson a phony whose "total incapacity" for leadership, government, and war would leave the republic "infinitely worse" than he found it. Jefferson's cronies, in turn, labeled Adams "a hideous hermaphroditical character [with] neither the force and firmness of a man nor the gentleness and sensibility of a woman." (I guess I can stop worrying quite so much about today's rancorous political rhetoric.) Understandably, the two men went more than a decade without speaking until New Year's Day 1812 when a mutual friend brokered a reconciliation.

"You and I ought not to die before we have explained ourselves to each other," Adams suggested.

Jefferson agreed, and the two old gray-haired frenemies began an extraordinary exchange of 158 letters on everything from their health to philosophy, religion, and the Revolution. Most of them were penned by Adams, who, in his day, churned out letters like the rest of us send text messages. Held by the Boston Public Library and the Massachusetts Historical Society, the Adams archives contain volume after volume of Adams's almost manic level of correspondence with Abigail, Jefferson, and countless others throughout his long life of public service.

But trust me, there is nothing in this vast, extraordinary collection quite like the 229-word note Adams penned to Jefferson on June 22, 1819.

Adams had always suspected Jefferson of being a lightweight, erudite poser who covertly cultivated far too much credit for authoring the Declaration of Independence, a project they had worked on together. Only now, with the discovery of the Mecklenburg Declaration of Independence, Adams had the receipts. And the proof he found might just upend our understanding of one of humanity's most important documents, not to mention Jefferson's gilded legacy. In other words, the MecDec was potentially earth-shattering. And Adams, stooped and bald and as gruff and passive-aggressive as ever, even at eighty-three, seemed downright giddy about it. Just a few days after perusing the *Essex Register*, in fact, Adams sat down at the secretary-style folding desk in the sunny northeast corner of his second-floor study in Quincy to fire off a letter to Jefferson, a communique that has to qualify as our nation's first—and finest—documented case of shade.

"May I enclose to you one of the greatest curiosities and one of the deepest mysteries that ever occurred to me? It is entitled the Mecklenburg Declaration of Independence. [And] the genuine sense of America at that moment was never so well expressed before, nor since," Adams breathlessly began. "How is it possible that this paper should have been concealed from me to this day? Had it been communicated to me in the time of it, I know, if you do not know, that it would have been printed in every Whig newspaper upon this continent. You know, that if I had possessed it, I would have made the hall of Congress echo and re-echo with it fifteen months before your Declaration of Independence. What a poor, ignorant, malicious, short-sighted, crapulous mass is Tom Paine's *Common Sense*, in comparison with this paper! Had I known it, I would have commented upon it, from the day you entered Congress till the fourth of July, 1776. . . . And yet history is to ascribe the American Revolution to Thomas Paine! *Sat verbum sapienti!* [word to the wise]."

After all this time it's still hard to pick my favorite part of Adams's letter, a document that would ignite a centuries-long global conspiracy that would reach the highest levels of power and government. (It would also be the source of what is clearly my own ongoing, unshakable obsession. And I thought donuts were a hard habit to kick.) Personally, though, I'm a big fan of the subtle ominous tones of *I know, if you don't know*, which sounds like a Biggie Smalls lyric and is Adams basically saying: "BUSTED" to his pal Jefferson. For sheer passive-aggressive artistry, though, you can't beat the cutting slight on Jefferson's Declaration, or the work of TJ's good friend Thomas Paine, when Adams writes: *the genuine sense of America . . . never so well expressed before, nor since. . . . What a poor, ignorant, malicious, short-sighted, crapulous mass.* Crapulous mass? I mean, come on. Forget the Treaty of Paris. This is Adams's true moment of genius. (It's not quite what you think, though. It means something closer to a gathering of drunks.) I'm also pretty fond of the part that goes: *I would have commented upon it . . . till the fourth of July, 1776*, which one Charlotte author and historian believes is Adams insinuating that Jefferson didn't just plagiarize the Mec-Dec, he suppressed it, not only delaying our freedom by a year but blocking Adams from the chance to lead our nation's movement toward independence all by himself.

Like I said, it's one helluva letter.

Adams was just getting warmed up, though.

He and Jefferson would go back and forth on the MecDec for some time. (At first glance, Jefferson believed it to be "spurious." Shocker.) But before Jefferson even had a chance to digest any of this, or spin it, Adams had already dispatched a second letter on the MecDec to the Reverend William Bentley of Salem, Massachusetts, in which he laid out his case in much, *much* stronger language.

"A few weeks ago I received an *Essex Register*, containing resolutions of independence by a county in North Carolina, fifteen months before the resolution of independence in Congress. I was struck with so much astonishment on reading this document, that I could not help inclosing it immediately to Mr. Jefferson, who must have seen it, in the time of it, for he has copied the spirit, the sense, and the expressions of it *verbatim*, into his Declaration of the fourth of July, 1776," Adams wrote. "Had I seen that declaration at the time of it, it should have been printed in every Whig newspaper on this continent. Its total concealment from me is a mystery. . . . [The Mecklenburg] Declaration would have had more effect than Tom Paine's *Common Sense*, which appeared so long after it. I pray you to intercede with the printers to transmit me half a dozen copies of that *Essex Register* which contains it, and I will immediately transmit the money for them, whatever they may cost."

This one doesn't require quite as much translation. *Mr. Jefferson, who must have seen it, in the time of it . . . has copied the spirit, the sense, and the expressions of (the MecDec) verbatim, into his Declaration of the 4th of July, 1776.* But just to be clear, in a follow-up letter to Bentley, Adams wrote: "The plot thickens. . . . Either these resolutions are a plagiarism from Mr. Jefferson's Declaration of Independence, or Mr. Jefferson's Declaration of Independence is a plagiarism from those resolutions. I could as soon believe that the dozen flowers of the Hydrangea, now before my eyes, were the work of chance, as that the Mecklenburg resolutions and Mr. Jefferson's Declaration were not derived the one from the other."

Now, we have no way of knowing, since Adams didn't sit for three more tortuous weeks to have another portrait done the moment he first learned about the Mecklenburg Declaration of Independence, but from his correspondence I can almost guarantee that an utterly dumbfounded Adams had the same physiological response that afflicts nearly everyone when they first learn about this incredible story.

His mouth gaped. His eyebrows pinched. His eyes flickered. And his flabbergasted, short-circuited brain began to riff on hydrangeas and wonder, "How in the WORLD did I NOT know about ANY of this?"

It's called "MecDec Face."

And it's quite common, actually.

Because, in addition to flat-out accusing a guy on Mount Rushmore of fraud, what Adams is suggesting in these MecDec letters is something almost beyond comprehension. The theory he's proposing is that the entire story of America's founding is, well, wrong and that for the past 248 years we've all been shooting off fireworks and scarfing hot dogs on the wrong Independence Day while celebrating the wrong freakin' group of Founding Fathers.

And an astonishing list of highly esteemed Americans and respected scholars believe Adams was absolutely correct.

No less than eleven US presidents have acknowledged the MecDec's authenticity, including five sitting presidents who visited Charlotte in person to honor the true Declaration and our first Founding Fathers. My personal favorite in that group, the 300-and-something-pound William Howard

Taft, once threatened to brain anyone who dared doubt the MecDec. While Billy Graham, arguably the most influential Christian leader of the twentieth century, once used his pulpit to enlighten a crowd of 105,000 acolytes on the MecDec.

"There is no question that the Mecklenburg Declaration of Independence happened," said Emmy award–winning journalist and author Cokie Roberts when asked about the MecDec in 2010. "There is not a question in my mind. First of all, there is plenty of evidence but secondly, when you have folk memory that's *that* strong, it's always right. Often people don't like that—as in with Sally Hemings and Thomas Jefferson—but that turned out to be right. There is just no question in my mind that [the MecDec] is true."

David McCullough, who won a Pulitzer Prize for his extraordinary work on John Adams, said, "All my instincts, all my experiences over the years incline me to believe it is true. And well worth exploring, worth commemorating and keeping alive." Ken Burns? "I think it's true," says the acclaimed historian and filmmaker. "There's too much historical triangulation to think otherwise." Even George Will has added a qualifier to the sacred text Jefferson presented in Philadelphia in 1776, calling it "a" declaration of independence but not "the" Declaration of Independence.

That one, says Will, "occurred on May 20, 1775."

Adams, of course, will always be the OG when it comes to the MecDec, and he must have had a pretty good sense of the trouble that had been stirred up. In his letters to Bentley, Adams first asserts that the MecDec "is of so much more importance that it should be thoroughly investigated" before pleading to any would-be donut-loving historians out there that the MecDec "must be more universally made known to the present and future generation."

As my time in Quincy draws to a close, that line, the one about the MecDec being made more universally known to future generations, repeats on a loop inside my head as I arrive at my final stop: United First Parish Church. Established in 1639 and constructed out of local granite in 1828 with funds donated by the Adams family, the stalwart Greek Revival–style sanctuary is located on the town's lovely urban mall. Known as the Church of the

Presidents, it serves as the family crypt for Presidents John Adams and John Quincy Adams, as well as their wives, Abigail and Louisa Catherine.

John Adams died in 1826 in his second-floor study at Peace field on the golden anniversary of the (second) Declaration of Independence, just moments after muttering to his granddaughter, "Jefferson survives . . ."

Actually, it was a tie.

Jefferson succumbed that very same day at his home in Virginia. He had woken up on the evening of July 3 and uttered, "This is the Fourth." Told "not just yet," Jefferson held on until morning.

Informed of the deaths, Adams's son, John Quincy, called it "Divine favor" that the two men had died together on the Fourth of July.

Beneath the church in Quincy, winding my way down to Adams's tomb, I get a general sense of where this whole quest is going when I spot a colonial-era bell clapper produced by Paul Revere, and, without prompting, inform my guide that the MecDec's Captain James Jack managed to ride 537 miles farther than Revere without, you know, ever getting caught by the British.

The locals would soon have their revenge, though.

To enter the Adams' crypt you have to duck through a gated doorway carved into the church's bedrock foundation. The space inside is tight—just big enough to fit the four identical coffins made from thick rectangular slabs of speckled Quincy granite. John Adams's tomb is the first one on the left. And although my natural instinct is to respectfully remain as far away as possible, I'm forced in close by the low ceilings and minimal space. It's hard to describe, but it's overwhelming and humbling being this near to such immense greatness. Adams's understated but dignified granite coffin is covered in a fifteen-star American flag (from the time of his presidency) with only his name etched into the stone in simple, newsprint-style lettering that features a distinct, deep curlicue "J."

The lettering is, oddly enough, very similar to the style I used on a family member's gravestone that I still visit often. Alone in the Adams' chamber, in a moment that's a mixture of reverence and habit, when I place my hand on the cold granite the tip of my forefinger just naturally finds the deep indentation made by the curly bottom part of the engraving.

It's cheesy, I know, but for a split second, I feel connected to Adams in some infinitesimal way. And that's when it happens, I guess. That's when I truly decide to go all-in on this crazy MecDec quest, just as Adams once requested.

Moments later, with my mind preoccupied as I step up and out through the crypt opening, I somehow manage to whack the crown of my head on an indented part of the bedrock ceiling. The *thunk* from my cranium is so loud I can imagine the parishioners in the pews one floor above all knowingly shaking their heads at each other in unison.

"Harry Truman once did the exact same thing," my guide giggles, "so I'd say you're in some pretty good company with that one."

I'm still fairly worried, though, that this might be a less-than-subtle warning sign from the great beyond. But then I reach up to rub the prodigious bump forming on my brain and realize that, instead, the swelling has taken on what I consider to be a very meaningful and symbolic form.

The exact shape of a donut.

Two

Brewed in Scotland. Bottled in Ireland. Uncorked in Carolina.

THE TRANSIT BUS HAS CREPT SO CLOSE TO MY BIKE THAT I CAN HEAR the *click-clack* of the orange right-rear blinker politely signaling my imminent demise. As the space between the bus bumper, the curb, and my life force begins to wink shut, the final exhaust-infused thought running through my brain is that, for the record, I had actually requested Gary Clark Jr. tickets for my birthday. Instead, when my MecDec obsession only continued to grow, my family decided this was a much more productive option: a guided bike tour through all the MecDec landmarks around Charlotte, starting on the south side of town with the Olde Mecklenburg Brewery, which has a delicious North German–style pilsner named in honor of Captain Jack. My guess is that Kim and our girls looked at the Facebook ad for this ride and just figured the words "MecDec" and "brewery" were all the incentive I needed. And, as usual, they were right.

Almost as important, though, was that the bike tour was being led by Scott Syfert, a corporate attorney in Charlotte who has become the foremost advocate, author, and expert on all things MecDec. Bearded and bald, Syfert is unlike any historian I've ever come across, meaning he's funny, athletic, open-minded, not the least bit territorial or condescending, and, on this particular morning, outfitted in wrap-around shades, socks with little doves on them, and a vintage Chelsea jersey.

Riding in Syfert's peloton of fabulous MecDec nerds, the first thing you learn—besides the fact that spandex really should come with an age limit—is the grand scale on which the Mecklenburg Declaration of Independence, potentially one of the most important documents in human history, still manages to hide in plain sight. Just five minutes into our ride, in fact, Syfert informs us that the road we're currently pedaling up is the very same one that pear-shaped British General Lord Charles Cornwallis marched on in 1780 before making the colossal mistake of underestimating the fighting spirit of the MecDecers' hometown. Although I'm guessing Cornwallis's dragoons never had to navigate any runaway commuter buses or endless minefields of empty Four Loko cans as they charged their way up Tryon Street into the heart of Charlotte.

More than twenty years ago, Kim and I moved here pretty much sight unseen just as I jumped from *Sports Illustrated* to ESPN and Kim was promoted to run MeadWestvaco's southeast region. Surely we must have noticed the curious May 20, 1775, date on the state flag and the FIRST IN FREEDOM mottos on the license plates, but like any Midwestern transplants (via New York City), we probably paid them no mind at all, too busy working on our tolerance for sweet tea and humidity. Pretty soon, though, as I dug a little deeper into the history of the area we now called home, everywhere I looked, I started seeing streets, villages, schools, churches, libraries, and parks connected to the MecDec. It's referenced on the state flag. On the license plates. On our beer. This MecDec story is even connected to our NBA team's mascot. It's behind the insignia of the giant youth soccer club, countless pieces of public art, even the police badges. There's a MecDec statue near the hospital where our girls were born and another landmark just down the street from where Kim had her successful cancer surgery. The college we live next door to has a motto—Let Learning Be Cherished Where Liberty Has Arisen—that's inspired by the MecDec.

Not surprisingly with its close association to Princeton, North Carolina, Davidson (our neighbor), and other temples of higher learning, there's an endless amount of scholarship available on the MecDec. Thanks to all that work, and starting in 1819 with the Adams and Jefferson letters, several times during the last quarter millennium the MecDec has risen to the level of national obsession, which leads to the greatest mystery of all. How in the world could the MecDec remain such a mystery? And what does that say about us, our founding folklore, and our peculiar American psyche—especially at this very moment in time?

The answers, Syfert says from his bike, are at the very heart of Charlotte.

Quite literally, it turns out.

After I expertly jump the curb to escape the murderous bus, Syfert pauses the bike tour for a long lecture at the intersection of Trade and Tryon, the very epicenter of Charlotte. Just a few feet behind his bike stands the elaborate glass, marble, and fresco-lined lobby of Bank of America's sixty-story world headquarters, a structure, we learn, that was built right on top of what was originally the front porch of Charlotte founder Thomas Polk.

Now, there are some extraordinary and wildly entertaining characters at the heart of this MecDec saga. A forgotten one-eyed surgeon who wrote circles around Thomas Jefferson. A Princeton lawyer who nearly killed a future president over a courtroom prank. A tavern owner who became the South's Paul Revere. A powerful, ruthless family known as the South's first mafia. A possibly bipolar revolutionary preacher who was, nevertheless, God's chosen vessel for American independence. And an unstoppable gang of whiskey-loving backcountry Scots-Irish pioneers who gave absolutely zero F's.

But none of them resembled a real-life, able-to-move-mountains kind of superhero as much as Thomas Polk, one of the driving forces behind the MecDec and a man who once braved the entire American frontier just for love.

Well, okay, and for some decent whiskey.

But mostly for love.

Charlotte's Thomas Polk was the great-uncle of future US President James K. Polk. "He was," recalled one historian, "a high-souled cavalier, full of dash and courage; rich, hospitable, and charming." Thomas and his fellow Scots-Irish colonists are credited with being part of the unwavering "backbone" of George Washington's army during its darkest days at Valley Forge.

15

(Legend has it that Polk also led the brigade that saved the Liberty Bell from being melted down into cannon fodder by the British.) As a close confidant to General Nathanael Greene, Polk helped turn the tide in the Southern Campaign of the American Revolution. In fact, when all seemed lost during the War of Independence, it was Polk's little town of badasses in Charlotte, outnumbered fifteen to one, that finally forced Cornwallis to do something he rarely did in America: retreat.

Not once, but four times.

Real superhero stuff. Which makes sense because even Polk's family history sounds like something straight out of a superhero comic book's origin story. The annotated legend, pulled from history books, begins nearly five hundred years ago in the Scottish Lowlands . . . *On a certain great occasion, away back in the misty past, a King of Scotland was marching at the head of an immense procession when a small oak appeared directly in front of His Majesty.* Blocked by the oak, a king's attendant by the name of Muirhead sprang forward and "with Herculean effort" tore the oak from the earth with his bare hands and chucked it aside so that His Majesty would not be delayed. Moved by this act of strength and gallantry, the King halted his procession, drew his sword, and knighted Muirhead on the spot, bestowing the man who had pulled the oak with the new, noble, Marvel-esque moniker of Pulloak, which was eventually shortened to just Polk.

"Some of those present argued that Pulloak was more than a Sampson," recalled Lyman C. Draper, the renowned Wisconsin historian who researched and wrote extensively about this period of history. "[That he] must have been imbued with supernatural aid."

Superpowers would have been a minimum requirement for the Polks or anyone else hoping to survive the Scottish Lowlands during the seventeenth century. That region was one of the poorest and most backward places in Europe with an overall vibe closer to barbarism. It was this environment, however, that forged a warrior class of Scots that would one day reshape not just America but the entire world. The lowland Scots were preternaturally tough, proud, and pushy people who had acquired what my high school guidance counselor once characterized as "serious issues with authority." Above all, as Calvinist-styled Presbyterians, they were religious and political radicals of the first and highest order. They believed that only God had the authority to rule, not monarchs, politicians, or any mortal man. And so, to them, resistance to tyranny was the highest form of obedience to God. This centuries-old doctrine—blended with a legendary obstinacy, a craving for confrontation, and an unrelenting, uncompromising demand for total freedom or death—made the Scottish Presbyterians more spiritually, politically (and, if possible, genetically) inclined toward independence than any group on earth.

Eventually, nearly half a million of them would cross the Atlantic to infuse the New World with their fighting spirit. And today, twenty-seven million Americans can trace their roots back to the Scots, the ancestral homeland of Barack Obama, Ronald Reagan, Mark Twain, Neil Armstrong, Dolly Parton, and nearly all the MecDec Founding Fathers.

As author and 2016 presidential candidate Jim Webb put it so perfectly, the Polks and the rest of these particular Scots didn't just come to America.

They became America.

THE CRAZY, TWISTED TALE OF HOW, EXACTLY, THE POLKS (AND THE SCOTS) ended up leading America to independence actually begins in Ireland. For nearly half a century Queen Elizabeth had tried in vain to domesticate her wild Irish subjects. As one overly diplomatic historian put it, the Queen simply wanted "to aid in ameliorating the natural turbulence of the Irish character." Which makes one wonder: *Had the Queen ever met anyone from Ireland?* Around 1610, her successor, King James I, thought he had come up with a single solution to "fix" both Ireland and the backward, rebellious Scots. James was quite the enthusiastic colonizer, you'll recall, starting with the Virginia colony in 1606 that was named in his honor. Four years later, James had an even wilder experiment in mind that would—in a slightly roundabout way—end up having as big an impact on America (and the world) as his Jamestown settlement. Rather than enlightening his Irish neighbors, James decided to simply transform them from the inside out by colonizing the north of Ireland with Scots. (This is what's known as a win-win, in the twisted mind of a king.) So, after confiscating nearly four million acres of land in the Donegal, Londonderry, Belfast region of Ireland, James renamed it the Plantation of Ulster and, like a used car dealer holding giant scissors in front of a red ribbon, he declared northern Ireland officially open for colonization.

By 1620, lured by the promise of cheap land and endless opportunity, nearly ten thousand lowland Scots ventured across the narrow Irish Sea to start anew as Scots-Irish. (You'll sometimes see them referred to as Scotch-Irish, but not here, since Scotch is a drink, not a people.)

Several decades later, that number of Scots-Irish would grow, by some estimates, to more than four hundred thousand, including Thomas Polk's ancestors who settled in the Irish town of Lifford near the River Foyle. Instead of solving everyone's problems, as King James had naively predicted, over the next century the Scots-Irish and Ulster Plantation experiment went horribly, epically wrong thanks to the endlessly cruel, oppressive mismanagement of the English authorities. (This kind of generational tyranny would become practically baked into the DNA of the Scots-Irish, who would recognize it and violently reject it far sooner than anyone else in America.) For starters, the people faced several years of drought, and endless taxes issued to support things like the Anglican Church led to widespread poverty, starvation, and illness. The final straw for the Scots-Irish, however, was the religious and political oppression legislated upon them by things like the Test Act of 1704, which made it illegal for Ulster Presbyterians to hold office or work in any of the country's more lucrative or influential professions.

To escape the disastrous Ulster experiment, starting in the early 1700s, a massive, biblical-level exodus of nearly four hundred thousand Scots-Irish set sail for one last shot at freedom and opportunity in America. Now, I don't want to get too far ahead of myself here, but it's worth noting that after being displaced, starved, and disrespected for a century, all of these Scots-Irish had built up an almost unfathomable degree of hatred for England, as well as an acute awareness of the Crown's dirty playbook on taxation and religious oppression. The Crown may have been oblivious to what it had incubated inside the failed Ulster Plantation, but an Anglican bishop from Londonderry tried to warn British authorities. "[I attribute] the rebellious spirit in the colonies in America to the emigration from Ireland of [around] three-hundred thousand fanatical & hungry republicans in the course of a few years." English historian James Anthony Froude agreed. "The resentment which they carried with them continued to burn in their new homes; and, in the War of Independence, England had no fiercer enemies than the grandsons and great-grandsons of the [Scots-Irish] Presbyterians from Ulster."

Small wonder, then, that twenty-five of the twenty-seven Signers of the Mecklenburg Declaration of Independence, and, by some accounts, 40 percent of the Revolutionary Army was of Scots-Irish descent. Some historians complain that we tend to "over-praise" the Scots-Irish for their role in creating America. And I get it. I do. I also recognize, up front, the possible eye-rolling that might occur from lionizing these particular folks for their courageous efforts to break the bonds of oppression with stirring declarations of freedom—endeavors, let's not forget, that pretty much excluded everyone who wasn't the same gender or race. But when it comes to the makeup of the army that fought and bled and died for our independence, well, the numbers just don't lie. If anything, they seem to be an understatement, especially to those who were there. British officers and loyalists regularly reported back to England that half the rebel army appeared to be Scots-Irish, whom they described as "the most God-provoking democrats on this side of Hell." In 1778, a Hessian captain wrote: "Call this war by whatever name you may, only call it not an American rebellion. It is nothing more or less than a Scotch-Irish Presbyterian rebellion." And at two of the most critical points in the war—Valley Forge and the Battle of Kings Mountain, South Carolina— the Scots-Irish were indeed the bulk of George Washington's fighting force.

"Of the different racial strains that mingled their blood with the earlier English—Irish, Huguenot-French, German, Scotch-Irish—the last was by far the most important," wrote historian Vernon Louis Parrington. "Armed with axes, their seed potatoes, and the newly invented rifle, they plunged into the backwoods [of America] to become our great pioneering race. Scattered thinly through a long frontier, they constituted the outposts and buffer settlements of civilization. A vigorous breed, hardy, assertive, individualistic, thrifty, trained in the democracy of the Scottish kirk, they were material out of which later Jacksonian democracy was to be fashioned, the creators of that western type which in politics and industry became ultimately the American type."

AFTER ESCAPING ULSTER FOR AMERICA, THOMAS POLK'S GREAT-grandparents settled near the eastern shore of Maryland. Polk was born there around 1730. As a young man, he and his family moved to Carlisle, Pennsylvania. With every ounce of his being Polk embodied the quintessential Scots-Irish American pioneer: he was a man's man, tireless, self-sufficient, and cunning, with a wiry, athletic build, leathery skin, a thick black widow's peak, and severe eyes. "[Polk] was plain and unassuming in his deportment," recalled nineteenth-century author Joseph Johnson. "More like a farmer or miller than a general." It was in Pennsylvania, while studying to become a land surveyor in Carlisle, that something happened to Polk that would change the course of human history and become one of my favorite parts of the MecDec story.

He fell madly in love with Susanna Spratt.

With thousands of fellow Scots-Irish still flooding into the port of Philadelphia each month, by 1750 the southern and central regions of Pennsylvania were bursting at the seams. "It looks as if Ireland is to send all its inhabitants hither," wrote James Logan, the provincial secretary of Philadelphia. In a constant search for cheap land and having been blocked from pushing farther west by mountains and hostile Native Americans, the Scots-Irish were encouraged to migrate south along the Great Philadelphia Wagon Road, where authorities secretly hoped they would act as human shields between the Indigenous people to the west and the more established colonies closer to the coast, which were populated by the far more couth and preferred English, German, and Swiss. (It's worth noting here, I think, that the Great Philly Wagon Road had to be one of the greatest misnomers of all time, seeing as how it was little more than a muddy path and often not wide enough to accommodate an actual wagon. I suppose the Crappy, Narrow Footpath Straight Down Through Hostile Territory just didn't have the same ring to it.)

As a young, astute land surveyor, Polk could not have been surprised when the lovely young Scots-Irish woman he hoped to court informed him that her father, Thomas Spratt, was moving their family to the Carolina frontier. I can't imagine it took the lovestruck Polk more than thirty seconds to decide to blow up his life in Pennsylvania and, in 1753, follow the Spratts south through Virginia and into a fertile, temperate region of the Carolina Piedmont that the Scots-Irish settlers had begun to call Mesopotamia. "Delicious country," is how one early explorer described the area's red-clay soil, crystal clear rivers, endless grasslands, and thick green forest canopy.

Back then, the Yadkin River would have served as a kind of de-facto northern border of North Carolina, and legend has it that the Spratts were the first white settlers to cross the Yadkin on four wheels. The second must have been Polk. Following right behind them on horseback, Polk was said to be carrying "only the knapsack upon his back and a goodly share of indomitable enterprise," along with a massive crush on Susanna, whom he would soon marry. Another reason the Scots-Irish moved south in search of more fertile land was for the purpose of farming corn, which, of course, is the main ingredient in the Scots-Irish artisan craft of whiskey distilling. So the way I see it, after his family crossed an ocean to be left alone, Thomas Polk then traversed through half an uncharted continent in search of love and whiskey before founding a town and taking on an empire with his patriotic pen.

How's that for a hero's journey?

In Polk's new home of North Carolina, the Yadkin River runs east from the mountains to the middle of the state before turning south toward Charleston. About sixty miles to the west, the Catawba River follows a similar trajectory. Between the two rivers, the Mesopotamia of Mecklenburg was originally inhabited some ten thousand years ago by the Catawba people, who traveled between the two key waterways by following animal trails carved mostly by buffalo herds. The trails led to natural, shallow crossing fords at each river. The Nations Ford was located below Charlotte on the Catawba with a path that moved northeast. Meanwhile, above the town was the Trading Ford, located on the Yadkin, with a path that wended southwest.

And on the elevated ridge where the two paths met—at the intersection of what is now Trade and Tryon streets—Polk set down his knapsack.

For all intents and purposes, Charlotte was born.

Technically, it would take Polk more than a decade of Herculean levels of hard work and cunning to make Charlotte official, but almost immediately upon his arrival Polk became the symbolic leader of what people originally called Charlotte Towne, or Charlottesburgh, in honor of King George III's new bride, Queen Charlotte, who was a native of the Mecklenburg-Strelitz region of Germany. Widely considered by historians to be "the most outstanding citizen of early Mecklenburg," Polk would go on to become the town's founder and treasurer, its militia commander, its first representative in the House of Commons, a trustee for the first college south of Virginia, and a critical force in the Revolutionary War as a close confidant of Nathanael Greene, the commander of the Southern forces. On top of all that, Polk was also a major source of population growth. He and Susanna had eight children. The two frontier lovebirds are buried together in a single plot in Settlers' Cemetery, which is less than five hundred feet from where Polk's knapsack first hit the ground.

And, of course, just a few feet away from this same spot at the center of town is where Polk would become the first American patriot to publicly declare independence from England.

"He thus became universally known and respected; no man possessing more influence in that part of North Carolina," says Draper, the historian. Another author says that Polk's contributions to Charlotte and the cause of freedom "were so numerous and so diversified, to mention them in detail would constitute a whole volume."

YET I STILL WONDER IF EVEN THE GUNG-HO POLK HAD SECOND THOUGHTS upon his arrival in the sparse, lawless Carolina backcountry. How could he not? George Washington himself famously called Charlotte "a very trifling place" and, honestly, early on that was something of an overstatement. Until the late 1760s, in fact, the muddy intersection Polk occupied featured only about a dozen primitive, unpainted, dirt-floor log cabins. There was a gaol [jail], a few taverns, a store or two, and that's about it. Squat. Dour. Unappealing. That's how Syfert described the Charlotte of yore on our bike tour, and I'm not sure I know anyone who's a bigger fan of the place. "In the summer the town stank of woodsmoke, manure, and hogs," Syfert says, "while in the rainy spring it was a mud pit. Nor was it very civilized."

Save for an occasional express rider from the north, communication with the outside world was practically nonexistent in Charlotte, which is exactly how Polk and his new tight-knit group of self-reliant Scots-Irish neighbors preferred it. Life expectancy here hovered right around forty years, and that actually seems generous. At one point there was so much random gunplay in town that a royal decree was needed to limit the use of firearms to only shooting cattle or hogs. Horse racing and gambling were rampant, especially a favorite local game called Long Bullets wherein men heaved and chased a twenty-eight-ounce iron cannon ball for miles through the woods on horseback. I mean, what could go wrong?

And there was drinking, of course.

Lots and lots of drinking.

The official Cornwallis Papers mention that "drunkenness, gaming, cheating, quarreling, and brawling were commonplace [in Charlotte]." I'm just spitballing here, but a contributing factor at the time may have been that most local residents distilled their own corn hooch, and the ones that didn't could still buy an entire gallon of whiskey or brandy for five shillings or a local beer categorized as "strong" for just six pence. (If, like me, you need a little help with the math, basically back then you could get four gallons of whiskey for a buck or two beers for a nickel.) And as anyone who has ever been to college or a bowling alley knows, cheap liquor often leads to fighting. County records at the time, uncovered by author and historian Daniel Patterson, were full of reports of eyes being gouged, bar patrons pulling swords on one another, and people getting shot. And then there was poor Joseph Avent whose "right ear was bit off by Henry Braswell." I'm not saying our man Polk also liked to drink, but after he died, records of his estate listed seventy-six gallons of whiskey stored in his house. Heck, even Polk's father-in-law, Thomas Spratt, was known to enjoy the occasional backcountry binge, including one legendary bender that took place on the very day of the Mecklenburg Declaration of Independence.

Booze by the gallon? Beers for a penny? Gambling? Crazy games? Fighting? Squalor? Lawlessness and fornication? Besides independence and patriotism, it sounds like Charlotte may have also invented spring break.

Not everyone was a fan, mind you. Charles Woodmason was an itinerant Anglican minister from South Carolina who traveled across the Carolina backwoods and kept a fascinating, exhaustive journal of his adventures. Most polite historians describe Woodmason as "acerbic," but a more accurate description is that he was just kind of a pretentious dick. And the Scots-Irish were having none of it. I don't know exactly when I fell in love with these folks, this town, and this incredible story, but this right here might have done it: to get back at the obnoxious outsider, the locals let their dogs loose during Woodmason's services, plied his would-be parishioners with free whiskey, and even stole his frock and lent it to the town's resident Casanova so that the single ladies would begin accusing his holiness of whoring around the Carolina frontier. The lesson seemed pretty clear: don't mess with Charlotte. "The Manners of the North Carolinians in General, are Vile and Corrupt," countered Woodmason. "The whole Country is a Stage of Debauchery Dissoluteness and Corruption. And how can it be otherwise? The People are compos'd of the Out Casts of all the other Colonies who take Refuge there. The Civil Police is hardly yet establish'd. . . . Polygamy is very Common—Celibacy much more—Bastardy, no Disrepute—Concubinage General—when will this *Augean* Stable be cleans'd!"

Now, if you think the wild dogs in church or the old frock switcheroo trick was too harsh, consider this: Woodmason's Augean Stable zinger is meant to compare the hometown of our true Founding Fathers to the stable in Greek mythology where King Augeas kept three thousand oxen for thirty years without ever cleaning it, which required Hercules to divert the River Alpheus in order to flush it out.

Maybe what Woodmason was trying to say was that Polk had his work cut out for him. But where others saw a tiny, dumpy, smelly backwater village full of heathens, Polk imagined America's Cradle of Independence, a kind of Scots-Irish Presbyterian paradise full of the ultimate symbols of elite colonial civilization: a courthouse, a college, a fearsome militia, and a network of churches teeming with feisty, truly free men eager to avenge their Ulster ancestors and fulfill their godly duty to combat the Crown's tyranny.

And not a second too soon. Because just as it did in Ulster, the enemy was about to reveal itself. Polk was tested and ready. He was the right man in the right place at the right time, surrounded by the right people. All he really needed was an irresistible, transcendent spiritual force powerful enough to light the fuse for freedom.

Luckily, Alexander Craighead was already on his way.

THREE

Son of Thunder: Sacrament in One Hand, Sword in the Other

THE CEMETERY CARETAKER IS ON THE PHONE WARNING ME, YET again, about the whores. I dutifully listen to the latest voicemail warnings about my plans to wander around one of the most notorious sections of Charlotte—but by now the caveats barely register. Because for me and my quest, this next adventure is a critical step: a road trip to the Sugaw Creek Presbyterian Church (founded in 1755) to see what must certainly be a towering, magnificent monument to Alexander Craighead, the radical Presbyterian preacher and spiritual father of American independence. Religion was, after all, one of the most important factors in the perfect storm that formed in the Carolina backcountry in the late 1760s that ultimately led to the creation of the MecDec. And from the very beginning, the "Son of Thunder," as Craighead was known, was at the center of the tempest, screaming himself hoarse with a fiery, take-no-prisoners style and a theology that perfectly suited his fellow hot-blooded Scots-Irish frontiersmen.

Of course, depending on which historian you ask, Craighead, who occasionally delivered his sermons with a drawn sword for effect, was either "the foremost American of his day in advocating for those principles [civil liberties under a republican form of government] for which the Revolutionary War was fought," or he was "quite possibly insane." The one thing we do know for certain is that Craighead was the product of a radical sect of

Presbyterians known as Covenanters who lived by a volatile mix of politics and religion based on a single tenet that dates back to the Scottish Lowlands: only God can rule, not monarchs or politicians, and resistance to tyranny is the highest form of obedience to God.

Craighead was almost two decades ahead of his time, preaching that all English kings had surrendered their right to rule over America as early as 1743, when Thomas Paine was all of six years old. Revolution supported by scripture was essentially Craighead's lifelong doctrine. And no one in American history delivered the message of freedom through faith (and force) with more evangelic fervor. No portraits of Craighead exist, but ever since I learned there was some red hair in his family I've always pictured him as a Jerry Lee Lewis type—albeit in knee britches and a cleric's collar—flailing around behind the pulpit in a way that challenged, scared, and excited his audience. And sure, like most geniuses and world-changers, Craighead was a little wacky, but that level of zealotry helps explain why nearly every one of the Scots-Irish that settled Charlotte, and especially the MecDec Signers themselves, were devoted and captivated by him and so eager to consecrate his beliefs with ink and blood. Without action, faith is meaningless. And by one estimate, 70 percent of the Revolutionary War troops from Mecklenburg County (which made up as much as 25 percent of North Carolina's entire army) were followers of the Son of Thunder.

"None of this happens without Craighead," says the Reverend Richard A. Ray, the chairman of the Presbyterian Heritage Center in Montreat, North Carolina, and an acclaimed theologian with a PhD from the University of St. Andrews in Scotland. "What did you call it? A perfect storm? Well, exactly, he was the perfect person, in the perfect place, at the perfect moment for the purpose of sparking independence. Craighead linked the two—the spirit and the politics—in a way, and with the kind of energy, that made all this move forward and become the defining moment in US history for the cause of independence. These men, inspired by Craighead, risked everything, yes they did; they very much risked their lives and their families' lives to put into writing their demand for independence.

"And when you put those thoughts to paper, there's no turning back, right? You get that? They were first. So that's the extent of what Craighead inspired and what this all means with the MecDec: that document is the germ, the seed, the spark . . . *the birth* . . . of American patriotism."

Hence the importance of today's visit to the Sugar Creek section of Mecklenburg County, just a few miles northeast of downtown, to see Craighead's church and his final resting place, which has the added distinction of being the first marked grave in all of Charlotte. It's an area of town, the cemetery caretaker reminds me several times over the phone, that hasn't changed all that much in the last quarter millennium. Once the most dangerous place on earth for the King of England and his representatives, Sugar Creek now has one of the highest crime rates in the state (a stat chronicled in lyric form by Charlotte native DaBaby who went to high school just a few miles away).

"Yessir, I've run into a lot of whores, drug dealers, and bad folks over there," confirms Lee, a retired Charlotte investigator and fire chief who now volunteers as the cemetery's caretaker. "Breaks my heart, but these days I wouldn't go to that place without a gun."

Pinching my iPhone between my shoulder and my ear, I yank open my nerdy black North Face backpack for a quick weapons check: there's a tote-sized umbrella that can barely fight off rain droplets, a few pens, a notepad, and a macadamia nut Clif bar, which won't necessarily kill anyone, but if they're hungry enough might just inspire them to take their own life.

Prompted by my jaw-gaping silence on the other end of the line, Lee suggests I meet him at the church so we can survey the Craighead site together. Lee's a lifesaver. In more ways than one. His family goes back half a dozen generations at the church, and his momma was born in a log cabin next to the original Sugaw Creek sanctuary. More importantly, for my purposes and my continued good health, Lee's also a retired firefighter and cop who has dedicated his life to Sugaw Creek's preservation and protection. When he was a battalion chief in the Charlotte Fire Department, Lee's only instructions to his men were that if they ever let his beloved Sugaw Creek Church burn, they'd all better die inside trying to save her.

Lee also happens to be the descendant of a few MecDec Signers. (A claim, I am quickly realizing, that is Charlotte's version of the Mayflower Society.) On May 20, 1916, President Woodrow Wilson visited Charlotte to celebrate MecDec Day, an honor the local paper said was "easily the greatest event ever held in North Carolina." Well, the cop who protected Wilson on his visit, the guy in photos standing just to the president's right with his baton drawn, that's Colonel Tom Black, Lee's great-granddaddy. In the 1980s, before Lee was promoted to battalion chief, he was asked by a commander how he'd handle the strong personalities that populate most fire companies. "You don't have to worry about me," Lee responded. "I've got Signers from the Mecklenburg Declaration of Independence in my family. Their blood runs through these veins, so you know I don't take shit from no one."

He got the job.

After fighting fires for decades, Lee, who is now a spry seventy-five, spent his last eight years on the force working undercover in the vice, narcotics, and drug interdiction unit in the Sugar Creek neighborhood. (The street, the creek, and the neighborhood have all been modernized, or "ruined" as Lee puts it, with an "r" spelling while only the church has remained authentic to the original "w" version, bestowed upon the creek by the Catawba Nation. And while we're at it: until 1737, Craighead himself was referred to in Presbyterian church records as "Craghead" or "Creaghead.") Working on a vice squad targeting prostitution in the area, if Lee ever lost contact with his partner or his tail car, they knew to rendezvous back at Sugaw Creek Church. On the job, Lee always kept an open radio channel inside his unmarked car and a pack of cigarettes in the shirt pocket over his heart. Behind his smokes, Lee would drop a straight razor into the pocket. "That way," he says, "I could slide my fingers down in there, looking like I was going for a smoke, and come out with it and come across the chest, if I ever got in a bind."

I'm starting to understand Lee's repeated warnings over the phone and why this exact area was once immortalized by DaBaby in the song "Tuesday" by Blacc Zacc. And today, after slicing through traffic on I-85 North, I follow DaBaby's instructions from the song, making a right to get off on Sugar Creek. The Shell station and the CookOut are right where he describes them, but instead of "cops" and "lookouts" and "blunts," what catches my eye is the Sugaw Creek steeple looming just above the treetops.

Once a glorious wagon-road landmark on the very outskirts of town, Sugaw Creek is now just a blip on a five-lane intersection between a tire shop and a grocery store. The people racing past on their way downtown, or out toward the NASCAR Speedway, pay little attention to the remarkable *Founded in 1755* footnote under the brick-framed Sugaw Creek sign. In front of the church, facing the intersection, there are also several carved, boulder-sized "off-in" stone blocks that parishioners once used to climb off horses and carriages. On the north side of the lot is yet another incredible landmark: a single-room, dusty brick schoolhouse, constructed in 1837 to replace the log cabin where, legend has it, Andrew Jackson learned his ABCs. After a few minor relocations, additions, and fires (but not on Lee's watch), today Sugaw Creek remains a traditional Southern-style (plain) red-brick structure. The church is elevated from the street (on a craig head, the Scots might have said), and it has a definite sense of grandeur that dissipates as soon as you pull into the deserted parking lot full of weeds growing through cracks in the crumbling pavement.

I park in the shade under a massive oak tree by the church hall, and a few minutes later Lee's small, well-used white pickup truck pulls into the spot to my left. Lee looks exactly as I had pictured him: a big, bushy Yosemite Sam mustache, an Indiana Jones hat covering his bald, liver-spotted head, brown slacks, a cop's belly, and a light green, Tommy Bahama–style short-sleeve button-up shirt with a bank envelope in the chest pocket where his razor and cigs used to go. (He quit years ago.) Together, we head down Craighead Road, a cut-through behind the church lined with apartment buildings and old row houses. Blue tarps cover a few of the roofs and a torn-up office chair teeters against the curb, ghost-spinning every time a commuter bus roars past. A daisy chain of little girls on bikes winds down the road, headed for a small but busy tienda carniceria with a kitchen exhaust that fills the area with aromas that make my stomach growl.

Whatever the crime stats, or DaBaby, might say about this place, the spiritual birthplace of American independence remains a vibrant, proud, working-class neighborhood built on a kind of cultural tapestry that's nearly impossible to find in most parts of Charlotte, or anywhere in the South for that matter.

"God only pulled off one creation," says Lee. "So we're all kin to each other 'round here is the way I see it."

As if to prove his point, a moment later when we get turned around deep inside the Sugar Creek neighborhood, Lee jumps out of the truck to ask for directions, creating one of my favorite memories from this day: a Yankee-transplant writer somewhat obsessed with twenty-seven mostly Scots-Irish patriots from the eighteenth century driving around in a beat-up pickup truck driven by a tender-hearted retired Southern cop, both of them stopping near the former site of an all-Black church to ask a young Latino man walking a labradoodle for directions to the gravesite of the holy father of American independence.

As it turns out, Craighead's cemetery is partly hidden behind an abandoned, dilapidated beer joint that's halfway through being reclaimed by kudzu vines. The small burial ground behind it, full of massive trees and a scattering of dandelions and disintegrating gravestones, is framed by a chain-link fence atop a rock wall that Lee says is mostly used as a local drinking stoop during the day and a guardrail for drunk drivers at night. We park off Craighead Road, by the abandoned beer joint, and walk around to the formal entrance on the south side of the lot featuring a massive bolder with the etching *SUGAW CREEK BURYING GROUND 1750–1825* and a six-foot stone pillar with a white marble slab that says:

MEMORIAL TO
ALEXANDER CRAIGHEAD
This wall restored and fence erected
By
Mecklenburg
Declaration
Of Independence
Chapter D.A.R.
1914

Lee locks us inside the burial grounds for our own protection (although I have yet to see any whores), and I wander for quite a bit before stumbling onto the final wish of Elizabeth Orr, who according to her marker departed this world on February 30, 1798, hoping that "worms devour my wasting flesh." And then there's the Campbell family plot, where the stones indicate that in 1781, four siblings, all under the age of thirteen, died within three days of each other—a story that is beyond sad, even for someone purposefully wandering around an ancient cemetery. In the fall of 1780, after joining the patriot army at sixteen, John Campbell was wounded at the critical Battle of Kings Mountain. He had also been unknowingly exposed to smallpox by his fellow soldiers, and when he was sent home to recover, the war hero infected his entire family.

John survived the war. None of his brothers or sisters did.

Moving toward the front of the cemetery, we finally reach Craighead's plot, which is facing east, Lee says, so the Revolutionary reverend will be looking St. Peter square in the eyes when he rises on judgment day. I hope they'll both be wearing sandals or some kind of protective footwear because this close to the street, the ground is littered with forty-ounce twist caps and shattered glass. Given Craighead's significance, I was at first a little underwhelmed by the size and state of this memorial, but then I remembered the twenty-five-foot marble obelisk meant to honor him inside the Elmwood Cemetery downtown—the one that somehow managed to misspell Mecklenburg *Decleration*. Originally, Craighead was delivered to this burial ground by his followers who used two sassafras saplings to carry his coffin. When the service was over, they stuck the tree limbs into the ground where they sprouted into two huge trees, towering over his grave for decades. About 125 years later, though, both trees were destroyed by a massive storm. Parishioners from all over the Carolinas made pilgrimages to the gravesite, chopping up the trees for souvenirs. And local legend has it that a gavel and the current pulpit at Sugaw Creek were carved from wood supplied by the Craighead trees.

Today, though, the grave's only distinguishing feature is a wobbly wrought-iron fence and a three-foot-tall gray, rectangular marble slab covered from top to bottom in biographical text. The wordy inscription takes up most of the stone, like a resume with margins awkwardly adjusted to fit everything on one page.

The etching includes where Craighead was born (Donegal, Ireland), his heritage (Ulster Scot), when he immigrated (1715), his style ("Fiery New

Side Revivalist Presbyterian"), where he preached (New Jersey, Delaware, Pennsylvania, Virginia, North Carolina), his famous friends (Ben Franklin and Great Awakening evangelist George Whitefield), and, of course, Craighead's greatest achievement in life (spiritual father of the Mecklenburg Declaration of Independence).

I stand at Craighead's feet, soaked in sweat and spellbound for an awkwardly long time until Lee finally walks up, hangs his hat on one of the fence spires, and worries out loud about the dark clouds and heat lightning looming to the north.

"I'm upta my ass in alligators," Lee also announces, fiddling with his phone.

Translation: I'm busy. Time to wrap it up, MecDec fanboy.

But I'm mesmerized and remain frozen in place, reading and rereading the thirteen lines of text covering Craighead's grave—words that feel almost like a treasure map, inspiring and prodding visitors to learn more.

The intrigue begins right there at the top of Craighead's headstone. He was born in March 1707 in Donegal, Ireland. But he wasn't Irish, not by a long shot. He was a Scot, of course. The Craigheads were originally from the Scottish Lowlands, where they were part of a militant sect of Presbyterianism founded in 1680 by Richard Cameron called Covenanters. This sect believed, as far as I can tell, that God was the only authority on earth, which meant monarchs were essentially, well, the anti-Christ. As one might imagine, this theology didn't sit well with King Charles II. Cameron and his followers were hunted down, according to church historians, "like wild beasts." His head and his hands were then torn off (presumably while he was still alive) and delivered as a gift to the English lords at Edinburgh Castle. Afterward, during a three-year stretch known as The Killing Time in Scotland, the rest of the Covenanters didn't fare much better.

Author Johannes G. Vos wrote that there was "chasing and killing upon the fields, many without sentence, and bloody butchering, hanging, heading, mangling, dismembering alive, quartering upon scaffolds, imprisoning, laying in irons, torturing by boots, thumbkins, fire-matches, cutting pieces out of the ears of others, banishing and selling as slaves old and young men and women in great numbers, oppressing many others in their estates, forfeiting, robbing, spoiling, pillaging their goods, casting them out of their habitations, interdicting any to reset them, under the pain of being treated after the same manner."

A thumbkin, by the way, was a finger-crushing vise made of iron, also known as the "thumbscrew." It was one of the most popular and effective torture tools of the time and could be customized with spikes driven under the victim's fingernails. While his thumbs remained intact, Alexander Craighead's father, Thomas Craighead, a third-generation Presbyterian minister, fled to the Ulster region of northern Ireland, where Alexander was born. Not exactly embraced by the Roman Catholic Irish landlords in Donegal, in 1723, when Alexander was just sixteen, the Craigheads joined the mass exodus of Scots to America—a group that over the next fifty years would grow to become the spark, the spine, and then the spear of the American Revolution.

"Brewed in Scotland, bottled in Ireland, uncorked in America" is how the saying goes.

This was especially true for the Craighead clan. In Lancaster County, Pennsylvania, where they settled, one scholar noted that even though he was a "fearless" and "useful" minister, "Thomas Craighead had the unhappy gift of discord and he led a somewhat stormy life." That's putting it mildly. After quickly gaining a reputation at the Pequea Church for being a miserable, intolerant, fanatical old fart (I added that last part), in May of 1736, Thomas was finally called in front of the Presbyterian leadership, a.k.a. the synod, after he barred his poor wife, Margaret, from receiving communion. Her mortal sin? Margaret simply didn't want her eldest son, John, and his family to move back in with them in Pequea. Which, for anyone who has housed their adult children, makes perfect sense, and so the church elders sided with Margaret. They found Thomas's actions "so excoriating and unconscionable, that we cannot forebear supposing that he is under some dreadful delusion of Satan, if not a delirium in his head as to this matter."

I mention this episode because, for one thing, it's pretty dang funny and oh-so relatable; secondly, *delirium in his head* is an awesome phrase that rivals even Adams's *Crapulous mass* catchphrase; and third, it's important to note the frame of mind Thomas was in while he was homeschooling his son Alexander on how to become a proper Presbyterian minister. While most of his contemporaries studied seminary at the Log College or back in Scotland at the University of Edinburgh—where they developed the skills, and learned the benefits, of interacting with different personalities and theologies—Alexander was trained at home by his extremist, loner father. A man once described as a "problem person" who, a few years later, literally preached himself to death. Witnesses at Pequea said that near the end of one of his sermons he waved his hands frantically and exclaimed, "Farewell! Farewell!" before expiring right there on the pulpit.

There's no official mention of applause, though.

Before we go any further, I should pause for a second to share the story behind where a lot of this Craighead information comes from. The comprehensive history of Craighead's Sugaw Creek Presbyterian Church was written in 1954 by Neill Roderick McGeachy, who had served as the Sugaw Creek pastor from 1941–1945 before moving to a larger church about an hour north in Statesville. The McGeachy name (pronounced: Muh-GAY-he) may sound familiar to some older, diehard ACC hoops fans. His son, Neill McGeachy Jr., coached the Duke basketball team for a single season in 1973–1974. Neill Jr. and his sisters, Elizabeth, Margaret, and Lila, grew up riding their bikes around the dusty, red-clay Sugaw Creek property where their father spoke of Craighead so often, and with such reverence, that until adulthood they were all convinced they were somehow kin to Craighead.

Neill Sr. died in 1979, and when his wife, Frances, passed away in 1998, Lila, while going through their belongings, came across a heavy box full of research marked "Craighead." It was clear from the content that her father had always dreamed of turning that box into a book, or even a novel. The research included a stunning find: copies of Craighead's sermons printed by Benjamin Franklin. Lila and her husband, Richard Ray, whom I quoted (extensively) at the beginning of this chapter, were about to move to Pennsylvania so that Dick could teach and study at the Pittsburgh Theological Seminary.

In her sixties at the time, Lila decided, *what the heck, I'll use my time on campus to get a master's degree.* She already had the topic of her thesis picked out. And two years later, in 2001, Lila published the 130-page, exhaustively researched thesis titled *Alexander Craighead: With Drawn Sword.*

In a crazy twist, Lila's niece turned out to be a former colleague of mine at *SI* and ESPN, so less than twenty-four hours after wondering how in the world I would ever find a copy of this obscure thesis, I was on the phone with Lila making plans to spend the day at her home in the Blue Ridge Mountains discussing all things Alexander Craighead over chicken salad sandwiches and sweet tea. A week later I was on her screened-in porch, about to dig in, when Dick bowed his head in prayer. He blessed me, my book, the MecDec patriots, and especially the scholar at the table—the remarkable woman he had met while lifeguarding almost seventy years before at a lake just down the street—who was "a true spiritual descendant of Alexander Craighead." (I thought this was about the most romantic thing I'd ever heard. But it was nothing for these two. Lila has trouble reading because of a worsening eye condition, so to prepare for my visit, Dick reread her thesis to her, a few pages at a time, every night before they went to bed.)

According to Lila, then, in 1735 when Alexander was given his own church near Lancaster, Pennsylvania, he picked up exactly where his father left off. Inspired by the Great Awakening revival and its top advocate, the young, popular evangelist George Whitefield, there were already growing divisions inside the Presbyterian faith between the traditional Old Side and New Side. While preaching to crowds of more than five thousand up and down the East Coast, Whitefield and the young Craighead became fast friends and something akin to religious rock stars. Whitefield's journals, in fact, even make mention of him riding through the woods with Craighead, singing and praising God on their way to a revival where people burst into tears upon hearing Craighead preach in his decidedly New Side style, a delivery that evoked "incidents of weeping, screaming, and fainting . . . and bodily commotions like epileptic fits."

It may sound a lot like Lollapalooza, but to the Old Side (or "Old Light") Presbyterians, preaching with any kind of flair or emotion, to anyone other than your own parishioners, was strictly verboten, which, I'm sure, only made it more appealing to someone wired like Craighead. As his preaching became more raucous, Craighead's theology became far more radicalized to the point that one Anglican described Craighead and his followers as folks who liked to receive "their Sacrament with a gun charg'd and a drawn sword." A prophetic Old Side minister added that Craighead and his New Lights were quickly becoming "foremost in propagating the principles of sedition and disobedience to authority."

Church elders believed that Craighead's growing influence needed to be curtailed. And they weren't entirely wrong. He was something of a religious fanatic, after all, and few things have proven to be as destructive throughout American history as the perceived moral high ground. An ecclesiastical trial was scheduled in December 1740 to be convened inside his church in Lancaster. All Craighead really needed to do was censor or humble himself just a little before church leaders. Instead, in what would become an escalating pattern throughout his life—with church elders and later governors, sheriffs, and ultimately the King of England, to whom he gave the MecDec middle finger—Craighead prepared to do what he did best: fight the power, or at the very least really, *really* piss it off. "Perhaps no ecclesiastical trial in colonial history was more thoroughly burlesqued than that of Alexander Craighead," author Leonard Trinterud wrote in 1949.

Church elders showed up expecting a chastened man and a quick, orderly trial.

What they got instead was a rebellion. The first of many from Craighead.

Rather than listen to the charges against him, the "mad fellow," as Craighead was now being called, had prepared a paper on the Presbytery and its ministers that accused them of "whoredom, drunkenness, swearing, Sabbath breaking, and lying." From the get-go, according to the extensive (and at times hilarious) minutes of the official Presbytery clerk, Craighead "utterly and absolutely declined our authority." Moreover, a large mob of his acolytes crammed into the meeting, and whenever the Presbytery attempted to make a point, Craighead whipped his followers into such a frenzy, "consuming our time by circumlocutions and harangues to amuse ye populace," that they had to abruptly end the meeting for their own safety and move the proceedings to a nearby home. One thing was clear: Craighead was in full Jerry Lee Lewis mode and thoroughly enjoyed the entire spectacle. But a very much shaken Presbytery clerk found Craighead's "notorious and disorderly conduct" to be "extremely irregular and disorderly, so that we have not known a parallel instance since we have been capable to mark anything on the world."

No known parallel instance in the world? The leaders of the Presbyterian Church, a group that once had its thumbs (and worse) torn off in Scotland, could not think of anything in the known universe to compare to this wild man Craighead. The Son of Thunder was truly one of a kind.

For this unforgivable sin, Craighead was promptly expelled from the synod. Repeatedly. All the church managed to do, however, was create a monster—and spark a revolution. Craighead's views on Christ's sovereignty over all civic affairs, and the use of armed resistance to defend this truth if need be, only grew louder, more frequent, and more incendiary. He called George II "the Head of Malignants and Protectors of Sectarian Heretics" who had given his power "to the Beast," and the idea that "No war is proclaimed without a drawn sword" kind of became Craighead's mantra. A shocked synod had no choice but to officially denounce his writings as "full of treason, sedition, and distraction and grievous perverting of the sacred oracles to the ruin of all societies and civil government."

And this was just Craighead's opening act.

He then published a pamphlet, one of several of his sermons printed by Benjamin Franklin, titled "The Reasons of Mr. Alexander Craighead's receding from the present Judicature of the Church, together with its Constitution." In it, Craighead swore he would no longer abide "the apostate, perjured, and blood-guilty Condition of the Church and State" and that it was their "duty to separate ourselves from the corrupt Constitution of both Church and State, and not to touch, taste, or handle these Abominations, lest partaking with them in their Sins, we be made Partakers with them in their Plagues."

On November 11, 1743, Craighead stood before his throng of supporters and asked them, just as their spiritual forebears had done, to draw their swords before renewing their hardcore beliefs known as the Solemn League Covenants. (The pledge's title pretty much sums up the entire Craighead vs. Everybody philosophy: "The Declaration, Protestation, and Testimony of a Suffering Remnant of the Anti-Popish, Anti-Lutheran, Anti-Prelatick, Anti-Erastian, Anti-Latirudinarian, Anti-Sectarian, true Presbyterian Church of Christ, in America.") With sword overhead, Craighead shouted: "Our renowned Ancestors were constrained to draw the Sword of Defense of their own lives. Our drawing the sword is to testify to the World, that we are one in Judgement of them, and that we are to this Day, willing to maintain the same defensive War in defending our Religion and ourselves against all Opposers thereof, although the Defense of these should cost us our lives. No war is proclaimed without a drawn sword and there is no Reason that this should be singular in this particular. Let King Jesus reign, and let all his enemies be scattered. Amen."

The whole thing was a stunning act of rebellion, if not full-on treason.

It was, as Lila summed it up to me with a knowing wink, "Craighead's *first* Declaration of Independence."

In his 1994 book titled *The Language of Liberty*, Jonathan Clark also puts Craighead in the highest of company—I mean, like, Mount Rushmore–level company—when he says Craighead's drawn-sword moment was "a vivid anticipation of that more famous renewal of a covenant which was . . . the American Revolution."

It wasn't long before Craighead caught the attention of the authorities. He promptly fled to Virginia, and after lying low for a few years, with the church and the law still on his back, Craighead (smartly) answered the call for preachers down at the North Carolina frontier where he'd be far, far away from the watchful eye of the Presbytery, the politicians, and the King's henchmen.

In 1758, Craighead arrived at Rocky River Church, a structure made of log and mud near a river ford just north of present-day Charlotte. There, he found a small scattering of fellow Scots-Irish scratching out a meager existence in the dense, hot, bountiful Carolina backwoods. To outsiders, it wasn't a pretty sight. "The individual traits of these [Scots-Irish] rose quickly to the surface," reported one historian. "Undisciplined, emotional, courageous, aggressive, pugnacious, fiercely intolerant, and hard-drinking, with a tendency to indolence, they nevertheless produce ambitious leaders with virtues of the warrior and politician."

But to Craighead, these were his kind of people.

And this place, where he'd answer to no one and he would be the only spiritual authority in the vast swath of land between the Catawba and Yadkin rivers—to him, this place was paradise.

There can't be a better description of Craighead's arrival in Carolina, and its deeper meaning, than the one from historian William Henry Foote:

Crossing the Blue Ridge, Craighead passed on to the more quiet regions in Carolina, and found a location among the settlements along the Catawba and its smaller tributaries, in the bounds of what is now Mecklenburg County. Here, Craighead found a people remote from the seat of authority, among whom the intolerant laws were a dead letter, so far divided from other congregations, even of his own faith, that there could be no collision with him, on account of faith or practice; so united in their general principles of religion and church government, that Craighead was the teacher of the whole population—and here his spirit rested. Here he passed his days; here he poured forth his principles of religious and civil government, undisturbed by the jealousy of the government, too distant to be aware of his doings, or too careless to be interested in the poor and distant emigrants on the Catawba.

The Charlotteans took to Craighead so quickly, and completely, it's said that he was installed at Rocky River in the morning and at Sugaw Creek Church in the afternoon and that he stopped to preach on horseback several times whilst riding between the two. Craighead would regularly speak to gatherings of fifty people or less in the shade of a giant oak tree or he'd ride deep into the woods down a single-track Indigenous path for miles just to reach a few more isolated souls. Craighead was flourishing in Mecklenburg County, to say the least. (Even in his happy place, though, his daughter said he was still occasionally "somewhat disposed to melancholy.") Over the next dozen years, the tireless (and unencumbered) Craighead would manage to indoctrinate just about the entire Carolina frontier as the chief shepherd, teacher, and moral authority of seven churches throughout Mecklenburg County. And his massive flock loved and revered him like a demigod. It's no coincidence, then, that the Seven Sisters, as they are known, eventually produced nearly all of the Mecklenburg Declaration of Independence Signers.

Truth be told, Craighead really didn't have to work all that hard to radicalize the Carolina backcountry. The British authorities did most of the work for him thanks to a series of regulations and taxes starting with the despised Marriage and Vestry Acts. Although there were practically no Anglican churches or priests in the region, after succeeding his grandfather King George III still insisted on an annual tax of ten shillings for every "taxable soul" to help build Anglican churches and support their clergy. The King was forcing the dirt-poor Scots-Irish settlers to bankroll a church they wholeheartedly believed was in cahoots with the devil. The law also required Anglican priests to officiate all weddings, which forced Presbyterian couples to either travel long distances or wait several months to be officially wed.

As a result, many frontier children of the "wrong" religion were born bastards with no way to legally inherit anything and no possible path to heaven. It seems laughable now, sure, but imagine, for a second, what this must have felt like at the time for new Scots-Irish parents: these were families that had risked their lives traveling across an ocean and two countries specifically to get away from this kind of tyranny, the kind that had been torturing their ancestors for generations, and now they had to stare down at the newborn miracle cooing softly in their arms and know it had already been condemned to a life of poverty on earth and then an eternity in the fires of hell because of the King's malfeasance.

Revolution and war? That must have seemed almost appealing to those parents. The casual and seemingly endless cruelty of the Crown enraged Craighead and his followers and helped solidify the Covenanters' incendiary and longstanding ideology requiring them to honor God by fighting back against such despotism. Craighead cultivated it for years, with every fiery word he preached, sharpening that weapon to a razor's edge until the question in Carolina was no longer *if* Craighead's followers would be gunning for the King.

But when.

"Craighead had the opportunity of forming the civil and religious principles, in no measured degree, of a race of men that feared neither the labor and hardship of the pioneer's life, nor the dangers of the frontier," historian and author Charles A. Hanna wrote in 1902. "It was a race that had sought and found freedom and prosperity in the wilderness. Under the teaching of Craighead, it is not strange that these people should be among the first to conceive the idea of Independence, to announce it to the world in their convention held in May 1775, and with their fortunes and lives to sustain that idea through the trying scenes of the Revolution."

A revolution that began, appropriately enough, with drawn swords and cracked skulls right in Alexander Craighead's backyard.

Four

A Pack of Brutal Sons-of-Bitches Wins the Sugar Creek War

Henry Eustace McCulloh arrived in North Carolina in 1761 an effete, lecherous wannabe aristocrat, and he died sometime around 1810 (no one's really sure) inside a British asylum penniless, humiliated, and driven mad by the "pack of brutal sons-of-bitches" he encountered in Charlotte. Poor Hank. Described by one historian as "almost the very stereotype of the rapacious English snot-nosed aristocrat," he was twenty-five and just entering the prime of his pampered life when his father, a wealthy London merchant and land speculator, dispatched him to the Sugar Creek region of the North Carolina frontier to survey his lands and collect rent. The task was essentially a suicide mission given the revolutionary frenzy Craighead had been stoking for years in the region and Hank's nonexistent qualifications that he described as "young in life, knowledge, and experience and totally unacquainted with the real circumstances of my father's affairs."

At the time, those affairs consisted mostly of land speculation in the New World. In 1737 the British Crown granted the rights to 1.2 million acres of land in the Carolina Piedmont—including nearly two hundred square miles that make up much of what is present-day Charlotte and its surrounding counties—to George Augustus Selwyn and Henry McCulloh Sr. The purchase option from the King, however, was contingent upon Selwyn and land agents like McCulloh luring six thousand settlers (the Crown preferred Protestants) to the backcountry and getting them to purchase, or mortgage, the land and then hand over an annual rental tax of four shillings per one hundred acres. (No foreign power would dare to charge the people of this region such outrageous fees, for so little in return, for another 250 years, until the IKEA opened two exits up from Sugar Creek.) It was a truly brilliant moneymaking scheme for Selwyn, McCulloh, and their cronies with the exception of just a few tiny logistical hurdles, such as, for instance, the inescapable fact that before anyone made a shilling, someone would be required to travel deep into the thick, muddy, treacherously hot Carolina backcountry to, well, actually survey the land and then somehow collect taxes from Scots-Irish settlers—quick-tempered folks who had a special enmity for the Crown and bloodsucking British landlords. In other words, the exact kind of English entitlement that oozed from every one of Hank McCulloh's pores, as well as his pen.

Upon his arrival, after whining that he had already aged twenty-five years in this dreadful, backward "strange country" as he wended his way west on crude wagon trails toward the patriots in Charlotte, Hank wrote to friends back in England to brag about all the bank and babes he was locking down in North Carolina. In a style of prose reminiscent of a Guy Ritchie ancestor, he wrote: "Now I doubt whether there is a Stockjobber in Exchange Alley that takes more pains about the Universal Catholicon (money) than I do. Of nights I follow good King David's example. Solace myself in the flesh way. I can't make up of the Scripture phrase and say that I have a Virgin to lay to my bosom, mine is an *improved* one. And although I lead here a life of absolute ease and freedom, I long after the flesh and money of thy Western regions."

Of course, "thy Western regions" of North Carolina had very different plans in store for McCulloh. The earliest Charlotteans had elevated English harassment to an art form—as Father Woodmason, the "whoremonger" knew all too well—but the locals had a truly special backcountry welcome wagon waiting for old Hank.

McCulloh had no way of knowing that he was trotting, with his compass, survey staff, and wineskins, straight into an area that General Cornwallis would one day categorize as a "veritable hornet's nest of resistance." Indeed, it was a populous that, for nearly a decade, had been whipped into an ideological frenzy by Craighead, who mixed religion and revolution so seamlessly that civic leaders in Charlotte, men like Thomas Polk and Abraham Alexander, could no longer tell them apart. What made the sword-waving Craighead different, though, especially among his audience of Scots-Irish, was his willingness to back up his sermons with action. In fact, when he found out that his original church, Rocky River, had been built on land awarded by the Crown to two local commissioners in exchange for their work surveying the state border, Craighead resigned in protest and marched west to a new, purer pulpit where his crowds swelled and his message of righteous resistance went from a simmer to a boil inside Sugaw Creek Church.

This was a house of worship that, by some form of divine providence, was constructed near a baptismal spring at the very center of McCulloh's lands. Meaning it was only a matter of time before Craighead's holy water and the oily McCulloh mixed—violently.

EVER THE DIVA, McCULLOH IS THE ONE WHO ORIGINALLY CATEGORIZED the events that followed as a "war." In a long, melodramatic testimonial to the North Carolina governor, he pleaded: "Shall not the War of Sugar Creek be handed down to posterity? Can the annals of the history of this country parallel this affair?" McCulloh's lyrical legal statement from May 9, 1765, describing the entire ordeal runs on for thirty-three eye-rolling pages. And, according to the Colonial and State Records of North Carolina, it's missing at least another eight full pages. Despite its occasional verboseness, Mc-Culloh crafted a truly amazing and timeless document. Hank had a way with words, I'll give him that. And no matter how many times I read it, I'm always left a little stunned by its time-machine qualities—the way it instantly transports you hundreds of years back to the center of a mob on the banks of a small, muddy, world-changing creek in the middle of the Carolina wilderness.

Although McCulloh was warned almost a year earlier that the backcountry was "infested" with Presbyterians, he managed to survey most of his best land in the Carolina Piedmont—the lush, fertile grassland between the Yadkin and Catawba rivers—without so much as a cuss word from the locals. McCulloh was feeling especially cocky upon returning to Sugar Creek. In early 1765, he wrote to a friend that he intended to ask for as much as twelve pounds per one hundred acres and to "outdo all my former Outdoings."

However, on March 4, when he arrived at the home of Abraham Alexander on the banks of Sugar Creek, 150 angry locals were there to greet him. Dressed in buckskin and bearskin, the mob was armed with axes, knives, clubs, and a few pistols. McCulloh's Spidey sense told him they were plotting "ill return to his kind intentions." It was nothing personal. It was, instead, what historians like to call "the long agrarian tradition of violent opposition to gentry domination in England." McCulloh, of course, handled the situation with his usual aplomb, waving the land grant from the Crown in everyone's face and threatening "forfeiture of all they possessed in the world," not understanding the land they were standing on *was* pretty much all they possessed in the world. Many of the locals argued that they had already paid a land grant to the King when they arrived. Those that didn't had been quoted a price of five pounds per one hundred acres for plots of land they had since greatly improved with years of back-breaking labor. Sounding a bit like a used carriage salesman, Hank countered with a three-year, money-back guarantee (honestly, he did) and reasonable financing terms, but he held firm on requiring one-third up front, which means buying a home hasn't really changed at all in the last quarter millennium. Finally, the Sugar Creek gang, a group led by Thomas Polk and others, made a counteroffer of ten pounds. But there was a catch. They wanted to pay in Proc, or proclamation money, the currency used in the colonies, which was valued at about 30 percent less than sterling.

A heated argument ensued and, at some point, McCulloh's way with words betrayed him. He slandered North Carolina Governor Arthur Dobbs before mumbling under his breath that the settlers were behaving like "a parcel of blockheads." McCulloh had failed to read the room. The intensely proud and easily triggered Scots-Irish were always looking for a fight.

Now they had one.

McCulloh wrote that the crowd closed in, pushing and shoving him, and—horrors!—"talking to him in the most insulting manner."

Up until that point, Thomas Polk, who held the prestigious office of justice of the peace, had been working with McCulloh to calm the mob and negotiate a compromise. McCulloh was no dummy. He partnered with Polk for a reason. Although they were about the same age, Polk was his exact opposite in just about every conceivable way: a plainspoken, self-made man, lean and leathery, with the sculpted jaw of an MMA fighter. He was the kind of man who seemed to have his own gravitational pull, a leader who embodied the cunning spirit of the impending American Revolution. Mc-Culloh, on the other hand, was preternaturally condescending, pale, portly, and fancied Victorian shirts with blousy collars and cuffs. He wrote that he had recruited Polk's help because he was "the only man who has any pretense to sense or weight among these deluded people."

That was most certainly true. Because the moment Polk sensed the crowd at the Alexander farm turning, he stepped aside and left McCulloh twisting in the wind.

Eventually, it was Polk who announced that henceforth no one in Mecklenburg would pay a dirty shilling for their land or allow it to be drawn out by the likes of McCulloh.

The war was on.

The seeds of the Mecklenburg Declaration of Independence had been planted, right there on the Alexander farm.

Having now morphed into a crowd acting "more like wolves than rational beings," the Charlotteans cackled in McCulloh's face and warned him that if he returned, "the best usage he should expect to meet with would be to be tied neck and heels and carried over the Yadkin, and that he might think himself happy if he got off so."

Brave, greedy, or just clueless, at nine the very next morning McCulloh returned to the banks of Sugar Creek only to find men armed with guns standing guard at a fence. Led by Polk, the mob of one hundred quickly converged on McCulloh who, again, was able to correctly surmise "the greatest probability of their design to injure my life or person." What clued him in, perhaps, was the snarky fellows asking McCulloh if he thought he'd have as many men at his impending funeral. You can almost hear the echoes of their laughter when McCulloh then "made a solemn and legal proclamation in the majesty's scared name to disperse the riot."

To which the crowd "paid no regard."

Instead, they seized his surveying chain and snapped it into several pieces. Knowing it was the highest of insults, Polk himself then snatched McCulloh's compass off his staff. (Many compasses were ornate, expensive heirlooms.) Outnumbered inside an angry, armed mob, this was the moment McCulloh says he was uncertain "whether that day was to have been the last of his life or not." He was saved by the always-two-chess-moves-ahead Polk, who offered fifteen Proc per one hundred acres. A shaken McCulloh used the distraction to retreat from Sugar Creek. He promised to consider the offer the following day. But not in person. Oh no. "In writing," he said. Hank was slowly catching on.

McCulloh had no intention of facing the Sugar Creek crazies ever again. He was now focused on a different tactic: using his political clout to destroy the traitor he referred to as "Our Sovereign Lord King Polk" and all of his disciples.

"Damn thee Tom Polk," McCulloh wrote, sounding a bit lovesick. "Damn thee Tom Polk if I don't conquer thee."

WHAT HAPPENED NEXT MIGHT BE CONSIDERED THE TRUE BIRTH OF THE current American spirit: everyone lawyered up.

Hank summarily rejected the fifteen Proc offer, even though it was close to his original asking price. Instead, he filed eviction papers on all the Sugar Creek property holders and a civil suit for one thousand pounds in damages against Polk while petitioning the courts (and all of Daddy's powerful friends) to strip Polk of his lucrative position as justice of the peace. In his forty-page argument, McCulloh went so far as to reference the English Black Act of 1723, which authorized the death penalty for the kinds of offenses he says he suffered on the banks of Sugar Creek. (This was no joke. A few years later in nearby Hillsborough, six farmers were hanged for their participation in a similar kind of rebellion.) Polk filed his own complaint to William Tryon, the royal governor of North Carolina. (Although Polk's testimony has been lost, my guess is it was something close to "kick rocks.") Tryon ordered McCulloh not to evict any residents until the matter could be settled by the next state assembly.

Emboldened by what they considered the governor's support, the Sugar Creek gang in Charlotte prepared to escalate their attacks on McCulloh and his crew. McCulloh must have taken the numerous death threats seriously. The next day he stayed behind to draw up his will while a group of locals he hired returned to Sugar Creek to continue the surveys.

The decision probably saved his life.

On May 7, 1765, McCulloh's surveyors were marking off Sugar Creek property claimed by a widow of the powerful, ubiquitous Alexander clan when a group of twelve armed men stormed the creek. There's no record of Craighead being a part of the mob. He was nearly sixty by then. But make no mistake, he was there in spirit. And his men moved with the ruthless ferocity of soldiers on a moral mission. This skirmish was different than the ones that preceded it. It was clear right away that the locals were no longer in the mood to negotiate. Using a technique that dates back to the earliest methods of agrarian warfare, the settlers had blackened their faces with tar and soot to avoid recognition—never a good sign. Their guns, they shouted, were for the specific purpose of murdering McCulloh. When he couldn't be found, less severe forms of frontier justice were meted out to his hired hands, all of whom were local men. Some were even members of the state assembly who were simply in the wrong place at the wrong time.

"I can hardly form an idea equal to the horror of their behavior and appearance," McCulloh wrote upon hearing of the bloody, inevitable escalation of the Sugar Creek War.

Several surveyors were immediately beaten unconscious with makeshift clubs as generations of pent-up anger and frustration boiled over. The brutal assault left John Frohock, the leader of the crew, with his nose and mouth split open and spewing blood. The men who tried to flee were dragged back to the banks of Sugar Creek to face their punishment. One of them was stripped "from the nape of his neck to the waistband of his breeches" and whipped until his back looked like a crimson-ink road map.

A local kid named Jimmy, working for McCulloh, got the worst of it. His skull was cracked open. "He very near had daylight let into his skull" reported one horrified witness. Somehow, he survived.

"Had I been present I most assuredly and without any ceremony, would have been murdered," a sullen, defeated McCulloh wrote. "Is not my life in the greatest of peril? My friends cruelly abused for being so? What am I to do?"

Nothing, it turns out. With pressure mounting from the McCulloh family's powerful allies in London, when word that the disturbance in Sugar Creek had turned violent reached Governor Tryon, he was forced to act before the North Carolina frontier fell into open rebellion. (It was headed that way eventually. All Tryon did was delay the inevitable.) In September 1765, Tryon formally charged Polk and his men with rioting. He then offered full pardons to any of the rioters who would step forward to admit guilt and provide names of the others involved, but in a show of solidarity that laid the groundwork for the MecDec, none of the Charlotteans came forward to take the governor's offer. Not a single one. And as long as the men remained anonymous, a trial would be impossible.

Ultimately, Polk and the Sugar Creek rebels were spared by fellow patriots protesting the Stamp Act. In the fall of 1765, in an attempt to raise money for the French and Indian War, the British Parliament passed a law taxing official business in the colonies by requiring all documents to be recorded on stamped paper imported from England. After the uproar, judges in North Carolina refused to hear any civil cases stemming from protests against the Stamp Act or any other forms of taxation without representation. When the judges were suspended, it created a backlog of one thousand cases, which ground the court system in North Carolina to a halt and essentially suspended, indefinitely, any judgment against the Sugar Creek defendants.

In January 1766, encouraged by Polk to strike a deal, the locals agreed to pay thirteen pounds Proc per one hundred acres, which was, of course, very near the midpoint of their initial negotiation that March morning on the banks of Sugar Creek. First and foremost, what the War of Sugar Creek really accomplished was to solidify Craighead's immense influence on the region. Charlotte now had a divinely inspired taste for independence. The bloodshed on Sugar Creek, and the solidarity shown afterward, was more than enough proof of the town's collective resolve. It was only a matter of time before the MecDec patriots would put it in writing for the rest of the world to see.

The "war" also helped establish Polk's power and status throughout the county. In his lengthy letters McCulloh makes it clear that the mob at Sugar Creek would have done whatever Lord Polk demanded, be it fight or pay up. Out of respect, or fear, McCulloh then made him the land agent for much of Mecklenburg County, allowing Polk to have the last laugh and deliver the final, fatal blow of the Sugar Creek War. In his new position, Polk secured from Selwyn a deed for 360 acres of prime real estate in Mecklenburg worth more than five thousand pounds that McCulloh gave away for just ninety pounds. (Proc, of course.) The following year, in 1768, the North Carolina assembly made Charlotte official. The assembly then appointed three of the main participants in the Sugar Creek War—Frohock, Alexander, and Polk—as trustees and directors for a new town to be called Charlotte located on the land McCulloh had just practically given away. What's more, according to the actual founding deed of Charlotte, the center of town was to be located practically in Polk's living room, "beginning at a white oak about 150 yards from Thomas Polk's line."

To help guarantee Charlotte's continued status as the county seat, Polk and others quickly built a courthouse (at their own expense) located just fifty feet from Polk's front door, right smack dab in the middle of where the two trading paths intersected.

This is the building where, a few years later, many of the same men, baptized by the waters of Sugar Creek into the cause for freedom and independence, would gather again to craft the Mecklenburg Declaration of Independence.

TODAY, HANK MCCULLOH WOULD BE HAPPY TO KNOW THAT IN THE LATE 1960s the original parcel of land fought over during the Sugar Creek War became home to C'est Bon, a strip club, and the first one in Charlotte to, according to a local reporter, "break the boobie barrier" before mysteriously burning down several years later. A quarter millennium after the Sugar Creek War there isn't a single trace of McCulloh in town today. All of his land was confiscated at the start of the Revolutionary War, a conflict he helped inspire and one that was declared at the very center of the land he had inadvertently donated to the cause. No wonder he went mad. Hank died bankrupt and alone in a British asylum probably muttering about the "unmannerly, ungrateful, brutal sons of bitches" from Sugar Creek who were living in his mind and on his land—rent-free, I might add. McCulloh's boss, George Selwyn, has fared much better. In 1990 he was awarded what I like to call the Southern Medal of Merit: both a pub and an elementary school in Charlotte were named in his honor.

By far, though, my favorite nugget from this entire Sugar Creek saga is that since 1910, the current tenant on Abraham Alexander's original homestead has been the Charlotte Country Club. The city's oldest and swankiest golf club with the (what else) classic white-columned, plantation-style clubhouse entrance, the CCC's course was originally laid out by famed golf architect Donald Ross. More importantly, according to the club's two-page Guest Policy—a masterpiece of passive-aggressive Southern charm—the Charlotte Country Club "wants you to feel comfortable at our club . . . by carefully adhering to our dress code." This means absolutely no denim or cell phones. Or, God forbid, denim-covered cell phones.

Although they don't currently possess the power to don a collarless shirt inside their own club, the folks who run Charlotte have occupied this land, one way or another, since the 1760s. In the beginning, the zealots of Sugar Creek happily risked their lives—and sowed the seeds of independence—by refusing to pay even a nominal fee for the right to toil and tame the unforgiving, red-clay soil they considered their sacred birthright. So you have to think that wherever he is, good ol' Hank McCulloh is laughing his ass off knowing that, today, potential members of the Charlotte Country Club happily line up to hand over $85,000 in initiation fees (about £386 in 1765) plus $12,480 in annual dues (another £55) in order to dress up in the kind of clothes he fancied and chase a tiny ball across the dirt he used to own.

Maybe McCulloh won the Sugar Creek War after all.

Five

Let Freedom Spring

MY PLAN IS PRACTICALLY FOOLPROOF, I TELL MYSELF AS I PULL INTO the church parking lot. All I have to do is convince this nice Baptist minister to break a few laws. Piece of cake. I should have the benefit of karma on my side, since today I'm in Huntersville, a town that was originally named Craighead. Located about ten miles north of the "battlefield" from the Sugar Creek War, Huntersville is now a booming, perpetually torn-up section of town near Charlotte's new six-lane outer loop highway. As I exit the highway and head south, the landscape looks a bit like the surface of Mars. Around here all traces of trees and vegetation have been strip-mined away by developers, leaving nothing but long stretches of flattened red clay dotted with orange barrels, twisted temporary fences, and oversized construction equipment rattling down dusty, impossibly narrow country roads.

Plopped down right in the middle of all this, Independence Hill stands out like a beacon. The quaint, immaculately landscaped 150-year-old Baptist church is perched, literally, above it all on a slight crest atop the rolling but now barren surrounding landscape. After arriving a few minutes early, I park in the shade of a giant, ancient oak tree facing the modest chapel. With my back to the construction across the street, I begin rehearsing the spiel I'm about to deliver that will, god willing, turn Pastor Todd into my accomplice. Mainly, my message today is that I am but a lone, humble, god-fearing scribe whose latest research into two key aspects at the epicenter of the Mec-Dec legend has led me on a pilgrimage right here to Independence Hill.

If need be I'll remind Pastor Todd that his church now sits on the exact spot where the legendary Alexandriana estate once stood. In the 1770s, at a time when the average farm in the Carolina backcountry was around one hundred acres, the land baron John McKnitt Alexander was said to own ten square miles of Mecklenburg. (He usually dropped the John and went by just McKnitt—pronounced: McKnight—and so we will too.) Records show McKnitt made something like thirty-five land purchases during his lifetime. But his favorite piece of property, by far, was always the 1,500 acres right here under our feet today, a family headquarters and plantation McKnitt dubbed Alexandriana. In its heyday the Alexander family was so powerful, and their holdings so immense, that Alexandriana was noted on area maps as if it were its own metropolis, which in many ways it was.

Although the Alexander family sold this sacred ground to the Baptists in 1868, I also plan to remind Pastor Todd that since its inception his church has been deeply connected to the MecDec. The church was originally dedicated as Oak Grove Baptist. But in 1875, just four years after its founding, the normally, shall we say, unwavering Baptists, who are, again, shall we say, not exactly big fans of the Presbyterians or impetuosity, actually agreed to rename their church Independence Hill in honor of the MecDec's centennial celebration.

"I don't know if you know this, but Baptists just don't change the name of their church," explains the red-headed Pastor Todd, who is, to my ever-loving surprise and delight, fairly young, built like a rugby player, wearing yoga shorts, and, if he's not careful, right on the verge of being downright sociable while showing me a glass case full of the church's oldest relics, photos, and historic documents. "For me, this has always been the best, strongest, really the *only* piece of proof I'll ever need about just how significant the MecDec was. Change the name of a church? Baptists just don't do that, like, ever."

To honor this area, Mecklenburg County has preserved a swath of woods to the west of the church as a kind of memorial picnic area and park called, of course, Alexandriana. With Independence Hill getting choked out on three sides by developers, including one of those massive, gleaming, Death Star–sized Amazon distribution centers looming to the south, the park is the only thing preventing this church from being metastasized into a strip mall Applebee's. Neglected and overgrown, Alexandriana Park is now deafeningly close to the traffic, giving it all the peaceful charm of a NASCAR pit row. Trust me, I spent several days traipsing around in here with my dog treasure hunting for MecDec clues. Instead of ruins or gravestones, though, all I found was an alarming amount of garbage indicating that these days Alexandriana, once the Monticello of Mecklenburg, has been reduced to a cell phone lot, a hook-up spot, and a shaded break room and toilet for itinerant construction workers and Amazon employees. The only thing left of any real note is a large stone and brass MecDec marker, a cobweb-covered bulletin board with information about the document and the Signers, and, out next to the two-lane highway, a national park–style, ten-foot wooden plank sign that reads:

ALEXANDRIANA
Birthplace of Mecklenburg
Declaration of Independence
May 20 1775

I've probably driven by this place a hundred times. (My old rec-league roller hockey rink was just down the street from here. During my final few years on the team, the deal I had made with Kim was that I was allowed a maximum of three emergency room visits per season, including the playoffs. So, most of the time on this road I was probably far more focused on how to hide puck contusions, pulled groins, and concussion symptoms.) Having switched unhealthy obsessions from cross-checks to MecDecs (or, if you can stand it, from pucks to Polks) it was only recently that I noticed the peculiar wording of the Alexandriana marker.

Birthplace?

There's no doubt that McKnitt was an immensely wealthy, respected civic leader and patriarch of an Alexander family that played a major role in the planning, creation, and preservation of the MecDec. Six of the twenty-seven Signers were Alexanders, including Abraham Alexander, the committee chairman. But it would be McKnitt, the committee secretary, who would become the principal character in this entire saga—from start to finish, and beyond. Even casual MecDec fans know that the document itself was crafted and signed ten miles south of here at the courthouse in the center of Charlotte. But as I explain to Pastor Todd, I keep uncovering clues challenging that notion. Along with a 1954 newspaper article and a 1960 textbook by a former newspaper editor, I also found the most wonderfully weird, historically accurate 1940 novel about the MecDec saga titled *Alexandriana* by renowned journalist, historian, and McKnitt descendant LeGette Blythe.

All three sources, and the *History of Independence Hill Baptist Church* written in 1972, make distinct references to a sacred, lost meeting place on McKnitt's property called Freedom Spring.

After the Sugar Creek War, during the rapid escalation of hostilities between the Crown and the Carolinas in the buildup to the MecDec and the Revolution, McKnitt would frequently host spirited discussions and strategy sessions with the region's most educated and prominent leaders at Alexandriana. These meetings were often held at a heavily shaded natural alcove that cradled a serene, bubbling, crystal clear spring just down the hill from his main house and very near where Independence Hill stands today. It was a colonial Curia, if you will, powered by McKnitt's homemade apple and peach brandy and famous corn liquor, which, according to one historian, was "hot enough to strangle an unwarned guest."

Craighead himself was perhaps the inspiration for these spring-side summits. He had a penchant for outdoor preaching (and revolution) and was close with the entire Alexander clan. At this secluded, picturesque spot, shaded from the suffocating Carolina heat, surely there were discussions about the major headlines of the day, things like the Boston Tea Party, the scuffle on Sugar Creek, the repressive Marriage and Vestry Acts, and the growing Regulator rebellion in North Carolina. So it makes perfect sense that the idea to formally declare independence from England was also likely inspired, debated, and formulated at this very place.

Which means the Alexandriana sign is accurate, and this is indeed sacred ground.

The spiritual birthplace of the MecDec.

Thinking out loud, I nervously blurt out to Pastor Todd how much I sort of love the idea that our country's creation may have partly been just an excuse for McKnitt and his buddies to sneak out of the house and get stran-gled on corn juice. Today we just call it Fantasy Football, I say with a laugh, before remembering that I'm currently speaking with a Southern Baptist preacher. After a long, awkward silence, Pastor Todd turns his back on me, and my fear is he's begun hastily locking up the cabinet, no longer interested in helping a degenerate like me find some mythical spring in the woods. He's not the only one. It seems like everyone else has pretty much given up on the Freedom Spring as well. "The famous 'Declaration Spring' where McKnitt and his compatriots often rendezvous, and it is said discussed the various phases of the Declaration before the convention in Charlotte, is now wholly obscured by dense underbrush deep in the ravine back behind the home," a nineteenth-century historian noted.

Before Pastor Todd sends me on my way, though, I at least want to con-fess, to someone, the deep significance of this Freedom Spring and why, at this stage of my quest, cannonballing into it would be transformative for both me and the story. "Imagine if it actually exists, though, right? I mean, like, holy cow," I stutter and stammer, pleading to Pastor Todd's back. In one long run-on sentence I explain that, to me, because McKnitt was the chief architect and eyewitness to it all, that makes Freedom Spring a bit like the holy grail of the MecDec: a physical validation and connection to the lit-eral and figurative wellspring of our freedom, independence, and patriotism.

"In my mind," I stammer, "it's, like, as close as we can get to the actual document . . . like standing among the Signers . . . like . . . like . . ."

At this point I'm just full-on blubbering when Pastor Todd slowly turns back around. Instead of cutting me off and locking up the cabinet, though, he's carefully reaching deep into the back, past an ancient, tattered Bible, to retrieve an antique, heavy pewter frame containing a grainy black-and-white photo from 1941 of an Independence Hill member being baptized . . . in a nearby spring.

"You mean this spring?" Pastor Todd says with a shrug so nonchalant that if I didn't know any better I'd swear this man of God was totally F'ing with me. Actually, his reaction makes it seem like he's been waiting years for someone from the MecDec world to finally come looking for the Freedom Spring.

But no one ever has.

"Yeah," he says, "I think I know where that is."

Stunned, relieved, and then so excited I have to resist the urge to sprint out of the church and into the nearest clump of woods to begin searching for the source. I practically yell, "Can you point me in the right direction?"

Pastor Todd exhales as if mentally clearing his afternoon schedule. Then he taps his phone and brings it to his ear. On the other end is the construction foreman from the massive apartment complex going up across the street who sounds like he's either a full-blown member of Independence Hill or, at the very least, an aspiring Baptist like me. The foreman puts us on hold for a hot second while he hollers at his sheetrock guy. Then, after some back and forth and assurances from Pastor Todd that we have the proper safety equipment, the foreman says, "Well, then, okay. Y'all come on over and have a look."

To this day, the Alexander family still gets the full rock star treatment from the Charlotte Museum of History. At the expansive, modern, glass rotunda–style museum just a few miles east of downtown Charlotte, the main attraction remains the 1774 Alexander Rock House. Built by Hezekiah Alexander (McKnitt's older brother and fellow MecDec Signer), this astonishing, expertly crafted five-thousand-square-foot mansion made from light brown and pinkish stones is, fittingly, the last remaining structure from the city's revolutionary history.

There are, of course, plenty of other interesting artifacts here. In a snarky tribute to Charlotte's revolutionary reputation, the entrance to the men's bathroom is marked by a life-sized portrait of King George III. In the courtyard behind the museum, a ginormous, 7.5-ton freedom bell (decorated with a tiny hornet) is proudly described as being four times bigger than Philadelphia's cute little Liberty Bell. But make no mistake, the stars of the show here are the Alexanders, one and all. An entire wall of the main exhibition space is taken up by a glass case featuring a collection of McKnitt's intricately engraved pistols and a long rifle. At the top of the lobby's grand staircase, the first thing you see is a pair of perfectly preserved Alexander family slippers. Outside, past the obnoxiously big bell, is a statue memorializing Hezekiah Alexander. Lately visitors have been shrieking and swooning at the square-jawed, ponytailed Scots-Irish pioneer in knee britches, mistaking him for Jamie, the hunky main character from the *Outlander* TV series.

For an extra eight bucks you can splurge on the VIP guided tour of Hezekiah's Rock House, conducted by a lovely local historian in cargo shorts and Asics who is overly fond of the Ben Stein/Ferris Bueller fill-in-the-blank tour guide style. "The most affluent feature on this house is the—anyone? Anyone? Offset indoor chimneys, yes. And the cash crop on Hezekiah's six hundred-acre plantation would have been—anyone? Anyone? Tobacco, yes. This is a plant known as Lamb's Ear that the Alexanders would have used for—anyone? Anyone? Toilet paper! These odd symbols carved into the home's two-foot-thick walls were probably put there by—anyone? Anyone? The Masons, yes!"

This goes on for what feels like hours until, finally, our guide blurts out his very own succinct and insightful description of the massive, wealthy, all-powerful Alexander clan.

"The Alexanders really were like their own Charlotte mafia," he says.

The comparison makes sense in more ways than one, and not all of them are good. An Alexander was a trustee on the original Charlotte town charter. And for decades afterward the family held the highest military ranks, filled the most powerful public offices, and served as the most influential judges and magistrates. During a 1779 trial in Mecklenburg County, four of the ten judges (and quite possibly the defendant) were Alexanders. This family had founders and elders in several churches, and Alexanders made up four of the fourteen original trustees for Queen's College, the first university south of Virginia. On top of all that, six of the MecDec Signers were Alexanders: McKnitt and Hezekiah; their cousins, Ezra Alexander and Abraham Alexander, a founder and elder at Craighead's Sugaw Creek Presbyterian Church; and their nephews Charles Alexander and Adam Alexander, who were both officers in the Revolutionary Army. After the war, the Alexanders ended up owning more than ten thousand acres near Charlotte, and McKnitt's will indicates that he had around half a million in cash (in today's economy) just laying around his estate when he died. At one point, the

Alexanders made up something like 20 percent of the town's population and probably had a hand in half its economy. They were even prominent enough to command a personal audience with George Washington, according to the first official history of Mecklenburg County, which was written by—yes, you guessed it—an Alexander.

As our tour guide points out, the Alexanders were also slave owners. At Hezekiah's Rock House home site and plantation there were twelve Alexanders and seventeen enslaved persons. Many of the Alexanders, Polks, and several other MecDec Signers also owned slaves. And as impossible as it is to understand, so did Reverend Craighead. In 1790, there were 1,608 enslaved people in Mecklenburg, which represented more than 10 percent of the county's population. At the time, most women, and other adults that did not own land, had next to no rights and no role in civic matters. So it's important to be clear that when the civic and religious leaders of Charlotte did first formally conjure the ideals of freedom and independence in America, they did so while purposefully excluding many people from sharing in the same God-given rights they had proclaimed for themselves.

A century earlier, in Ulster, Ireland, seven Alexander brothers, hoping to escape the famine and religious persecution that had overtaken the region in 1679, were preparing to set sail for America on the ship *Welcome*. On the eve of their departure, the Alex bros sent for their Presbyterian minister for a final blessing before the treacherous voyage. On his way to the ship, however, the priest was arrested and jailed. The historian Draper says that a respected old Alexander family matron commanded the brothers, "Gang ye away, take our minister out o' the gaol and take him, good soul, with us to Ameriky." Led by Joseph Alexander (McKnitt and Hezekiah's grandfather), the Alex bros armed themselves and hustled off the ship. They broke the priest out of jail, fought their way back onboard, and managed to set sail with their clerical castaway before royal authorities could blockade the ship.

Many of the Alexander descendants from that crew eventually settled on the eastern shore of Maryland, where Joseph's son James Alexander gobbled up massive real estate holdings in the tidewater area and as far south as the Carolina Piedmont. In 1754, James tabbed his son, the twenty-one-year-old John McKnitt Alexander, to move to Mecklenburg and take possession of the family's lands. The choice of McKnitt for this extreme adventure was no accident. One Charlotte historian described him as lean, stern, acorn-hard, and blessed with a preternatural abundance of the Alexander family traits of toughness and character.

A McKnitt descendant once told a Charlotte reporter that for centuries the Alexanders have had a "Three Day" rule about being spoiled or sick. In the Alexander family, after three days the choice is simple: "Get well or die." My other favorite Alexander descendant story comes from a friend of a friend who recalled being on a school field trip to the Alexander Rock House, where he tried to impress his middle school crush by telling her he was part of this powerful family. "Everyone in Charlotte is," was her cold-blooded reply. The best firsthand source on McKnitt has always been his grandson Dr. James Ramsey, a nineteenth-century historian of some repute and, for the record, an unapologetic, lifelong supporter of the Confederacy, to put it mildly. Ramsey idolized his grandpa, and he especially loved the idea that Southern men were the first to declare independence. (He named his Tennessee plantation "Mecklenburg.") In his massive autobiography Ramsey describes McKnitt as "self-reliant and energetic . . . a man of great public spirit and enterprise . . . [with] a vigorous intellect . . . and the most brilliant black eyes I have ever seen." When it came to his grandpa, Ramsey was absolutely certain of a few things: McKnitt was a true Founding Father as well as a ruggedly handsome man of the highest character, intellect, and physical strength. And, wouldn't you know it, Ramsey also believed himself to be an "exact facsimile" of his amazing grandpa. Go figure.

The truth is, McKnitt thrived on the frontier because as a young man he was a natural-born hustler. And I mean that in the highest sense of the word, the way kids use it today to show admiration for a resilient, shrewd entrepreneur. Self-educated and trained in Maryland as a weaver and tailor, when McKnitt landed in Charlotte, family records indicate he stitched and sold everything from linen nightgowns to buckskin breeches and nine-button mohair coats. "When the deer and the buffalo furnished not only viands for the table, but a portion of the apparel of the people, a leather-breeches maker was not probably a sufficiently profitable occupation for the enterprising young Marylander," Draper concludes. With nearly all the land in the region still unmapped and unsold, McKnitt keenly jumped from tailor to the far more lucrative profession of surveyor. As a side hustle during his wide travels mapping properties, McKnitt would collect food, tobacco, and various other hard-to-find products that he'd mark up and resell to his neighbors.

From what I can tell, though, McKnitt's first love, and his true gift, was always as a master distiller. It seems like every critical scene in Blythe's *Alexandriana* novel involves the most powerful men of the day deciding America's fate while sipping McKnitt's latest superb batch of whiskey. Other family members still have sales receipts for McKnitt's brandy and whiskey, and some of them are for more than five pounds (or roughly $250 in today's economy), which would have made him the colonial version of Pappy Van Winkle. Regardless of the cost, people came from all over Mecklenburg to imbibe in McKnitt's craft booze, which was so amazing (and potent) that it earned a unique claim to fame and its own place in history.

It was so good it helped start a revolution.

And as every serious bootlegger knows, McKnitt's secret ingredient was his water source, which just so happened to be Freedom Spring.

WEARING OUR MATCHING FLUORESCENT SAFETY VESTS, PASTOR TODD AND I begin making the trek through the massive construction site. It's an obstacle course of torn-up ground, twenty-foot-high stacks of prefab attic eaves, active cement trucks and backhoes beeping everywhere, garbage dumpsters and the endless *pop-pop-pop* of a hundred nail guns. After about a half mile of following the property's gradual downward slope, we reach the deserted northern end of the site that's bordered by a series of freshly built retaining walls and drainage ponds, all of it framed by long stretches of black silt fencing. Six months ago this was all thick, tall forest. Now, only a thin, bare minimum section of trees has been left standing to act as a natural buffer between the future tenants and a highway off-ramp.

Seeming a little disoriented, Pastor Todd stands at a dead end on top of a high embankment and stares intently down into the woods. Nearly seventy-five years ago, when Independence Hill regularly used Freedom Spring as its baptismal font, the church dug out and framed a small wading pool for submersion. And for several minutes, Pastor Todd silently surveys the woods for these remnants, searching back and forth like the captain of a ship leaning out over his bow, desperately looking for land.

My sense is he's feeling a little sad, or angry, seeing this once sacrosanct spot reduced to a parking lot and storm drainage for millennials.

Until finally he stops and points.

"Ha! There it is!" he shouts.

In a flash, I'm surfing down the loose embankment, hand over fist, up to my waist in dirt, dust, and brambles. When I approach an orange plastic construction fence marked with numerous warnings, I realize Pastor Todd is still right beside me and now, just as I predicted, my partner in crime. While we game-plan how to manage the fence, the initial wave of joy and excitement is replaced by a strange and suddenly overwhelming sense of urgency to get to the small, reflective brook just thirty feet away.

I want to fly there in one giant leap, like in a dream.

Because, at this distance, John McKnitt Alexander's Freedom Spring—the actual wellspring of our country's patriotism and independence—appears to still be alive and flowing.

But just barely.

Feeling the same way, Pastor Todd simply stomps on the waist-high plastic construction fence with his foot and waves me onward like an usher. As we approach through the thick woods, the spring looks more like a small mud puddle. It's underwhelming and sad, at first, like finding sections of the actual Berlin Wall behind the urinals at the Main Street Station Casino in Las Vegas. (True story.) Just below the spring, though, I see the remnants of the wood-framed baptism reservoir. It's about five feet wide and fifteen feet long, with steps on one end, and must be about four feet deep. For safety's sake, it looks like someone years ago tried to cover it with a chain link fence that has been pulled back to reveal the tank is mostly full of sediment and leaves.

Now at the spring's edge, as soon as I stand still the sound of bubbling water tickles my ears.

I exhale and chuckle in disbelief.

We found it. We actually found it. Incredible.

When I look up, I'm shocked to realize that we're at least one hundred feet practically straight down from the top of the ravine. As soon as the natural secret-alcove features of this place begin to take shape, it becomes easy to picture McKnitt and the rest of the MecDec brain trust gathered around here, sitting on log benches, cups in hand, in the middle of some spirited debate about how best to proclaim our independence.

Without thinking, I drop to my knees at the water's edge and reach into the crystal-clear pool. I cup a tiny amount of water from the Freedom Spring in my palm. As the liquid leaks through my fingers, I realize I don't really have anything clever or meaningful prepared for this moment. The old-timers in Charlotte are fond of the Revolutionary-era toast of "Huzzah!" Instead, I just kind of salute the spring with my hand and then repeat what I think is the most important revolutionary phrase from the MecDec.

It's something the Freedom Spring crew probably first uttered and toasted to right here at this exact spot 245 years ago, as tensions with England escalated beyond repair.

"Free and independent," I whisper before taking a tiny sip of the water.

Good lord. This is completely nuts.

I've just shared a drink with our Founding Fathers.

Well, that, or I've just given myself a historic case of Alexandiarrhea.

JUST FIFTEEN YEARS AFTER ARRIVING AT THE EDGE OF CIVILIZATION, Mc-Knitt Alexander had become one of the largest landowners and most influential leaders in the region. That success paved the way for multitudes of Alexanders to migrate south and join forces to become Charlotte's first family. And as his extended family and wealth grew, McKnitt's estate at Alexandriana grew along with it. Described as "princely," Alexandriana had expanded to more than one thousand acres with several buildings decorated with the finest furnishings, like a Queen Ann–style parlor table; expensive, hand-crafted clocks from William Gillespie of Pennsylvania; and a burgeoning library. "[McKnitt] was exceedingly fond of books," wrote his grandson, and he "read early and late with intense avidity." Syfert, the Charlotte author and bike tour guide, notes that McKnitt would sign each book on the top right inside corner using his customary *JMkAlexander* signature, under-lined with an elegant flourish in a style reminiscent of John Hancock. It's a fitting comparison for the ultimate self-made man like McKnitt, who by the early 1770s had transformed himself into Mecklenburg's most ardent patriot and sought-after statesman.

I realize that because I'm so fond of the colorful, quick-tempered, and hard-nosed Scots-Irish frontiersman stereotype (I guess it's the former D1 college wrestler in me), it would be easy to assume that the MecDec was cre-ated on some crazy whim by a gang of impulsive, uninformed backwoods-men. And the perfect storm that created the MecDec did, certainly, contain more than a few of these colorful (and awesome) personalities. Remarkably, though, the gatherings at Alexandriana's Freedom Spring, where the Mec-Dec was first conceived, would have much more closely resembled a Prince-ton reunion.

In the 1960s, noted MecDec author V. V. McNitt concluded that these early summits would have included Abraham and Hezekiah Alexander along with Craighead, whom the author called "one of the most militant ministers of the colonial period, [a man] still revered for his leadership in re-ligion, education and the crusade for liberty." (My guess is that before Craig-head fell ill it was probably hard for anyone to get a word in edgewise at the spring. More time to drink, at least.) Even though Craighead was educated by his father, based on his theological leanings in the 1760s, he could have easily passed for a Princeton man. Although he eventually found it not quite radical enough for his tastes, Craighead had been, for a time, a member of the New Light Presbyterians—the same slightly more modern and open wing of Presbyterianism that was all the rage at Princeton.

So it's no coincidence, really, that McKnitt was later joined at the Free-dom Spring by Princeton alums and fellow MecDecers Hezekiah Balch (class of 1766), Dr. Ephraim Brevard (class of 1768), Thomas Reese (class of 1768), the son of Signer David Reese, and Waightstill Avery (class of 1766). Years later, both McKnitt's son, Joseph, and Craighead's son, Thomas, would also attend Princeton.

At Princeton, Balch was a founder of the Cliosophic Society, America's oldest (and still functioning) college debate and political club that was also an early training ground for James Madison and Aaron Burr. A "tall, handsome young man with fair hair which he wore long and curling," Balch understood, firsthand, the fury and frustration created by the Marriage and Vestry Acts. At the ripe old age of twenty-three he was ordained as the minister at both Rocky River and Poplar Tent churches in Mecklenburg County. First, though, he had to survive the scandal of censure for having his marriage performed by a minister from the Church of England. The Presbytery forgave Balch, eventually. In the written history of the Rocky River Church, though, the incident reads like something straight out of *The Handmaid's Tale*. In the text, church historians actually refer to Balch's better half as "the wife thus acquired under such allegedly reprehensible circumstances [who] bore the given name of Martha."

Balch's classmate Reese also earned a doctorate in divinity from Princeton in 1794 and was the longtime pastor of Salem Presbyterian in South Carolina. During his time in Mecklenburg, though, author V. V. McNitt says Reese was "active in indignation meetings in Mecklenburg County before May 1775 and wrote papers so influential in rousing public opinion [about independence] they were remembered as late as 1830."

Meanwhile, Ephraim Brevard and his seven brothers grew up in Cecil County, Maryland, near the original Alexander clan. (All eight Brevard brothers would serve in the Revolutionary War.) "John Brevard, the father, was a distinguished man—a Christian and a patriot," the Reverend Charles Sommerville wrote in the history of Hopewell Presbyterian Church. "His home was noted for its culture and its piety." Ephraim was three when his family moved to North Carolina. A few years later, he and his little sister were watching a neighbor burn off an old field when the roaring flames shifted suddenly, and Rebecca's clothes caught fire. Ephraim was able to save his sister, but flaming debris blinded him in one eye during the rescue. Despite the injury, Brevard excelled in school and graduated from Princeton in 1768. "He was a man of undoubted genius and talent . . . an exalted patriot," concluded Draper. After teaching school in Maryland, Brevard became a surgeon, studying medicine under fellow Princeton grad and well-known historian and independence advocate Dr. David Ramsay. "It was easy to see the source, in these schools and teachers, of the principles Ephraim Brevard stood for and [would later write] in the famous Declaration of May 20, 1775," reads the history of Hopewell Church.

It was the same with Waightstill Avery.

A Latin Salutatorian at Princeton (which, I should point out, was actually called Nassau Hall at the time), he roomed with Oliver Ellsworth, the future chief justice of the Supreme Court. Avery himself went on to become North Carolina's first attorney general and a renowned attorney and political scholar in his own right. According to nineteenth-century historians in Chapel Hill, he was "the patriarch of the North Carolina bar, an exemplary Christian, a pure patriot, and an honest man." In one of his early, prescient treatises against the Crown, Avery used the phrase "natural and inalienable rights," which would show up again in a famous document, or two.

He was also a frequent couch surfer at Hezekiah Alexander's Rock House, where a re-creation of his Murphy bed remains right at the top of the stairs. Avery and the Alex bros must have hit it off right away. In Avery's diary from 1769, he notes that Hezekiah only charged him twelve pounds for eight months' rent. Of this match made in MecDec heaven, the *North Carolina University Magazine* surmised that Avery "could not probably have found upon the face of the earth, a home and a people more entirely congenial to him, and those who desire to understand, why the earliest movements in favor of American Independence were made in Mecklenburg, may well examine the . . . peculiar character of the people with whom he was about to unite his destinies."

Avery's diary is an absolute trip and includes what I think might be the first-ever play-by-play breakdown of a barroom brawl.

Making his way toward Charlotte on February 22, 1769, Avery had stopped at a friend's home near Hillsborough to eat and rest when all hell broke loose.

"I soon perceived the neighbor drunk," he penned. "And there being but one room in the house, he reel'd and staggered from side to side thro' it, tumbling over stools and tables. He was soon accompanied in the staggering scheme by the landlord and travelers who all blunder'd, bawl'd, spew'd and curs'd, and broke one another's heads and their own shins, with stools and bruised their hips and ribs with sticks of the couch pens, pulled hair, lugg'd, hallo'd, swore, fought and kept up the Roar-Rororum till morning. Thus I watched carefully all night, to keep them from falling over and spewing upon me. Without shutting my eyes to sleep, I set out at day-break, happy that I had escaped."

If you can't tell, Avery had what one historian described as a "quick wit and a sharp tongue" and a habit, he once confessed to a family member, of being "more sarcastic, perhaps, than the occasion warranted." It was an affliction that nearly cost him his life.

Later in his career, while appearing in the district court of western North Carolina, when faced with a legal challenge, Avery loved to make a show of announcing that he was going to "refer to Bacon" before reaching into his saddlebag and pulling out Matthew Bacon's highly regarded legal textbook *New Abridgment of the Law*. Now, according to one version of the legend, before arguing against Avery in court, a young, hotheaded lawyer (and future president) named Andy Jackson thought it would be funny to secretly replace Bacon's book with an actual hunk of bacon. (And he was right; it was pure genius.) An embarrassed Avery blasted Jackson for his unrefined courtroom behavior and, for good measure, also ridiculed his poor understanding of the law. Jackson responded the way he seemingly responded to even the tiniest perceived slight when he was young and insecure: by challenging Avery to a gun duel. (It was the first of many duels for the short-fused, Scots-Irish future president.)

When no immediate reply from Avery was forthcoming, Jackson took the odd extra step of submitting his request for a duel to the death . . . in writing. *Sir: When a man's feelings and character are injured he ought to seek a speedy redress; you received a few lines from me yesterday and undoubtedly you understand me.* Avery must have known Jackson was serious because in Jackson's note, which is on display at the North Carolina Museum of History, he demands that Avery skip dinner to meet him for their pistol fight.

After court that day the two men met at a ravine next to the Jonesborough Court House. There are, of course, several versions of what happened next. Avery's granddaughter, Mary Avery Chambers, believed Jackson immediately fired first and nicked Avery in the ear. The older, wiser Avery then deliberately discharged his pistol into the air, walked over to Jackson, and gave him some fatherly counsel on the dangers of pride and temper before the men shook hands and parted as friends.

Now, keep in mind this is the granddaughter's version of events, but years later when Waightstill Avery's nephew John Avery of Owego, New York, called on Jackson at the White House for a political favor, upon hearing the last name Avery the president stopped cold in his tracks.

"Did you know your uncle and I once had a duel?" Jackson exclaimed. "We did fight and your uncle delivered me a lecture which caused me to esteem and reverence him more than any man I ever knew; and I have ever cherished the highest regard for him."

WE SHOULD ALL DO THE SAME, REALLY, BECAUSE IT WAS AVERY AND THE rest of his Princeton classmates gathered at Alexandriana's Freedom Spring who would become the brain trust and catalyst behind the MecDec. This collection of theologians, lawyers, scholars, patriots, and, yes, hotheads, would have rivaled any similar type of intellectual gathering in pre-Revolutionary America, including Philadelphia. There was a kind of Dream Team aspect to the MecDec Signers, according to Draper, who believed the Mecklenburg Declaration to be a uniquely American-style, brains and brawn mixture of the "classical attainments" of Brevard, Avery, and Balch and the "native enthusiasm of Thomas Polk."

The free-flowing whiskey at the Freedom Spring probably had something to do with it as well. In the buildup to independence, at McKnitt's Freedom Spring there was never a shortage of topics to debate, actions to ponder, or corn liquor to share.

"[They] drank brandy near the spring at McKnitt's home and asked one another: *What is to be done?*" wrote Syfert. "Hard choices faced them on every side."

At Freedom Spring, and from every pulpit he could reach, Craighead had railed against the English Crown's dreadful Marriage and Vestry Acts, and the Sugar Creek War in 1765 was a direct result of Craighead's spiritual handiwork. By the late 1760s, though, these kinds of skirmishes had become so common in Carolina that the Crown felt compelled to institute the Riot Act, which treated rural uprisings like full-blown insurrections, punishable by death.

At this point there was little else to threaten the colonists with. North Carolina had suffered through several droughts, which led to failed crops, widespread poverty, and rampant disillusionment. All the while, taxes, fees, and tensions continued to rise, unabated. The Stamp Act was a disaster. But still needing to pay its massive war debts, England felt perfectly justified in piling taxes onto Americans wherever it could. There were fees to get married, fees to draw up a will, fees to ship items, and, probably, fees to create fees—all of which folks in Carolina may have tolerated.

But then, several layers of taxes drove the price of imported rum to nearly twenty shillings a gallon.

I'm guessing that was the last straw.

After losing everything, including the chance to drown their sorrows in rum, a few thousand destitute colonists joined forces in the Carolina back-country. Known as the Regulators, the colonists around Hillsborough, North Carolina, about one hundred miles northeast of Charlotte, began to fight back against royal Governor William Tryon and his shady secretary, Edmund Fanning. By the summer of 1768 the Regulators' numbers had grown to more than three thousand men, and they were now threatening to attack the courthouse in Hillsborough.

Tryon called on the powerful Polk and begged him to bring the Mecklenburg militia to help thwart the angry farmers. The always-shrewd Polk agreed, but on two conditions: he wanted the Marriage and Vestry Acts rescinded, and he wanted the Crown's approval for a new college in Charlotte. Going back to the very founding of Charlotte, nobody could work an angle like Polk, and he would have known that religious freedom and educational opportunity were two of the most important things to his neighbors. Lawful Presbyterian marriages would mean local children would not burn in hell or be denied their legal inheritance. And at the time, a college instantly conveyed status and respect on a colonial town.

The shrewd Polk must have known he had Tryon over a barrel, because he pretty much asked for the moon—and got it. Or so he thought. Polk's militia helped quell the Regulators (for the time being), and in 1770 Tryon approved an act that allowed Presbyterian ministers to perform marriages and another for the "founding, establishing, and endowing of Queen's College, in the Town of Charlotte in Mecklenburg County . . . as near as may be agreeable to the laws & customs of the Universities of Oxford & Cambridge or those of the Colleges of America." The decrees were provisional, however, pending the approval of London's Board of Trade and, ultimately, the King. With Tryon's backing, though, they seemed like practically a done deal.

As a result, the spring 1771 wedding season in Mecklenburg must have been the greatest in history. We're talking, like, in your mid-twenties, five-years-after-college-epic-weddings-every-weekend kind of great. And if there was one thing the Scots-Irish knew how to do besides fight, it was throw a party. Most weddings featured ungodly amounts of whiskey drinking, gunfire, wrestling, and a game on horseback called gander pulling, which, well . . . I looked it up, and let's just say it will haunt my dreams forever.

It was also immediately clear just how proud, excited, and hopeful the town leaders in Charlotte and at the Freedom Spring were about the possibility of Queen's College and the thought of higher education for their kids. Polk, Avery, McKnitt, and Abraham and Hezekiah Alexander were all named college trustees. Joseph Alexander and Brevard were tabbed as professors. Avery donated a collection of thirty-five volumes of books he titled "Mecklenburg Library." Queen's opened in 1771 in a building erected by Polk—on what is the current southeast corner of South Tryon and Third Street in downtown Charlotte—and it operated in collegial bliss for the next two years while awaiting final approval from the Crown.

In the meantime, the Regulator rebellion in North Carolina had gotten totally out of hand. When the group's civil protests against corruption and oppression were met with (what else) condescension and indifference, the frustrated Regulators became increasingly violent. In May 1771, a full four years before Lexington and Concord, the conflict escalated into the Battle of Alamance, which is sometimes referred to as the "first" battle of the American Revolution. Yes, they like their "firsts" in Carolina, but the Regulator rebellion is another key moment in the constant escalation of hostilities from 1765–1775 that ultimately led to the creation of the MecDec. It's fair to wonder why in the world the leaders in the remote village of Charlotte would be the first patriots to take the bold step of formally declaring independence. Until you realize that with the religious persecution, the taxation, an impending, indefensible double-cross by the Crown, and especially the Regulator rebellion, these men were pretty much already at war, fighting for their freedom and their very survival.

All of this must have spawned some lively debates at Freedom Spring. In 1768 Polk's militia had backed Tryon, but since then the relationship between the Crown and the Carolinas had fractured beyond repair. In a 1769 petition, Avery railed against the Marriage Acts by not-so-subtly reminding the King that "there are about one thousand freemen of us, who hold to the established Church of Scotland, able to bear arms in the County of Mecklenburg." Complicating matters further were reports about a group of men from Rocky River and Sugaw Creek churches who had disguised their faces with black soot and blown up several wagonloads of British gunpowder and ammunition intended to be used on the Regulators. I'm sure it was just a coincidence but one of the ambushes of the British supply chain just happened to take place on the plantation of John Phifer, a future MecDec Signer.

A few weeks later in Alamance, Tryon's troops cut down the overmatched Regulators with relative ease and took fourteen prisoners. Tryon offered to pardon anyone who would swear allegiance to the Crown. Eventually, twelve Regulators were found guilty of treason and condemned, and six were ultimately hanged. Even with a noose around his neck, Regulator leader James Pugh tried one last time to simply address his grievances against the governor. As he began listing the misdeeds, Fanning, the secretary, gave the order for the barrel to be kicked out from under his feet.

Before his final breath Pugh prophesied that his death "would be as good seed sown on good ground, which would produce a hundredfold."

He was wrong, of course.

In a few years, not hundreds but *thousands* of North Carolinians would be the first to declare and then fight for their freedom from Tryon's England.

For the MecDec men of Freedom Spring, the final breaking point came in June 1773.

Although it was decreed in 1772, word didn't reach North Carolina until the next year that King George III had ruled on Polk and Tryon's supposed deal. His Majesty's decision? Thumbs down. On all counts. KG3 said "No" to revoking the despised Marriage and Vestry Acts and probably "Hell no" to the idea of a bunch of rabble-rousing Presbyterians in Carolina starting their own college.

"We don't have any record of Polk's reaction on receiving the news," Syfert writes. "But we can guess."

Oh, I'm almost certain that once he realized Tryon and King George III had played him, there could have only been one thing on Polk's mind.

Revolution.

And the otherwise dignified and noble men of higher learning gathered at the Freedom Spring? They were right there with him.

"The seeds of revolution were sown in Mecklenburg by the . . . repeal of the charter of Queen's College," historians at the University of North Carolina concluded in 1855.

The double-cross by the Crown was a devastating, humiliating gut punch delivered to a proud, patriotic, and united pack of Scots-Irish men in Charlotte who simply knew no other way but to hit back and hit back hard. In rapid succession after the Queen's College fiasco in 1773, news arrived in Charlotte of the Boston Tea Party and of Parliament declaring the Massachusetts colony in "actual rebellion" before making good on its threat of using force to restore order in Boston. Shortly thereafter, British warships blockaded the port and redcoats occupied Boston, which was now under British martial law. Tales of the extreme suffering and starvation in Boston quickly spread throughout the colonies. Meant to be a warning, instead, Boston became a symbol and a rallying cry that bonded all of the colonies—especially the Carolinas.

Summing up the incendiary atmosphere of June 1775 in a series of editorials, the *South Carolina and American General Gazette* wrote:

> One general fact runs through all the colonies from Boston to Charlestown, which is that of resistance; the spirit of opposing the pretensions of the mother country is uniform through them all. . . . The cause of America [has] now become so serious that every American considers it as a struggle from which they shall obtain a release by an ample redress of their grievances, or a redress by the sword. The only alternative which every American thinks of is Liberty or Death.

Once you consider the perfect storm of myriad, escalating circumstances that had been brewing in the region since Craighead arrived, as well as the background, education, and temperament of the leaders who founded Charlotte—men like Polk, Avery, Brevard, and the Alexanders ad infinitum—the idea that this group would take the bold, dangerous (but scholarly) step of formally declaring their independence in writing doesn't seem incredible at all. It seems inevitable.

In fact, it would have been far stranger and much more out of character if the Founding Fathers of Charlotte had decided to bite their tongues, politely bide their time, and wait for others to sort this whole mess out. That just wasn't who these men were. These particular patriots in Charlotte, for better or worse, were simply incapable of inaction or subservience. "Politicians would have recommended forbearance, and pointed to some future and more propitious period for action," surmised one nineteenth-century author. "But in the simplicity of their hearts [the MecDec men] appealed to the law of nature indelibly stamped upon the human bosom that when power becomes tyranny, resistance is a duty and the God of battles must decide." I mean, Avery, for one, was perfectly willing to kill a future president for simply replacing his favorite law textbook with nature's most salty and delicious add-on item. So what do you think he was prepared to do to a king and his corrupt representatives who had condemned his religion, taxed his neighbors into starvation, hung his friends, and robbed his children of a shot at both college and heaven?

By the spring of 1775, powerbrokers in England like Lord Dartmouth already considered the American colonies to be in a "state of general frenzy." And in the fall of 1775, George III would declare before Parliament that America was in "open and avowed rebellion." After generations of tyranny dating back to the Scottish Lowlands and the Ulster Plantation, after the Regulator rebellion, the Queen's College/Vestry Act double-cross, and the military occupation of Boston, on April 7, 1775, the royal governor of North Carolina just flat-out dissolved the state's General Assembly.

For a decade, the Scots-Irish patriots in Charlotte had been pushed into a corner by the Crown. At long last it was time to push back.

"John McKnitt Alexander and men of his kin, Dr. Ephraim Brevard, Waightstill Avery, the Rev. Hezekiah James Balch, the Rev. Thomas Reese, and others living nearer, were apt to gather at the spring on warm days and consider the alarming state of affairs," wrote Massachusetts newspaper editor V. V. McNitt in his seminal 1960 work *Chain of Error and the Mecklenburg Declaration of Independence*. "They worried over reports that Boston was short of food in consequence of English occupation, and talked of plans to send a hundred beef cattle. They hadn't liked the Boston Massacre, or the closing of the port. The story of the Tea Party had interested them. Mostly, they talked of independence. Eventually, it was decided at one of the gatherings [at the spring] to hold a county convention, and to ask Colonel Polk to have two delegates selected from each of the Mecklenburg militia companies. These men, and a few others . . . were to convene in [Charlotte's] log courthouse."

A date was set and a summons from Polk was soon dispatched to each militia captain throughout Mecklenburg County ordering them to elect, or appoint, two representatives to attend an emergency convention on May 19, 1775, in Charlotte.

The American spring of independence was about to flow forth from the Freedom Spring of Alexandriana.

Six

First to Freedom

THE HISTORIC EVENT BEGAN JUST AFTER SUNRISE, IN THE COOL, QUIET morning of Friday, May 19, 1775. Out on the rolling hills at the edge of Alexandriana, a solitary John McKnitt Alexander turned his horse south onto a narrow dirt trail for the nine-mile journey to the courthouse in Charlotte. All over the region the scene at Alexandriana repeated itself as duty-bound leaders from across Mecklenburg County honored the summons from Polk with their own pilgrimage to Charlotte's courthouse.

Constructed in 1768 and located at the exact epicenter of town, the courthouse was a rugged, log cabin–style rectangular structure, roughly eighty by forty feet and perfectly described by a visitor as being, well, "tolerable." (Not bad, really, especially if you remember how the always-hustling Polk threw it together in a sneaky, successful ploy to keep Charlotte's designation as the county seat.) Polk built it on top of ten-foot pillars, and the area underneath had become an open-air market and horse parking lot. Primitive as it was, it was still the commercial and governmental center of the county and the Carolina frontier. The courthouse was the mustering point for the militia, and all legal notices were nailed to the front door, as was the occasional wolf pelt for bounty-seeking hunters. Besides the smell of livestock from the open market underneath, the building's one true defining characteristic was a classic, Southern petticoat–style double staircase that led to an elevated speaking platform just outside the entrance to the court.

On the morning of May 19, 1775, as word of the impending convention spread, this natural gathering spot at the foot of the courthouse steps was buzzing with excitement and crowded with supporters, bystanders, and the steady arrival of a who's who of Mecklenburg's finest—a group that was about to make history.

"In recounting the causes, the origin, and the progress of our Revolutionary struggle," stated an 1831 government report on the MecDec, "whatever the brilliant achievements of other States may have been, let it never be forgotten that at a period of darkness and oppression, without concert with others, without assurances of support from any quarter, a few gallant North Carolinians, all fear of consequences lost in a sense of their country's wrongs, relying, under Heaven, solely upon themselves, nobly dared to assert, and resolved to maintain . . . independence, of which, whoever might have thought, none had then spoken; and thus earned for themselves, and for their fellow citizens of North Carolina, the honor of giving birth to the first Declaration of Independence."

Of the twenty-seven men who attended the convention, Polk and Brevard were likely the first to arrive since they both lived just across the street from the courthouse. Hezekiah Alexander and Avery probably rode in together from the Rock House roughly five miles east of town. Attorney William Kennon had come in all the way from Salisbury. A bit of an outcast as an Anglican, Kennon was nevertheless a vocal critic of the Stamp Act and the tea tax. He was joined inside the courthouse by land barons, magistrates, militia officers, farmers, merchants, college grads, a surgeon, and a minister. (There was also a traitor in their midst.)

There were class distinctions in Charlotte at the time, of course. Only white male landowners were summoned to the courthouse. But one of the unique factors that made the MecDec possible only at such a time, and at such a place, was that the far more rigidly defined class distinctions in Pennsylvania and Virginia had not yet reached the Carolina frontier. And so, among those privileged enough to be invited, each attendee was afforded an equal voice in the process of creating the MecDec, regardless of education, wealth, or status.

With the exception of Kennon, the Anglican, a Swiss descendant, and an attendee with ancestral ties to the French Huguenots, the rest of our true Founding Fathers were all Scots-Irish Presbyterians. Along with the Alexanders and the Freedom Spring crew, the most influential group inside the courthouse was the Craighead Caucus made up of nine Presbyterian church elders, all of them spiritual disciples of Alexander Craighead. Even though Craighead had died in 1766, there's no doubt about his direct influence on the events of May 1775 inside the Charlotte courthouse. The *History of Mecklenburg County* "attributes the zeal and undaunted courage of these men, and others like them, from the Sugaw Creek congregation, who labored so earnestly for freedom and who fought so valiantly in its cause, to the teaching of Alexander Craighead, though he had been dead for nine years." Centuries after the MecDec's creation, Craighead was still being celebrated in sermons by Billy Graham and other preachers as "that illustrious hero [who was the reason] that Charlotte occupied the front rank more than a year in advance of Philadelphia, on May 20, 1775, declaring independence so Mecklenburg became the leader of the land." The *Charlotte Observer* says that "Craighead should have been there that morning when they signed the Mecklenburg Declaration. He should have been the first signer. And in a way, he was."

Friday would have been a day of fasting for devout Presbyterians at the time, so most of the attendees, including Abraham Alexander, David Reese, John Davidson, McKnitt, and Balch, would have been among the last to arrive and the most ravenous for action after attending morning services that reaffirmed and reignited their solemn commitment to keeping God above any and all earthly kings or governments.

"Besides the two persons elected from each militia company [usually called Committee-men] a much larger number of citizens attended in Charlotte than at any former meeting—perhaps half the men in the [area]," recalled one of several MecDec eyewitnesses, General Joseph Graham. An American hero from the Revolutionary War who nearly died defending Charlotte during Cornwallis's attack, Graham had a gift for leading men in battle—and for understatement.

As proof, on the morning of May 19, 1775, in Charlotte, Graham described the mood thusly: "There appeared among the people much excitement."

I learned firsthand of Graham's amazing account, and just about everything else that transpired over the next forty-eight hours in Charlotte, thanks to several long but invigorating days buried deep inside the Southern Historical Collection archives at the University of North Carolina's Wilson Library. It took months to secure a spot inside Wilson, a process that included several formal written requests, two Zoom interviews about protocols, several days scouring the extensive research catalog, and, of course, the most exhausting, mentally challenging obstacle of all: finding a (legal) parking spot anywhere near the Bell Tower in Chapel Hill.

But it would all turn out to be worth it. And then some.

Really, the biggest problem for me was that I arrived on an absolutely picture-perfect fall day, the kind of day where the last place on earth you want to be is stuck inside a dusty, windowless archive chopping it up with a bunch of librarians. The quad in front of Wilson was domed by one of those endless Carolina blue skies. Framed by trees exploding with color, every available inch of grass was filled with students warming themselves in the sun and feasting on food truck fare while contemplating life's great mysteries. Standing at the foot of the library, in fact, was a pale, bearded philosophy student holding a sign that asked: *Do humans possess an immaterial soul?* I was probably just looking for an excuse to delay entering the archives, but the question stopped me in my tracks. And after a minute or two, I confessed to the kid that I was actually experiencing, in real time, the answer to his existential riddle. Do our souls exist apart from our physical bodies? Well, they must, I explained. Because at this very moment while my entire being wants to grab a taco and take a nap out on the sun-baked UNC quad, my brain, on the other hand, knows all too well that I should probably just keep moving toward the stately, monument-style steps of Wilson Library.

Atop those steps, past the marble-columned, Smithsonian-style entryway, a security guard ordered me, like a kindergarten teacher, to wash my hands with soap and water before entering the special collections room. The hallway to the bathroom is lined with massive, ornately framed portraits of every UNC chancellor, and as I slinked off to the john, I swear I felt the eyes of those berobed academic titans judging me and my apparently filthy hands. At the entrance to the archives I was stopped, again, for more instructions and told to store all my stuff in a locker that would be subject to search upon my exit. Finally, the archivist, who couldn't have been more pleasant or helpful, escorted me across a stately reading room and past more oil paintings and glimmering chandeliers to a large, glass-topped mahogany table.

Next to the table stood a blue metal book-shelving cart fully loaded with what I recognized as my requested items. There were old books and manuscripts, reels of microfilm, letters from presidents, family scrapbooks and genealogies, and endless folders of yellowing newspaper clippings and manuscript pages. Over the next few days, I would eventually get to them all during several marathon sessions in which the hours blurred together and blinked by. At the end of one particularly long stretch, I was so deep in thought down a rabbit hole from 185 years ago—stretching across the globe and into the depths of the Office of British Records in London—that the archivist had to wave gently in my field of vision, like she was waking a sleepwalker, to politely tell me it was well past time for me to get the hell out. She then apologized for the loud student protest that had gone on most of the afternoon across the street at the Bell Tower, and I pretended to know what she was talking about but, truthfully, I had been so absorbed in all this incredible MecDec stuff that I hadn't heard a word.

"I'm sure this place is totally haunted, but can I just spend the night in here?" I begged.

That made her laugh, which, if you know any archivists, is kind of a monumental accomplishment in and of itself. I wasn't joking, though. I needed the extra time after spending the entire first day completely geeking out over a single gray cardboard box/time machine labeled: *MECKLENBURG DECLARATION OF INDEPENDENCE PAPERS.*

Inside was sworn testimony on the events of May 1775 from more than a dozen eyewitnesses. But not just any old random, no-name onlookers. The MecDec Papers include detailed affidavits from a large group of men with what I would consider unimpeachable character: a governor, a judge, attorneys, ministers, scholars, businessmen, and decorated military veterans of every rank, all the way up to general. Several of the witnesses, like

Humphrey Hunter, had earned more than one of these titles. Taken prisoner after the Battle of Camden during the Revolution, Hunter survived to become a Presbyterian minister as well as a highly respected historian and author. His detailed account of the catastrophe at Camden remains an oft-quoted resource of historians and scholars to this day.

Still, for me, one of the most heart-stopping moments of this entire quest came while reading the MecDec testimony of Major John Davidson. It wasn't until I was done obsessing over this powerful affidavit and was carefully refiling it in its gray cardboard box when I caught a glimpse of the dateline: Beaver Dam Plantation.

What?

When I read that, I swear, the hair on the back of my neck stood up, and the feeling that I was being watched inside the archives was so strong it spun me around in my seat like there was a spider on my back. Beaver Dam is two freakin' minutes from my house and still operates as a small scenic park and party facility we have frequented often over the years. I don't know exactly how to best describe this incredible moment of discovery and coincidence—or fate. Imagine: deciding to do a book about searching for the Holy Grail and realizing halfway through that it was buried in your neighbor's backyard . . . where a few summers ago during an oyster roast you did tequila shots and tried to form an old-person mosh pit during a cover of "Sweet Child O' Mine."

Anyway, I had seen Davidson and Hunter's incredible accounts (and many others) referenced before in countless books and articles, but somehow the visceral experience of holding the evidence in my hands elevated these words to gospel. Not just because of the quality of the witnesses but the realization that they were collected independently and at a time when these people would have had virtually no way of communicating with each other to compare notes or corroborate their stories. Yet they all match the written records and are all unfailingly consistent on the details of that historic day. What's more, some of the most detailed and thorough testimony surrounding the creation of the MecDec is from Graham and Hunter, two war heroes and highly respected civic leaders whose other accounts of the Revolutionary War are considered the gold standard of historic annotation.

Put it this way: if the MecDec were ever put on trial, it would have more than a dozen of the best possible witnesses available—men who had lived their lives sworn to a higher truth by their trade, their faith, their honor, or often all three. And any prosecutor dumb enough to attack the document would have to base their entire case on the notion that the same selfless veterans who risked their lives to establish our freedoms turned around a few years later and perjured themselves while coordinating with judges, priests, and the actual governor of North Carolina to manufacture a massive hoax for their own self-aggrandizement.

"The combined testimony of all these individuals prove the existence of the Mecklenburg Declaration, and all the circumstances connected with it, as fully and clearly as any fact can be shown by human testimony," North Carolina Governor Montford Stokes wrote in the state's official 1831 report. "It is not hazarding too much to say, that there is no one event of the Revolution which has been, or can be more fully or clearly authenticated."

Inside Wilson, the mystery behind why the MecDec has remained such a mystery only deepens. It's such an important, inspirational document, and there's so much proof. Yet it remains largely unknown, which strikes me as someone in this day and age having to go on some epic quest to discover the first, true patriotic protest known as the Boston Tea Party. I had barely recovered from poring over these testimonials when I pulled out another folder and suddenly realized I had something even more sacred in my hands: the torn, tattered, and yellowing pages of actual MecDec meeting notes and recollections, handwritten and signed by none other than John McKnitt Alexander himself. Usually referred to as McKnitt's "Rough Notes," for centuries these pages have been the Rosetta Stone for MecDec researchers and enthusiasts.

Even though they're sealed inside protective coverings, the MecDec Papers look and feel like old tissue-thin treasure maps that might disintegrate in your hands. It's a truly surreal sensation holding something so weathered and frail that still contains such power and significance. According to McKnitt's own preserved words, the men who had arrived at the courthouse that morning were "clothed with ample powers to devise ways and means to extricate themselves and ward off the dreadful impending storm bursting on them by the British Nation."

SEVERAL OTHER WITNESSES ALSO NOTED THAT THERE WAS SOMETHING DE-cidedly electric in the air on May 19, 1775, in Charlotte and that the timing of the meeting felt almost preordained. Just moments after the entire group was assembled and called to order inside the crowded courthouse, in fact, a roar went up out on the street below when an express rider raced into town with urgent news from Lexington and Concord.

"To all friends of American Liberty!" is how most of the dispatches from Massachusetts began.

Because it is so central to the MecDec story, the exact timing of the express rider's arrival in Charlotte was painstakingly authenticated decades ago by the University of North Carolina's Archibald Henderson, a prominent historian and biographer with his own folder at the Wilson archives. Without knowing it Henderson also uncovered the earliest-known game of "Telephone"—because the farther south the express riders progressed, the more the atrocities by the barbarous British at Lexington and Concord seemed to grow in scope and horror. Colonial news usually traveled down the coast first, and when it reached Charleston, the cold-blooded "lobster backs" had even bayoneted old and infirmed colonists as they lay helplessly in bed. By the time the shocking news finally reached the MecDecers in Mecklenburg, Lexington and Concord had become the spark that would ignite a powder keg more than two decades in the making.

New Englanders had a stoic, stubborn, independent streak the Scots-Irish patriots in Mecklenburg felt a special kinship to. After the Boston Tea Party, citizens of Charlotte were willing to drive one hundred head of cattle north to help feed their fellow patriots, an offer of such generosity and goodwill that it prompted a thank you card from the people of Boston. By the summer of 1775 the rallying cry in the Carolinas had become: "The cause of the town of Boston is the common cause of the American Colonies!"

And so, when the express rider in Charlotte shouted out the horrific details of The Shot Heard 'Round the World and the American bloodshed from a month earlier at Concord's North Bridge, the news especially enraged the men who had gathered in Charlotte on this day and all hell broke loose in the Mecklenburg courthouse.

We were now essentially at war, and it was time to pick sides.

"We smelt and felt the blood & carnage of Lexington, which raised all the passions into fury and revenge," McKnitt noted. In his Rough Notes he also added, "After a short conference about their suffering brethren besieged and suffering every hardship in Boston and the American Blood running in Lexington & Concord the electrical fire flew into every breast."

The electrical fire flew into every breast . . .

To preserve order inside the courthouse, the first act of business was to name McKnitt committee secretary and his cousin, Abraham Alexander, committee chair. Given the size of the convention and the fervor drummed up by the news from Massachusetts, Abraham was the obvious and smart choice for MecDec chair. At fifty-seven, he was the group's elder statesman and an established, well-respected leader in Charlotte. More importantly, as a founder and elder at Sugaw Creek Presbyterian, Abraham was a spiritual stand-in for Craighead and unambiguously in favor of cutting ties with Britain. Based on their choice for chair, there was no mistaking what the committee had in mind. As an added bonus, after surviving the Sugar Creek War, it was also clear that Abraham could take a punch, which was not an insignificant attribute for the MecDec chair, given how the Scots-Irish often liked to settle their scholarly disputes.

With Abraham squarely in charge, the convention wasted little time getting down to business. McKnitt describes the committee engaged in a free and open discussion about the most impactful way they could "give relief to suffering America and protect our just & natural rights." And after much "animated discussion," General Graham says, plainly, "the question was taken, and they resolved to declare themselves independent."

Just like that.

Given the circumstances of the day and the long series of discussions and debates that preceded them at the Freedom Spring, perhaps the next step was just a formality at this point. But, man, let's not forget what these guys in Charlotte were actually proposing on this day: Revolution. Or, more importantly, what they were risking by even voicing these opinions out loud, let alone in writing: death. Yet they seem so certain, so freakishly calm and businesslike about, well, their decision to blow up the world.

(I sat at my table inside the Wilson archives, staring off into space for a long time and trying to figure out if this made the MecDec Founders total badasses or just flat-out crazy, until I realized, as with most revolutionaries, that it was probably a little of both.)

"Every delegate felt the value and importance of the prize and the awful and solemn crisis which had arrived, [and] every bosom swelled with indignation at the malice, inveteracy, and insatiable revenge developed in the late attack at Lexington," states a record from the MecDec proceedings. "The universal sentiment was: let us not flatter ourselves that popular harangues, or resolves; that popular vapour will avert the storm, or vanquish our common enemy; let us deliberate; let us calculate the issue—the probable result; and then let us act with energy, as brethren leagued to preserve our property, our lives, and what is still more endearing, the liberties of America."

Wow. This passage is a pretty good reminder that the eloquence of the MecDec, and the language it inspired, was every bit as poetic and powerful as what was coming out of Philadelphia and Virginia around the same time.

The patriots in Charlotte still needed something to formally vote on, though, so a subcommittee was formed made up of a doctor (Brevard), a preacher (Balch), and a lawyer (Kennon) and tasked with drafting the potential resolutions of independence. That this Dream Team of young, highly educated, articulate, and independence-craving minds would all end up together in a courtroom on the Carolina frontier exactly one month after Lexington and Concord seems almost beyond fate. Brevard, you'll remember, had been mentored in med school by one of the South's leading historians and most outspoken advocates for independence. And after all those discussions at the Freedom Spring, Brevard seems to have been journaling on the idea of the MecDec for some time, anticipating just such an opportunity. A year later a family member found what appeared to be a rough draft of the declaration among Brevard's papers at Queen's College. Historic work that would all be lost, or destroyed, during the war.

Few had more riding on the MecDec than Balch, however. For the "elegant and accomplished scholar," helping to craft the document would prove to be the final, and greatest, accomplishment of his life. He died, suddenly, just a few months later, and the large flat marble stone placed over his grave read: "He was distinguished as one of the committee of three who prepared that immortal document the Mecklenburg Declaration of Independence, and his eloquence the more effectual from his acknowledged wisdom, purity of motive and dignity of character, contributed much to the unanimous adoption of that instrument on the 20th of May 1775." (The beautiful cursive etchings are still visible and oddly moving, and, in my mind at least, totally worth the trip to Balch's grave just north of Charlotte.)

Kennon, meanwhile, was perhaps the region's most well-versed legal mind in this area, having already authored many of the state's most notable anti-British resolutions. In one final bit of perfect providence, the trio recused themselves from the courthouse and repaired a few blocks south to draft the country's first formal declaration of independence inside the library of Queen's College, an institution the King had flatly refused to even acknowledge.

That was about to change.

While the authors toiled away inside the Queen's library, Graham reports that back at the courthouse the committee continued to vigorously, and thoughtfully, debate the idea of independence and, especially, their previously sworn fealty to the Crown. Below is a particularly insightful excerpt from Graham's written testimony that is unaltered except for the few paragraph breaks I have (mercifully) added to the original text from the Wilson archives.

One circumstance occurred I distinctly remember:

A member of the committee, who had said but little before, addressed the Chairman as follows: "If you resolve on independence, how shall we all be absolved from the obligations of the oath we took to be true to King George the 3rd about four years ago, after the Regulation battle, when we were sworn whole militia companies together. I should be glad to know how gentlemen can clear their consciences after taking that oath."

This speech produced confusion. The Chairman could scarcely preserve order so many wished to reply.

There appeared great indignation and contempt at the speech of the member. Some said it was nonsense; others that allegiance and protection were reciprocal; when protection was withdrawn, allegiance ceased; that the oath was only binding while the King protected us in the enjoyment of our rights and liberties as they existed at the time it was taken; which he had not done, but now declared us out of his protection; therefore was not binding.

Any man who would interpret it otherwise, was a fool.

By way of illustration, (pointing to a green tree near the court house,) stated, if he was sworn to do any thing as long as the leaves continued on that tree, it was so long binding; but when the leaves fell, he was discharged from its obligation.

This was said to be certainly applicable in the present case.

The discussions went on like this inside the courthouse well into the early morning of May 20 until Brevard appeared with five written resolutions. The first and second ones formally dealt with the cessation of British rule in Mecklenburg County. "That whosoever . . . in any way, form or manner, countenanced the unchartered and dangerous invasion of our rights, as claimed by Great Britain, is an enemy to this country, to America, and to the inherent and inalienable rights of man. . . . [And we] do hereby dissolve the political bands which have connected us to the mother country, and hereby absolve ourselves from all allegiance to the British Crown."

This was bold, beautifully crafted, world-changing stuff from Brevard, Charlotte's one-eyed visionary.

But the heart and soul of the document, and our entire revolution, really, could be boiled down to ten simple words proclaimed publicly in America for the first time in Brevard's third resolve:

"We do hereby declare ourselves a free and independent people."

To which Brevard added: ". . . and to the maintenance of which independence, we solemnly pledge to each other, our mutual co-operation, our lives, our fortunes, and our most sacred honor."

Translation: our fates are now tied together.

We are one, to the end.

It was, in essence, the founding definition of American patriotism.

Although the Founders had been at it all day, the MecDec Papers say they were "neither sleepy, hungry, nor fatigued." Moved by Brevard's two world-changing passages on independence and patriotism, perhaps, they decided to push through to a vote.

"The deliberations and speeches continued through the day and into the night," states a biography of Robert Henry, a pioneering attorney and professor in the western part of North Carolina who was wounded in the Battle of Kings Mountain during the Revolutionary War. "That night, Robert slept on his father's great coat behind the door just inside the Charlotte courtroom where the assembly was in session. Robert's curiosity was aroused. He asked what these men were doing and was told in reply that they were "declaring for liberty" and "passing resolutions of freedom" and that what they were doing "would bring on war."

Knowing full well what was at stake, the role was called.

"By a *solemn* and *awful* vote," McKnitt states, "[we] Dissolved [abjured] our allegiance to King George and the British Nation."

McKnitt used the word *awful* to express the heavy burden on the Signers who must have known their vote would certainly lead to bloodshed and sacrifice. Yet no one wavered. Just below this in his notes, McKnitt scribbled the Latin phrase "Nem-Con" regarding the outcome of the MecDec vote:

Unanimous.

Humphrey Hunter, another eyewitness to the proceedings, also confirms, "The resolves, bye-laws and regulations were read by John McKnitt Alexander. It was then announced from the Chair, are you all agreed? There was not a dissenting voice."

Then, around 2 a.m., the committee asked Brevard to prepare "a more correct and formal draft of the Declaration of Independence . . . the proceedings having been thus arranged and somewhat in readiness for promulgation, the Delegation then adjourned until tomorrow, at 12 o'clock."

Word spread quickly overnight across the region about what was taking place in Charlotte, and by the next morning a large, shall we say, spirited crowd had gathered outside the courthouse. The scene in downtown Charlotte on May 20, 1775, must have been something to behold. Look,

I'm sure during the last few millennia there have been countless groups that have changed the course of human history just like our Founders in Charlotte, but I'm guessing none of them had more fun doing it than the MecDecers.

Polk's oldest son, William, who was a student at Queen's College at the time, was an eyewitness to all the day's historic events. A few months later, at seventeen, an inspired William joined the Continental Army and, although he was gravely wounded several times, served for the next six years, rising to the rank of lieutenant colonel under Thomas Sumter at the conclusion of the war. Decades later, as a trustee at UNC, the grand master of the state's Masonic order, and a nationally recognized Federalist, William Polk was formally declared "Raleigh's Most Illustrious Citizen."

His little brothers?

Not so much.

Legend has it that several of the younger Polk boys were deemed worthless as potential eyewitnesses to the day's events because they had celebrated being "free and independent" in the classic Scots-Irish fashion of getting blackout drunk on whiskey. (Described by one historian as "wild and frolicsome," one of the Polk boys went by the sobriquet "Devil Charley.") Also leading the festivities of May 20, 1775, was Charlotte royalty Thomas Spratt. Polk's father-in-law and the first European settler in Mecklenburg, Spratt went by "Kanawha," the honorary title bestowed upon him by the Catawba Nation elders.

"My grandfather and several of the Catawba rode up the old National Road to Charlotte, where a much-heralded event was to occur, on the 20th of May, 1775—the signing of the Mecklenburg Declaration of Independence," Thomas Dryden Spratt wrote in his 1875 family memoir. "However, Thomas 'Kanawha' Spratt did not, himself, sign this famous, historic paper, because, instead of dipping into an inkwell, he dipped into a gallon jug. In fact he, himself, became so vivacious that an officer of the law put him in the little city's place for the confinement of those who committed some penal offence, the county jail."

He wasn't there for long. When word spread that Spratt had been arrested, his friends quickly devised a plan to spring him from the hoosegow.

"The Catawba got on their horses, rode up to the jail . . . ripped off two or three planks and took 'Old Kanawha' out," Dryden Spratt recalled. "They put him on his horse, then they raced their steeds around the Court House Square several times—yelling and whooping."

Inside the courthouse just before noon, "under the shouts and huzzas of a very large assembly of the people of the county, who had come to know the issue of the meeting" the formal document prepared by Brevard was signed by the delegates. "It was unanimously adopted," Graham adds. "And shortly after it was moved, and seconded, to have the proclamation [pronounced] and the people collected, that the proceedings be read at the courthouse door, in order that all might hear them."

But who should have the honor of reading the historic document?

There was only one choice.

With paper in hand, Thomas Polk took the final steps on a journey toward true freedom and independence that he and his ancestors had been traveling for centuries. Walking through the dark courthouse doorway, he stepped out into the bright midday sun that cast his shadow across the town he had carved, with his own hands and deeds, out of the frontier and into the paragon of American history. "At the breaking out of the Revolution," wrote Draper, "Polk was . . . the most prominent man in Mecklenburg; and all his influence was exerted in behalf of the popular cause."

At the edge of the courthouse platform, Polk unfurled the Mecklenburg Declaration of Independence and proclaimed:

RESOLVED! That whoever directly or indirectly abetted, or in any way, form or manner, countenanced the unchartered and dangerous invasion of our rights, as claimed by Great Britain, is an enemy to this country—to America—and to the inherent and inalienable rights of man.

RESOLVED! That we the citizens of Mecklenburg county, do hereby dissolve the political bands which have connected us to the Mother Country, and hereby absolve ourselves from all allegiance to the British Crown, and abjure all political connection, contract, or association, with that nation, who have wantonly trampled on our rights and liberties—and inhumanly shed the innocent blood of American patriots at Lexington.

RESOLVED! That we do hereby declare ourselves a free and independent people, are, and of right ought to be, a sovereign and self-governing Association, under the control of no power other than that of our God and the General Government of the Congress; to the maintenance of which independence, we solemnly pledge to each other, our mutual co-operation, our lives, our fortunes, and our most sacred honor.

RESOLVED! That as we now acknowledge the existence and control of no law or legal officer, civil or military, within this country, we do hereby ordain and adopt, as a rule of life, all, each and every of our former laws, wherein, nevertheless, the Crown of Great Britain never can be considered as holding rights, privileges, immunities, or authority therein.

RESOLVED! That it is also further decreed, that all, each and every military officer in this county, is hereby reinstated to his former command and authority, he acting conformably to these regulations. And that every member present of this delegation shall henceforth be a civil officer, viz. a Justice of the Peace, in the character of a 'Committee-man,' to issue process, hear and determine all matters of controversy, according to said adopted laws, and to preserve peace, and union, and harmony, in said county,—and to use every exertion to spread the love of country and fire of freedom throughout America until a more general and organized government be established in this province.

The Founding Fathers in Charlotte had just produced and proclaimed America's first, true declaration of independence, a document that, one could argue, rightfully deserves to stand alongside the Magna Carta, the Preamble to the US Constitution, and the Gettysburg Address.

And yet, my favorite part of this entire crazy, fascinating twenty-four hours in Charlotte might just be the adorable way the newbies of North Carolina initially reacted to the news that they were finally "free and independent" from Britain.

A local tavern owner said that the MecDec was "received with every demonstration of joy by the inhabitants." And then, for whatever reason, Graham and several others all distinctly remember one particular detail regarding what transpired next.

"It was then proposed by some one aloud to give three cheers and throw up their hats," says Graham. "It was immediately adopted . . . and the hats thrown."

For decades, our original American patriots in Charlotte had bravely, and expertly, maneuvered through every last obstacle leading up to this historic moment.

With one delightful exception.

The hats.

"Several of them lit on the courthouse roof," Graham reported. "And the owners had some difficulty to reclaim them."

The hats would prove to be just the beginning, though.

Nothing about being first to freedom was going to be easy.

SEVEN

THE SOUTH'S PAUL REVERE, ONLY MUCH BRAVER

ONCE EVERYONE RETRIEVED THEIR HATS FROM THE COURTHOUSE ROOF, the celebration surely continued a few blocks west inside Pat Jack's Tavern. Like any respectable colonial town, the true heart of Charlotte in 1775 wasn't the courthouse or a church, but the cramped, lively, log cabin–style pub on the dirt path that eventually became West Trade Street. Opened around 1772, the tavern was owned by James Jack, forty-four, a respected leader in the Mecklenburg militia who everyone affectionately called Captain Jack, and his father, Patrick Jack, a beloved barkeep who was said to "crack many an Irish joke to the infinite delight of his numerous visitors; and by his ready wit, genial good humor and pleasantry, greatly contributed to the reputation of his house and inculcated his own patriotic principles."

Those principles of liberty had been hardwired into the Jacks' Scots-Irish family for more than a century. In 1661, the Reverend William Jack of the Laggan Presbytery in northern Ireland was evicted and put on trial by King Charles II for not conforming to the Church of England. Patrick Jack was likely his grandson. Born in Ballykelly, County Derry, Ireland, in 1700, he emigrated to America around 1730 and initially settled in Lancaster County, Pennsylvania, in the same region as Alexander Craighead and many of the future Charlotte patriots. Similarly, around 1760 the Jacks also moved south to a Presbyterian community near Salisbury, North Carolina, before settling in downtown Charlotte and building a home that doubled as Pat Jack's Tavern.

With an uncomplicated drink menu of rum, ale, cider, whiskey, and, on rare occasions, wine, chroniclers say Pat Jack's was "the favorite place of resort" for the college students attending the nearby Queen's College "and of other ardent spirits of the town and country, to discuss the political issues of that exciting period, all foreboding the approach of a mighty revolution."

Anyone who is the least bit familiar with where most revolutions are launched (or where most committee work gets done) knows a good portion of the details and debate behind the MecDec were ironed out over many, many drinks inside Pat Jack's, where the proprietors made no secret of their support for independence. Although Captain Jack was not an official member of the Mecklenburg Committee of Safety, he did confirm that "for some time previous to [the MecDec] I was privileged to a number of meetings of some of the leading characters of that county." And, Captain Jack continued, "When the resolutions were finally agreed on, they were publicly proclaimed from the courthouse door in the town of Charlotte and received with every demonstration of joy by the inhabitants."

If you read between the lines of McKnitt Alexander's Rough Notes, once the MecDec was signed and sealed (and the hats were coaxed off the courthouse roof), there seems to have been what historians technically refer to as an "Oh sh*t" moment. When the excitement and bravado wore off and the weight of what they had just done hit the Signers, a slight panic must have set in. It's as if they looked at the MecDec, then around at each other, and wondered, sheepishly: "What have we done?" Alexander even mentions the word "rash" in his notes. A few days later, before those second thoughts had any time to fester, members of the committee reconvened (more than likely inside Pat Jack's Tavern) to decide what to do next with this ticking time bomb in their hands.

For the MecDec men the choice was obvious: they doubled down. In the days following the MecDec celebration, leaders in Charlotte realized now that Mecklenburg County was officially no longer under British rule, they would need to establish some kind of basic, temporary framework of self-governance—at least until the Continental Congress in Philadelphia could get up to speed. McKnitt's Rough Notes say that following the Mec-Dec, "many other laws and ordinances were then made . . . merely to protect the association from confusion, and to regulate their general conduct as citizens." The result was a collection of twenty additional resolutions that came to be known as the Mecklenburg Resolves. Unlike the eloquent bravado of the MecDec, the Resolves read more like an HR memo: a laundry list of direct, businesslike guidelines that mostly deal with legal and administrative issues and the job of preparing for war, or whatever his royal highness KG3 had in mind in the way of payback. According to nineteenth-century scholars George Bancroft and Hugh Blair Grigsby, Brevard's incredible range as a writer—from the soaring words of the MecDec to the sensible tone of the Resolves—was unmatched at the time. Brevard, they said, should be "remembered with honor by his countrymen" for having "digested the system which was then adopted, and which formed in effect a Declaration of Independence, as well as a complete system of government." And when it came to the two revolutionary documents Brevard crafted, Bancroft and Grigsby believed that "the beauty of their diction, their elegant precision, the wide scope of statesmanship which they exhibit, prove incontestibly that the men who put them forth were worthy of their high trust at that difficult crisis."

With the administrative work out of the way, McKnitt's notes say the Signers concentrated on what exactly to do next with the MecDec. "Share it with the world," came the overwhelming response. Charlotte would send a messenger "to go express to Congress with a copy of all said resolutions and laws and a letter to our 3 members there, Richard Caswell, William Hooper & Joseph Hughes, in order to get Congress to sanction or *approve* them."

A conscription was quickly raised in town to pay for the express rider's food, lodgings, river ferries, and, should he get captured, his funeral. The MecDec had the power to change the world, but not without a volunteer brave enough to deliver it. The MecDec Founders needed a strong horseman and navigator who was also trustworthy, brave, and just brash enough to carry the country's first declaration of independence (and his own death warrant, should he be caught) nearly six hundred miles to Philadelphia.

Luckily, they didn't have to look far.

He was right behind the bar.

No one knows for sure why Captain Jack, at forty-four, was chosen for the hero's trial of riding the top-secret and treasonous MecDec to Philadelphia. As a respected member of the Mecklenburg militia and a de-facto associate of the Safety Committee, his experience and loyalties were beyond question. As a tavern owner seeking supplies, and with relatives in Lancaster County, Pennsylvania, Jack would have had experience with the Great Wagon Road, not to mention a great cover story for why he was on it. And as Syfert points out, although Waightstill Avery or Thomas Polk seemed like the obvious choice, they were both fairly well-known in the region, and the sight of either one racing by toward Philly would have likely aroused suspicions.

Jack, on the other hand, was a nobody. For the time being, anyway.

His anonymity was his armor. His selfless sense of duty, his superpower.

Captain Jack downplayed the whole thing, of course, saying plainly that he was "solicited to be the bearer of the proceedings to Congress" and he "set out the following month, say June."

The scene was captured in a painting by Charlotte's Chas Fagan, a world-renowned painter and sculptor, who decided to focus on the moment the die was cast: when an intense, resolute Captain Jack first brings his horse to full gallop on his way out of Charlotte. In the distance you can just make out the courthouse and the Signers. And as the larger-than-life Captain Jack and his horse thunder by in a cloud of dust, a small crowd of Charlotteans pay tribute from the side of the road. Under their bonnets and tri-cornered hats their faces are full of awe, fear, and hope.

THE MECDEC COMMITTEE'S HOPE WAS THAT WITH A COOPERATIVE HORSE and decent weather Jack could cover up to fifty miles a day on his way to Philadelphia. But this was June in Carolina, where the weather options remain threefold: torrential rain, scorching heat, and oppressive humidity. On most days, Jack was up to his boots in the kind of heavy, gooey red clay that used to turn our yellow Lab a deep shade of pink after every rainstorm. We know there was a ton of rain at the time thanks to the local Moravians' annoyingly cute habit of taking notes on literally *everything*. And their journals from June 1775 include endless, detailed reports about the treacherous weather. (Don't get me wrong, though, thank goodness for the pioneer-nerd Moravians and their obsessive emo-teen-like journaling habits, which would eventually provide one of the most important and irrefutable accounts of the MecDec and Captain Jack's ride.)

Carrying what is believed to have been four copies of the MecDec in his saddlebag (one for each North Carolina delegate of the Continental Congress and another for the House speaker), on his first day Jack covered more than forty miles to Salisbury, North Carolina. Today the town is mostly known as the headquarters of beloved Cheerwine soda, a century-old, family-owned regional brand of cherry soda. Or, at least, I think it's cherry soda. The brand was originally called Mint Cola, but when World War I created a sugar shortage, the company's founder, L. D. Peeler, fought off bankruptcy by experimenting with different flavors to create the still top-secret formula. I, for one, am very glad he did. Cheerwine is a marvelous virtue signal for Southern transplants, and it's awesome in poke cake, barbecue (honest), and with a splash of bourbon.

In 1775, Salisbury was an affluent town, the Rowan County seat, and home to MecDec coauthor and Signer William Kennon, a prominent local lawyer. "In passing through Salisbury, the General Court was sitting," Jack recalled in his affidavit for the 1831 North Carolina Governor's Report. "At the request of the court I handed a copy of the resolution to Col. Kennon, an attorney, and they were read aloud in open court."

Jack says that MecDec Signers John Davidson and Waightstill Avery called upon him later at his lodgings in Salisbury to say that they had heard of only one local official who did not approve of the MecDec. At the time, though, one accusation of high treason could still be a death sentence. According to the papers of General Joseph Graham, when the purpose and destination of Jack's trip became known around Salisbury, a couple of Tory-leaning lawyers (British loyalists) threatened to have him arrested.

Captain Jack handled the dust-up in the most Captain Jack way imaginable.

"He drew his pistols and threatened to shoot the first man who dared to interrupt him," Graham's account states.

No one dared.

Jack then climbed back up on his horse and continued toward Philadelphia.

His next challenge would have been navigating the three-shilling ferry crossing of the Yadkin River just north of town. "On the next morning," a North Carolina historian writes, "Captain Jack resumed his journey from Salisbury, occasionally passing through neighborhoods, in and beyond the limits of North Carolina, infested with enraged Tories, but, intent on his appointed mission, he faced all dangers."

My sense, though, is that the stop in Salisbury changed the ride's vibe entirely. "Long, lonesome, and perilous" is how one historian describes the rest of Jack's journey north. It was clear now that a large percentage of colonists, outside of Charlotte at least, remained steadfastly loyal to the Crown. (Throughout America the number may have been as high as 20 percent.) It was easy for Jack to risk his neck in theory while planted on a barstool in the safety and comfort of his Charlotte tavern, basking in toasts to his godlike bravery. After narrowly escaping Salisbury with his life, though, the full distance and danger (and sheer insanity) of his actual mission must have hit him like, well, that first gulp of Cheerwine. Salisbury, then, was Jack's true superhero moment: an ordinary person thrust into extraordinary, potentially world-changing circumstances realizes his life is now in serious danger . . . and decides to ride on anyway. Maybe I'm being sappy, or overstating it, but when James Jack, the father of four young children, saddled up in Salisbury with the full knowledge of what he was risking, it was the authentic (and often forgotten) definition of patriotism: the acknowledgment that the cause of freedom is bigger than any one man's life.

Because of this, people like to refer to Captain Jack as the Paul Revere of the South. But I find that comparison utterly ridiculous. Captain Jack rode nearly six hundred miles. Revere? A mere thirteen. By my calculations that alone makes Jack forty-six times braver. But there's more. Jack rode alone (not with a group of other riders). He actually completed his mission and never fell off his horse or got caught (ah-hem). And, as others have pointed out, Jack never had the great public relations boost of being immortalized in a (largely fabricated) Longfellow poem. In yet another case of history-isn't-quite-what-we-think-it-is, as far as I can tell, Paul Revere's greatest accomplishment was that his name was easier to rhyme than the other riders screaming *the British are coming!* all over New England that fateful night.

Jack never got his poem, or any publicity for that matter. For his own safety he pretty much stayed off the grid the rest of the way to Philadelphia. And with good reason, because once word got out about his Declaration Derby, his life literally depended on it. "It's understandable why they might have concealed what they had done," says historian David McCullough. "They would have been committing an act of treason. . . . It was an extremely risky thing."

In fact, loyalist "spies" along the Great Wagon Road to Philadelphia had already informed high-level British authorities, as well as North Carolina governor Josiah Martin, of Jack's operation. And the correspondence these informants inspired among our British rulers at the time is flat-out stunning—especially the way it seems to confirm, well, everything about the MecDec. It's all right there in *The Colonial and State Records of North Carolina*. In the summer of 1775, Martin, the last royal governor of North Carolina, wrote several letters to the Earl of Dartmouth in London to tell him he had learned "of a set of people stiling themselves a Committee for the County of Mecklenburg most traitorously declaring the entire dissolution of the Laws, Government and Constitution of this country" and that these "Resolves of the Committee of Mecklenburgh" which "surpass all the horrid and treasonable publications that the inflammatory spirits of this Continent have yet produced" were "sent off by express to the Congress at Philadelphia as soon as they were passed in the [Mecklenburg] Committee." Martin then called upon his remaining loyal subjects in North Carolina to keep an eye out for these "seditious Treasons and Traiterous Conspiracies" and to bring the King's justice to any of the "principals and accomplices therein" behind the MecDec. If they couldn't do it, Martin vowed to take matters into his own hands: "Your Lordship may depend [the MecDec's] Authors and Abettors will not escape my due notice, whenever my hands are sufficiently strengthened to attempt the recovery of the lost authority of Government."

This correspondence is so revelatory it requires a second, and possibly a third read. It's extraordinary, really. This is the highest-ranking British authority in North Carolina repeatedly confirming, in writing, that a committee in Mecklenburg had just crafted the most treasonous, inflammatory document ever produced by American colonists. And then, the governor confirms, to make matters worse, as soon as the MecDec was voted on and signed, these freakin' ingrates actually dispatched their declaration straight to Philadelphia on an express rider.

Translation: *The bollocks on these MecDec guys.*

And for all this trouble, the English governor vowed, they would pay dearly.

The stakes were set.

Now, all Captain Jack had to do was stay alive for the next 550 miles.

I CONFESS: I MIGHT HAVE JUST BEEN LOOKING FOR AN EXCUSE TO ATTEND the annual Cheerwine Festival in Salisbury, which was being headlined by the Spin Doctors (swear to God). But to better understand the epic scope of Captain Jack's ride, my original plan was to retrace the route in my old—my kids call it "vintage"—Mini Cooper. The only difference being my Mini may have proven to be a slower, far less comfortable ride than Jack's steed.

But then I was hit with my own case of MecDec Face.

This is truly what I've come to love about investigating the MecDec story. There's always—*always*—another twist, or another level, and each one is usually more jaw-droppingly *wait-how-the-frick-did-I-not-know-that?* nuts than the last. This time, while charting my ride, every time I Googled something close to . . . *Retracing Captain Jack's Mecklenburg Declaration of Independence ride to Philadelphia* . . . references to a different Charlotte legend named Humpy kept appearing on my screen. Of course Humpy's connected to this, I giggled to myself, pushing back from my desk. It makes perfect sense. These two Charlotte legends were absolutely made for each other.

H. A. "Humpy" Wheeler was the longtime and beloved former president of the Charlotte Motor Speedway and a man who single-handedly pushed NASCAR to its peak popularity in the early 2000s with his own unique approach to PR. (A method that was, shall we say, equal parts pro wrestling, patriotism, and Ringling Brothers.) When I first moved to Charlotte, I did a lot of local sports radio, which meant endless "arguments" on air with cohosts like Humpy about my outrageous NASCAR takes on issues like, you know, increasing driver safety and banning the Confederate flag. Once, during a commercial break, the silver-haired and self-deprecating Humpy confessed to me in his classic Carolina drawl that he had actually inherited his nickname from his dad, who got caught smoking Camel cigarettes when he was a kid. I have no earthly idea if that's true or if Humpy made that up on the spot. What I can confirm is that Humpy is impossible not to like. He was 40-2 as a Golden Gloves boxer as a kid, and in the late 1950s he played defensive line for the University of South Carolina Gamecocks before carving out a Hall of Fame career in PR in Charlotte.

To this day people still talk about Humpy's insane pre-race publicity stunts. Like the time one Memorial Day weekend when he staged a full-scale military reenactment of the invasion of Grenada on the infield at Charlotte Motor Speedway, complete with a squadron of Apache helicopters. It was so authentic, in fact, Humpy had to call the local sheriff and convince him we weren't experiencing a Red Dawn–style incursion.

But even Grenada couldn't top Humpy's greatest PR stunt of all time: Jerry Linker.

In May 1975, as vice chairman of the committee in charge of Charlotte's bicentennial celebration of the Mecklenburg Declaration of Independence, Humpy, then thirty-six, came up with the brilliant (and slightly deranged) idea of promoting the event by having a local equestrian dressed in authentic Revolutionary garb recreate Captain Jack's *entire* six-hundred-mile ride to Philadelphia, where he would then deliver the MecDec, for a second time, on its bicentennial anniversary. This was Humpy the PR Hall of Famer at his absolute best, bringing one of America's original true patriots back to life in spectacular fashion for a country chomping at the bit to start its own bicentennial celebration in 1776.

So, it turns out, there was no need for me to jump in my MINI and retrace Captain Jack's adventure myself.

Someone far crazier had already attempted it.

For Humpy and the 1975 MecDec Bicentennial Committee, picking the horse was the easy part. A local owner and trainer was happy to provide a seven-year-old blood-red Arabian bay stallion. Named Sharek, the horse became an instant celebrity in the buildup to the bicentennial. At 850 pounds and fourteen hands high, every day in preparation for his marathon ride to Philly, Sharek consumed two gallons of oats, barley, and corn along with two bales of hay laced with calf manna protein. Expected to average twenty-five miles a day, Sharek, whose face was split by a racing strip of white hair, was outfitted with custom, diamond-strength tungsten carbide horseshoes for better grip on the pavement.

Finding a rider was another story.

There would be a small support crew riding along with "Jack" in a classic 1970s Partridge Family–style RV. To keep the ride as authentic as possible, however, Captain Jack 2.0 would be required to stay in period garb and tack, and all lodging and stabling would be done by 4-H groups along the route. As grueling and unglamorous as that sounds, Humpy still received seventy-two applications for the role of Captain Jack. When it came time for the live auditions, though, most riders struggled with the American Saddlebred horse that was chosen specifically for the tryout because of its unruly size and demeanor.

Things were looking rather bleak, and the entire stunt seemed to be in jeopardy, when, in a scene straight out of a movie, in sauntered twenty-two-year-old Jerry Linker, a third-generation farrier who had been shoeing horses and riding bulls since he was nine. Oozing Rip Wheeler *Yellowstone* vibes, without asking permission Linker tore off the saddle, tossed it aside, and leapt up on the massive, stunned horse. After effortlessly commanding the suddenly submissive beast around the ring, Linker stopped on a dime in front of the judge's dais, stood up on the horse's back, and, to a chorus of gasps, dismounted with a backflip.

Humpy Wheeler was in love.

He had found his Captain Jack.

"Jerry was brash and totally bad to the bone, which is kinda how I had always imagined what Captain Jack must have been like," says Karen Linker, Jerry's eighth (and final) wife. "To just stand up in a bar and go, 'Sure, I'll ride five hundred miles and risk my life for this cause. Why not?' That was Jerry too. He was unnaturally strong. He was a frontier justice, Let's

Freakin' Go kinda guy too. They totally picked the right guy for this ride—*both times.*"

In some ways Captain Jerry was every bit the legend Captain Jack was. He was supposed to grow a full beard for the 1975 ride but couldn't because his cheeks were covered in scar tissue from a fire when he was sixteen. At eighteen a bull fell on him and crushed his spine. Scheduled for surgery, Jerry waltzed out of the hospital with the back of his gown flapping in the wind. He let his back heal on its own, which resulted in a curved and calcified spine that shrunk him by a full two inches.

Today, Jerry lives in a tiny apartment in Georgetown, Kentucky, with a long-since-retired horse trailer and truck parked out front. He's only seventy. But just like that banged-up, rusted-out pickup of his, Jerry packed a ton of miles into those seventy years, and they seem to have finally caught up to him. After months of back-and-forth scheduling, we finally found a window to talk in person in between his bouts of Covid-19, a stroke, and surgeries to place a shunt in his brain. "Back then I didn't believe in fear, and I didn't believe in pain," Jerry tells me. "Back then if it didn't have two legs and was hot, or four legs and was wild, I didn't want nothing to do with it."

In the weeks leading up to his 1975 ride, Jerry was described by reporters as a trucker, a college student, a rodeo rider, a blacksmith, a horse trainer, and a salesman—none of which was completely true. A third of his family members back in Texas were said to be in jail, except his grandma, who was locked away in an asylum. Jerry was a standout quarterback in high school. But when he begged to skip his farm chores for a day to attend his football team's award ceremony, family legend says his father decked him just for daring to make the request. Jerry got up, walked to the banquet, and never returned home. Of his seven marriages before he met Karen, the longest one lasted two years. The shortest, two weeks.

"At times, like with the MecDec, he did seem like a larger-than-life superhero, just a slightly deranged, schizoaffective, not necessarily all that pleasant superhero," says his daughter Valerie Linker who, if you couldn't tell, is studying psychology at the University of Kentucky. "He was very much the center of attention everywhere he went. So, naturally, he loved being Captain Jack. And he was great at it, he really was. I'm his daughter and I wouldn't say I necessarily like him all the time, but even I have to admit he was pretty darn charming."

From the moment that backflip literally landed him the job, Linker was all-in on the role of his lifetime. For two months, he rode Sharek through downtown Charlotte to acclimate him to traffic, noise, and well-wishers. In preparation for his press conferences and public speaking along the route, Linker read all he could on Charlotte and the Mecklenburg Declaration of Independence. And to help him recover from the extreme heat, the committee stuffed his saddlebag with salts, potassium pills, and extra vitamins, which Linker may have occasionally supplemented with his own stash.

It was the '70s, after all. And this poor guy had to sleep in farmhouses and ride an 850-pound horse down a highway shoulder for a *month* while looking like a member of the Village People in wool knee britches, a tri-cornered hat, and a puffy shirt. "Hated the outfit," says Valerie. "Said it made him look like a sissy." A new, up-and-coming Vegas oddsmaker named Jimmy "The Greek" Snyder gave Linker and Sharek only a fifty-fifty chance of completing the MecDec mission. "It's hard to grasp how deadly it was what Captain Jack did. The British woulda killed him in a heartbeat, no questions asked," says Jerry, who today looks like an older version of John Adams if he were on vacation at a dude ranch. "I just wanted to make it so that people could get a grip on what Captain Jack did for his country. I needed people to know that."

As part of the bicentennial celebration, Humpy's committee built a full-scale re-creation of the original Charlotte courthouse featuring a staircase identical to the one where Thomas Polk formally proclaimed our independence on May 20, 1775. Two hundred years and eleven days later, in front of fifty local dignitaries and the marching band from Independence High School, Linker stuffed a copy of the MecDec in his saddlebag and trotted off north on Tryon Street to Route 29 where, a few miles up the road, he and Sharek passed Sugaw Creek Presbyterian Church on their way to Winston-Salem.

Moments earlier, in a press conference before his departure, Linker, looking (and sounding) like a Revolutionary version of Lynyrd Skynyrd's Ronnie

Van Zant, told reporters, "Now there'll be some people who'll think this is great. And they'll be some people who'll say, 'Who in the hell is this turkey?' But the people I'm worried about are the lunatics that don't believe in the Mecklenburg Declaration of Independence. There's no telling what they might do."

He'd find out soon enough, just as soon as he and Sharek stepped foot into Thomas Jefferson's home state of Virginia.

Both Captain Jack and Captain Jerry crossed into Virginia via the Dan River, but their routes diverged from there. Jack had no choice but to follow the only path available and ride northwest toward Big Lick (Roanoke) and then, following what's I-81 today, up the Shenandoah Valley and through a loosely connected trail of Irish and Quaker communities toward Staunton and Winchester. In northern Virginia, when he reached the main section of the Great Wagon Road, about 150 miles west of his destination, Jack would have finally been able to exhale a tiny bit, blending in with the crowds of merchant wagons and livestock and making good time on what was the 1775 version of a superhighway. From there he would have headed east through Gettysburg, York, and Lancaster, Pennsylvania, where his family first settled after fleeing Ireland.

After Linker crossed the Dan, he rode northeast through Halifax and Charlotte Court House, Virginia, where, soon enough, the herculean task of what he (and Captain Jack) had signed up for began to sink in. With fifteen appearances scheduled in Virginia, the sunburned Linker was spending up to fifteen hours a day in the saddle (more on days when he got lost, which was often), and he had already gone hoarse from spreading the news about the MecDec. Sharek was in similar shape. He had already worn through a set of tungsten horseshoes, was limping slightly after tripping in a pothole, and had begun to struggle with the increase in altitude.

"Jerry always said when the ride got rough, that's when he really could feel Jack's spirit right there with him," says Karen Linker. "Jack was nothing special; what I mean is he was just a normal person who volunteered to do a job and risk his life for his country. Jerry really related to that. You talk about walking a mile in someone's shoes? Try five hundred. Every day that passed he had more respect and admiration for what Captain Jack did and what he represented, and one of the reasons Jerry never even thought about quitting was it angered him so much that the world didn't recognize and appreciate what Captain Jack had done."

Trying to correct that would push Linker to the brink. The next obstacle came on June 11 when he arrived in Palmyra, south of Charlottesville, Virginia. In the morning he and Sharek were scheduled to ride eighteen miles for a ceremony at Monticello, Thomas Jefferson's mountaintop plantation and national historic site. The detour was explained to reporters as a gesture of goodwill. Truth be told, Humpy couldn't resist the chance to parade the first, true declaration of independence all over the manicured grounds of Jefferson's beloved Monticello.

"That Humpy Wheeler, he's slicker'n snot on a doorknob," says Jerry.

When Linker arrived in his Revolutionary finest, the Monticello curator informed him of an obscure rule (perhaps written that morning) that prohibited people in colonial costume from entering the site or even being photographed with the president's home in the background. Unwelcome at Monticello, Linker and a large crowd of local government officials, representatives from the Daughters of the American Revolution, and close to fifty 4-H members and MecDec groupies found refuge across the street in Michie Tavern, a place far more suited to Captain Jack and Captain Jerry anyway. (The pub opened in 1784 when Corporal William Michie returned from a tour at Valley Forge. And, says Valerie, "bars and bar fights were kind of my dad's thing.") Standing in the rain, Linker calmly read his copy of the MecDec to the assembled crowd of Virginians who then awarded him with two replica quill pens. The same kind of quills, one would assume, that Jefferson would have used while copying passages from the MecDec over to his own declaration draft.

The dust-up at Monticello didn't quite garner the national attention the Charlotte MecDec bicentennial committee was hoping for. Two days later, near Culpeper, Virginia, with almost no press coverage, the ride halfway over, and Sharek badly in need of rest, Humpy Wheeler performed one of the greatest PR resuscitations of all time.

With its rolling green hills and endless white-fence ranches, Culpeper is the unofficial capital of Virginia horse country. Acting anonymously, it wasn't that hard for Humpy to convince a local busybody and horse-loving humane officer to swear out an arrest warrant on Linker for "overriding" Sharek. "Whenever you needed dirt, Humpy knew exactly where to dig," says Jerry. Linker and Sharek were both taken into custody. The local sheriff then confirmed for the growing throng of media that the name on the arrest warrant was "John Doe Captain Jack." (Humpy must have been dancing on top of his desk at this point.) Released after an hour in jail, Linker defiantly jumped on a borrowed Appaloosa and, facing a $1,000 fine and a year in prison, rode off triumphantly toward Leesburg, Virginia, on the Potomac. Meanwhile, a district court judge in Culpeper ordered that Sharek had to rest and recuperate until an independent veterinarian could examine him. The following day, when the doc reported the horse to be in good physical condition, the now-refreshed steed was put in a trailer and driven north to be reunited with Linker before he reached Gettysburg. The charges were then dropped.

"Humpy only told him later that he was the one who had him arrested because the ride wasn't getting enough attention," says Karen Linker. "I don't think Jerry was very happy about that, but it sure worked. By the time he reached Pennsylvania it had reached national notoriety. For a while Jerry was famous-famous, ya know? Put it this way: he was famous enough to know that he hated being famous."

After the Associated Press picked up on the saga—*Arrest Delays Captain Jack's Declaration of Independence Ride*—Linker, Sharek, and the Mec-Dec were front-page news across the country for several days. "The South returned to Gettysburg Tuesday, but this time there was no battle," proclaimed the *Evening Sun* in Hanover, Pennsylvania. "It returned in the form of Capt. James Jack, portrayed by Jerry Linker." Bags of fan mail, mostly from school kids, started arriving in Charlotte for Sharek and Captain Jack. Now, when Linker stopped in Gettysburg or Chambersburg, where he laid a wreath on the grave of Colonial Army Colonel Patrick Jack, a relative of

Captain Jack's (and a fellow bar owner), there were several hundred fans waiting to greet him.

The ride was featured in *Sports Illustrated*, *The Mike Douglas Show* requested an appearance, and Linker was now on a first-name basis with President Gerald Ford. More importantly, the correct version of the MecDec story was finally being shared far and wide.

That week on the popular game show *Hollywood Squares*, one of the stars was asked "if a Declaration of Independence had been signed before the one in Philadelphia?"

They got it wrong.

The correct answer was "yes."

With Linker's six-hundred-mile journey nearing its end, a newspaper in Lancaster, Pennsylvania, noted that he was carrying copies of the MecDec, "the first declaration of independence by any Americans from Great Britain." And in covering Linker's arrival, even the *Philadelphia Inquirer* went on record, declaring, "Because Captain Jack was successful in his long ride, many of the Mecklenburg ideals were expressed in the Declaration of July 4, 1776."

When Linker finally reached Independence Hall at 2:30 p.m. on June 29, 1975, a raucous crowd of 1,500 was there waiting in a steady rain to welcome Captain Jack 2.0 back to Philadelphia. Linker's arrival was delayed slightly by an urgent pit stop at a Philadelphia hotel that tried to charge Captain Jack twenty-five cents to use the bathroom. "Me? I climbed over," Linker laughs. Afterward, members of the 2nd Pennsylvania Regiment of the Continental Line, dressed in authentic red and blue colonial uniforms, saluted Linker with a deafening cannon blast. An emotional history buff in the crowd, using the lexicon of the times, put the entire scene perfectly into perspective. "This is really far out!" the guy shrieked as Linker climbed off Sharek, reached into his soggy saddlebag, and presented the MecDec to a handful of Philadelphia dignitaries.

Gentlemen . . . bear it in mind, the original Captain Jack declared in this same spot two hundred years earlier, *Mecklenburg owes no allegiance to, and is separated from the Crown of Great Britain . . . forever.*

Linker was then presented with an eight-inch replica of the Liberty Bell, which sits in his living room to this day. It was an appropriate gift since it was Thomas Polk who likely saved the Bell during the Battle of Germantown. In front of the media, whenever Linker could he deflected praise and attention back to the OG, Captain Jack himself. "He did it alone," Linker reminded reporters. "And he could have lost his life at any minute." It's true, Jack had to constantly be on the lookout for Tories, whereas Jerry's biggest concern was tractor trailers. Jack also had to turn around and ride all the way back home. A car would speed Linker back to Charlotte where he would be "knighted" for his service, and one of Sharek's horseshoes would go on permanent display in City Hall. Another stark contrast between the two rides? While Sharek had lost some weight, Linker actually gained ten pounds thanks to the countless parade of people along the route who "were waiting in their yards with beer and lunches."

But the most touching moment of the ceremony at Independence Hall in 1975 came when the rain started up again after Linker's arrival. In a gesture that was indicative of the overwhelming gratitude and pride swelling up back home in North Carolina, when the skies opened up, Charlotte mayor John Belk quietly moved next to Linker and used his own umbrella to keep his city's favorite son dry.

Mayor Belk's act of brotherly love had accidentally blocked local press photographers from getting any good shots of Captain Jack, and before long someone in the press pool in front of the stage yelled out:

"Hey, you with the umbrella! GET OUTTA THE DAMN PICTURE!"

Linker and Belk shared a laugh at the authentic Philly-style welcome, the kind only Santa Claus at an Eagles game could truly appreciate.

It was a perfect and historically accurate ending to Linker's adventure.

Two hundred years earlier, in the same spot, the original Captain Jack had been given the exact same kind of welcome when he arrived in Philadelphia with the actual MecDec.

IN THE NORTH CAROLINA GOVERNOR'S REPORT ON THE MECDEC, THE sons of William Alexander testified about their father "frequently" proclaiming that in June 1775 he was in Philadelphia on a "mercantile business" trip when he bumped into Captain Jack, who then told him he had been sent on behalf of the committee of safety in Mecklenburg "as the agent, or bearer, of the Declaration of Independence made in Charlotte on the twentieth of May 1775 by the citizens of Mecklenburg." One of more than a dozen witnesses to Jack's ride, William Alexander even knew the exact date he met with Captain Jack—June 23, 1775—because it was the same day the town was abuzz with news that General George Washington had departed Philadelphia to take command of the Northern Army.

Coincidentally, a few days earlier Thomas Jefferson had made what author Joseph Ellis describes as his "grand entrance" to Philadelphia in a plush, cushy phaeton (a.k.a. a carriage) along with four horses, three slaves, and probably enough expensive Madeira wine to drown the entire British Army. By Ellis's description, Jefferson seems to have arrived on a cloud of velvet in a manner befitting what the newspapers called the "haughty sultans of the South." His arrival was perfectly contrasted by a dusty, half-starved Captain Jack, who was hellbent, as he testified in 1830, on delivering the MecDec to the Second Continental Congress at Independence Hall, which was then called the Pennsylvania State House.

Unfortunately, Captain Jack's timing could not have been worse. The language and views expressed in the MecDec were way ahead of the political sentiment in the rest of the colonies. (That's the danger of being first, I suppose.) In fact, just as Jack arrived in Philadelphia with a statement from the citizens of Charlotte declaring them "free and independent" from the King, and all British laws and authority null and void, the Continental Congress was busy preparing the "Olive Branch Petition" for King George III. Dispatched on July 8, 1775, just a few weeks after Jack arrived, the rather pitiful letter shows Congress groveling for reconciliation and denying any wish at all for independence.

I'm going to let historian C. L. Hunter, author of 1877's *Sketches of Western North Carolina*, take it from here on the full account—actually, "re-creation" is probably a better way to describe it—of Jack's ultimately frustrating visit to Philadelphia:

Upon his arrival [Captain Jack] immediately obtained an interview with the North Carolina delegates (Caswell, Hooper and Hewes [*sic*]), and, after a little conversation on the state of the country, then agitating all minds, Captain Jack drew from his pocket the Mecklenburg resolutions of the 20th of May, 1775, with the remark:

"Here, gentlemen, is a paper that I have been instructed to deliver to you, with the request that you should lay the same before Congress."

After the North Carolina delegates had carefully read the Mecklenburg resolutions, and approved of their patriotic sentiments so forcibly expressed, they informed Captain Jack they would keep the paper, and show it to several of their friends, remarking, at the same time, they did not think Congress was then prepared to act upon so important a measure as *absolute independence.*

On the next day, Captain Jack had another interview with the North Carolina delegates. They informed him that they had consulted with several members of Congress, (including Hancock, Jay, and Jefferson) and that all agreed, while they approved of the patriotic spirit of the Mecklenburg resolutions, it would be premature to lay them officially before the House, as they still entertained some hopes of reconciliation with England. It was clearly perceived by the North Carolina delegates and other members whom they consulted, that the citizens of Mecklenburg county were *in advance* of the general sentiment of Congress on the subject of independence; the phantasy of "reconciliation" still held forth its seductive allurements in 1775, and even during a portion of 1776; and hence, no record was made, or vote taken on the patriotic resolutions of Mecklenburg, and they became concealed from view in the blaze of the National Declaration bursting forth on the 4th of July, 1776, which only re-echoed and reaffirmed the truth and potency of sentiments proclaimed in Charlotte on the 20th of May, 1775.

Captain Jack finding the darling object of his long and toilsome journey could not be then accomplished, and that Congress was not prepared to vote on so bold a measure as *absolute independence,* just before leaving Philadelphia for home, somewhat excited, addressed the North Carolina delegates, and several other members of Congress, in the following patriotic words:

Gentlemen, you may debate here about 'reconciliation,' and memorialize your king, but, bear it in mind, Mecklenburg owes no allegiance to, and is separated from the crown of Great Britain forever.

No wonder Captain Jack was pissed.

I mean, he had just battled through six hundred miles of heat, rain, mud, hunger, snakes, bears, and horseshit and had risked drowning, arrest, arrows, and the noose—all to ensure the swift, safe delivery of America's first, true Declaration of Independence to Philadelphia. And, in the end, the one obstacle Captain Jack and the MecDec Signers were not able to overcome was the collective absence of a spine among their congressmen. (Sounds frustratingly familiar, ya know?) Desperate for reconciliation with the King and having deemed the wording and spirit of the MecDec far too incendiary to share publicly, it appears the North Carolina delegates simply ghosted Captain Jack and the Charlotte Founders. In his Rough Notes, McKnitt Alexander noted, "Congress never had our said laws on their table for discussion, though a copy was left with them by Captain Jack." Which confirms they could have shared the document or debated it publicly. Or, at the very least, they might have simply entered it into the Congressional record for posterity's sake to honor the Charlotteans' courage and foresight as the first patriots in America to declare independence.

Instead, in a cruel twist of fate, one of the bravest, boldest documents ever produced was delivered nearly six hundred miles straight into the trembling hands of the feeblest congressmen imaginable for such a historic mission. At worst, Caswell, Hughes, and Hooper actively conspired to hide or destroy the MecDec. At best, believing they were following the wishes of Congress and protecting their constituents, they simply pretended it never existed.

And the rest of the world followed suit.

So as tortuous and tragic as it may seem, in the end it was this cowardice and complete abdication of duty by North Carolina's own representatives that ultimately prevented our Founding Fathers in Charlotte from claiming their rightful place in history.

In their correspondence, Adams and Jefferson were certainly very clear about whom they blamed for the MecDec remaining a secret. Writing to his pen pal in 1819, Adams confessed, "[The MecDec's] total concealment from me . . . can only be unriddled by the timidity of the delegates in Congress from North Carolina." To which Jefferson replied (with shrugged shoulders it would seem), "You remember as well as I do, that we had not a greater Tory in Congress than Hooper . . . and Hughes was very wavering, sometimes firm, sometimes feeble, according as the day was clear or cloudy."

Ouch.

In his home state's encyclopedia, the very first line of Hooper's biography describes him as "an unusually delicate, nervous child." At fifteen, after studying at the staunchly Loyalist Boston Latin, Hooper was admitted into the sophomore class at Harvard. No less an authority than Adams himself would eventually note that "Richard Henry Lee, Patrick Henry, and Hooper are the orators of the congress." But his loyalties always remained in question. Getting dragged through the streets by your britches will do that to a fella. In 1769 when Hooper was appointed deputy attorney general of the Salisbury court, he ran afoul of the violently pro-independence Regulator clan in North Carolina. A group that, from time to time, enjoyed dragging the delicate, nervous Hooper through the streets of Salisbury. As late as September 1775, months after Lexington and Concord and even after reading a copy of the MecDec, Hooper was still publicly arguing against his constituents. "We have been told that independence is our object; that we seek to shake off all connection with the parent state. Cruel suggestion!" he sniveled at the Provincial Congress in Hillsboro, North Carolina. In 1776, though, when the tide had turned and Revolution was inevitable, Hooper was politically savvy, and enough of a weasel, to correctly read the room. He signed Jefferson's Declaration of Independence (on August 2, 1776), and by all accounts served the cause of freedom tirelessly and honorably. But after the war, when he immediately began defending Loyalists who had their lands and property confiscated, Hooper was voted out of office, and, the encyclopedia says, "chose to drown his increasing disillusionment in rum." He died at forty-eight the night before his daughter's wedding.

"Given their temperaments and political views it is inconceivable that [Hooper and Caswell] would have brought Jack's message before the general congress," writes Syfert. As for Hughes, in an 1813 letter Adams cites him by name as an example of a member of Congress overcome with "terror and horror" at the very thought of independence who later signed Jefferson's declaration with "regret" and "much lukewarmness."

"If the Mecklenburg document arrived [at the Continental Congress in June 1775] it would have been squelched because [Congress] didn't want any talk of independence," confirms historian David McCullough.

And so, Captain Jack returned to Charlotte in July 1775 to little fanfare, recalled McKnitt Alexander, and "carrying a long, full, complacent letter from the 3 members recommending our zeal, perseverance, order, and forbearance."

In other words: *chill the F out, you guys.*

On his way back to Charlotte, Jack passed through the Moravian settlement near what is today Winston-Salem, North Carolina. Already that summer the always-journaling Moravian pastor Johann Michael Graff reported to his church elders in Europe about a number of area groups that had dispatched "addresses" to the government. Several weeks later, on July 7, 1775, Graff's diary again states: "This afternoon a man from Mecklenburg, who had been sent from there Express to Congress in Philadelphia, and is now returning, brought a circular, addressed to Mr. Traugott Bagge." (Bagge was a well-known Moravian merchant and community leader.) In another 1775 entry, Graff had managed to accomplish what North Carolina's Three Stooges in Congress couldn't muster the courage to do: acknowledge (and corroborate) the timing, completion, and purpose of Captain Jack's courageous ride and the brave MecDec patriots. Although Graff's diary from 1775 never mentions him by name, a footnote in the records of the Moravians leaves no doubt about who was the subject of that all-important diary entry.

"Undoubtedly Captain Jack," it says.

Captain Jack returned home and lived out the rest of his days in a manner not quite befitting the South's Paul Revere. One can only imagine how many times over the next several years Jack retold the tale of his wild ride to Philadelphia over sterling pints of cider from behind the bar at Pat Jack's Tavern. When the Revolutionary War began, Jack says he served "from commencement to close." And as a captain in the Mecklenburg militia, Jack was said to be so beloved by his troops that they begged him not to take promotions in rank and break up their regiment. His obituary in the *Raleigh Register* confirms that Jack "spent the prime of his life and his little all in the glorious struggle for independence" and ends with confirmation that "in the spring of '75 he was the bearer of the Mecklenburg Declaration of Independence to Congress."

At war's end Jack's claim of 7,646 pounds for his service and expenditures ($1.9 million in today's economy) was approved by Colonel Matthew Locke, and paid in full, but in an ironic twist the express rider responsible for delivering the payment is said to have perished before reaching Captain Jack. As a result, Jack was forced to move his family to Tennessee and then to Wilkes County, Georgia, where he reinvented himself as a farmer. The Jacks had a daughter and three sons, including Patrick who became a colonel in the US Army and, later, after helping the state gain its independence, a member of the Texas Supreme Court. Captain Jack ended up with so many prominent Texan descendants that there is still an active chapter of the Daughters of the American Revolution in New Braunfels, Texas, named in his honor. In his book, Hunter concludes that Captain Jack enjoyed pastoral bliss late in life and "met his approaching end with calm resignation, and died on the 18th of December, 1822, in the ninety-first year of his age."

Hinting at the fame and fortune Captain Jack had earned—but never received—the *Register* concluded its rather artful obituary by noting that a few of Jack's old comrades were still alive and "should this notice catch the eye of any of them, it may draw forth a sigh, or elicit a tear, to the memory of their friend, more to be valued than a marble monument."

It would take nearly two centuries for Charlotte to bestow upon Captain Jack the kind of monument he deserved.

But it would be well worth the wait.

EIGHT

THE MONSTER OF MONTICELLO'S
INDECENT EXPOSURE

OUR TOUR ENDS AT THE FOOT OF THE ROTUNDA, THE DOMED LIBRARY designed by Thomas Jefferson as the centerpiece of his beloved University of Virginia and the spot where, our student guide informs us, we should leave all of our clothes. As an occasional guest lecturer at UVA and a dad with two college-aged daughters, I've become something of an expert on campus tour guides, and right away in Charlottesville I could tell our backward walker-talker was going to be amazing. Within the first ten minutes, a UVA undergrad we'll call Lisa revealed that she despised her roommate, had "thrifted" her entire outfit, cried her eyes out during her first chemistry lab, loved the school's renowned a capella clubs (mostly because they threw the sickest parties), and had once blown through $400 at Starbucks in less than a month. (My daughter Kate's response to the Starbucks confession suggested she took it as a challenge, not a warning.) Somehow, though, Lisa managed to save her best material for last. At our final stop, on the pastoral Lawn, just below the Rotunda, she shared the intimate details behind UVA's strangest graduation requirement: streaking.

Of course, Lisa explains, here at UVA—where they insist on saying "grounds" instead of "campus" and Jefferson's original set of student rules ran ninety-five pages—they also have very strict and long-held traditional guidelines for any and all acts of spontaneous nudity. Sometime before they graduate, students are expected to strip naked and leave their clothes at the top of the Rotunda's expansive steps, just as Lisa described. They must then run 740 feet down the perfectly manicured Lawn to the statue of Homer (it's okay, he's blind), kiss the bard on his backside, return to the Rotunda's portico (all without being "spotlighted" or pelted with snowballs by seniors living nearby), and then whisper through the keyhole "goodnight, Mr. Jefferson" to the massive 160-year-old marble statue of the school's founder on display under the Rotunda's oculus.

The UVA streaking tradition, like all streaking traditions, I suppose, began in the 1970s. It peaked in 2019 after the Cavs won the NCAA hoops tournament when that same night hundreds of students celebrated with their own naked fast break across Jefferson's front lawn. Standing here now at the foot of the Rotunda, though, I can't help but wonder if the streaking endures, in part, as a kind of protest—a celebration of the ultimate form of equality, openness, and transparency conducted at the temple of Thomas Jefferson, a man we now know was notorious for covering things up.

Over the last ninety minutes Lisa has expertly detailed every conceivable aspect of life at UVA. There have been deep dives into cafeteria food, secret societies, Edgar Allen Poe, and dorm sinks doubling as toilets. But she has yet to mention UVA's founder, you know, the former president and the guy up on Mount Rushmore. "To me, UVA was like the one thing Thomas Jefferson did that was good, and I guess, honestly, I don't really like any of the rest, I just don't," Lisa explains. "I always think about this one thing with Jefferson: he was literally, like, the person known for a style of architecture, called concealment architecture, used for hiding things. I always think about that. Jefferson hid so much stuff and got so good at knowing how to hide so much stuff, he accidentally invented his own style of architecture."

Jefferson simply combined two of his passions—building things and hiding things—into a single hobby. "Architecture is my delight," he once said. And he was so prolific and talented in a kind of Americanized neoclassical style that one architectural historian referred to him as "the father of our national architecture." Apparently, that passion for building stuff was extraordinary. One so-called Jeffersonian scholar actually tried to argue that TJ was so totally obsessed with architecture, he couldn't possibly have had any energy left for an illicit affair with one of his slaves. It is intriguing, though, how so many of the structures Jefferson built seemed to become manifestations of the man himself, windows into his soul. And now, thanks to the tip from Lisa, everywhere I look in and around Charlottesville I see proof that even this part of Jefferson was corrupted by the man's shady side and his need to cover it all up.

Just behind where we're standing on the Lawn, the area's gardens are separated by a seemingly magnificent series of serpentine brick walls. The guidebook refers to them by the cutesy name of "crinkle-crankle walls" and claims they were created by Jefferson because he "admired the practicality of the design," when the truth is that Jefferson designed the original versions to creatively conceal the school's expansive slave quarters. Jefferson's concealment architecture is even more prevalent at his nearby mountaintop plantation, where author Henry Wiencek says, "The labyrinths of Monticello mirror the ambiguities of its maker." Jefferson owned 607 slaves (although, he did free two of them during his lifetime, or .0003 percent), and he built his mansion atop a long, subterranean corridor that kept his enslaved workforce completely out of sight.

Despite Jefferson's best efforts and his strange architectural gifts, everything eventually came to light. It always does. When it happened, Jefferson's standing as an American icon plummeted more precipitously than perhaps anyone else in history. In 1998, on the heels of groundbreaking work by author Annette Gordon-Reed, DNA testing concluded, finally, that Jefferson had indeed secretly fathered at least six children with his slave Sally Hemings. He did this all, of course, while declaring in his only book *Notes on the State of Virginia* that racial amalgamation was a horrific, disastrous idea. In *Notes*, Jefferson also wrote that because Black people were inferior, with intellects more like children, they had no place in America, slavery was probably their own fault, and Black women had likely copulated with "Oranootans" (Orangutans). I napped a lot during high school history, but I'm pretty certain this side of Jefferson was never covered in class. (Although, I suppose TJ referring to Indigenous people in his declaration as "merciless Indian Savages, whose known rule of warfare, is an undistinguished destruction of all ages, sexes and conditions" might have been a pretty good clue.) Trust me, Wiencek was not exaggerating when he described *Notes on*

123

the State of Virginia as "the Dismal Swamp every Jefferson biographer must sooner or later attempt to cross." It's not just biographers who have to slog through it, though. It's all of us. They say you can't pick your parents; well, that applies to countries as well. "There can be no question that Thomas Jefferson was deeply and profoundly racist," Gordon-Reed concluded in 1998. Although, decades earlier, in his book *White over Black*, it was Winthrop Jordan who first noted Jefferson's founding role in American racism and just how deeply messed up it is that we all still celebrate *this* guy for proclaiming: "All men are created equal."

Jefferson's disgusting declarations in *Notes* caused Stanford's John Chester Miller to assert in 1977 that if the rumors of the affair with Hemings were true, Jefferson "deserves to be regarded as one of the most profligate liars and consummate hypocrites ever to occupy the presidency." Indeed, after the DNA results came back, in a 2001 Gallup poll on the Greatest Presidents in American History, Jefferson garnered 1 percent of the vote, or one-tenth of the votes Bill Clinton received. And it seems unlikely he'll ever poll that high again. By 2012 Wiencek and others had discovered that Jefferson wasn't quite the reluctant, benevolent slave owner so many scholars had made him out to be. Instead, his highly touted early efforts on emancipation "virtually ceased" once Jefferson learned that profits from holding Black children (as young as ten) in bondage, and motivated by the whip, were keeping his extravagant lifestyle and his beloved Monticello afloat. Responding to Jefferson's lasting reputation as a would-be emancipator, Virginia abolitionist Moncure Conway hissed, "Never did a man achieve more fame for what he did not do." In its review of Wiencek's book, the *New York Times* referred to Jefferson as The Monster of Monticello, and that's about the nicest thing anyone's said about him since. Not too long before our tour of UVA, Jefferson was grouped in with the tiki torch–wielding white supremacists marching in Charlottesville. That day, counter protestors hung a sign on a Jefferson statue that read: "TJ is a racist and rapist." A few months later New York's city hall removed its Jefferson statue altogether.

Initially, my entire argument on Jefferson and the MecDec was going to be, basically: the dude enslaved his own children, so I doubt borrowing from the MecDec was a step too far for The Monster of Monticello. But my trip to Charlottesville made it clear that in recent years, our new insight, understanding, and attitude toward the real Thomas Jefferson have changed so significantly that it merits another look into John Adams's original accusation. For centuries the Mecklenburg vs. Monticello debate often came down to a simple question of character. Only now, after one of the most remarkable pendulum swings in history, that's a contest Jefferson loses in a landslide. And in light of that change, the question requires one more look: Did this guy actually commit the intellectual crime of the millennia? Did he plagiarize the MecDec while drafting his own Declaration of Independence? And then, did he and his cronies respond to these charges in what we now recognize as truly classic Jeffersonian style—by concealing the truth?

We shall see.

THE MECDEC AND JEFFERSON ARRIVED IN PHILADELPHIA TOGETHER IN June 1775.

This is what TV lawyers call "opportunity." When Jefferson sashayed back into Philly, all the talk around town would have been about the King, Lexington and Concord, independence, revolution, and the prospect of war. So it's not a stretch to imagine that tales of the brave, bold pioneers in Carolina and copies of their just-delivered secret, treasonous MecDec would have been gossiped about in every tavern and every corner of Independence Hall. Jefferson knew the North Carolina delegates by name and reputation. And at least one other member of the Committee of Five tasked with drafting the 1776 statement for independence—let's call it the JeffDec—was also aware of the MecDec. Draper writes that in 1775, McKnitt Alexander "visited Philadelphia, where he communicated to Dr. Ben Franklin the facts and the circumstances of the preceding Mecklenburg Convention, when they were fresh in his memory" and that Franklin "expressed his approbation of their act."

Years later, upon first learning of the MecDec's existence, it bears repeating that John Adams's initial response was to attack Jefferson in writing, several times, for daring to "conceal" (there's that word again) such an important document. "How is it possible that this paper should have been concealed from me to this day?" Adams asks in a letter to Jefferson. Still waiting on a satisfactory explanation, a month later Adams confided to William Bentley that he remained "struck with so much astonishment on reading this [MecDec] document, that I could not help inclosing it immediately to Mr. Jefferson, who must have seen it, in the time of it. . . . Its total concealment from me is a mystery."

After nearly a year together with the MecDec in Philadelphia, on May 23, 1776, Jefferson famously moved "out" of the city to the second floor of a brick building on the corner of Market and Seventh streets to attempt a first draft of the JeffDec. We all want to believe in the romantic notion of this event, when, as author Joseph Ellis puts it, Jefferson's quill captured the very soul of America. Even Abraham Lincoln, the ultimate straight-shooter, bought into the myth that somehow the fresh air and pastoral tranquility of the Pennsylvania countryside transformed a thirty-three-year-old Jefferson into some kind of oracle who sat down and channeled the eternal truths of man and the entire, perfectly formed Declaration of Independence all in one magical flutter of his wrist. (Like how *every* book gets written in the movies.) In reality, though, Jefferson's second-floor office was swarming with nasty, biting horseflies from the stables across the street and was probably a bit loud thanks to a nearby tavern where he kept a tab. And if the gods *were* speaking directly through Jefferson's hand, well, they could have used a proofreader. Jefferson's initial version required eighty-six edits and was cut down by 28 percent during what Pauline Maier, author of *American Scripture*, describes as "Congress's magnificent editing job." Any writer can certainly empathize with Jefferson, who was "extremely sensitive to any criticism of his prose," having to undergo such a tortuous editing process. (Franklin tried to soothe him during this time with the story of the hatmaker who edited his shop's fancy and wordy sign over and over until it was just a picture of a hat. It didn't help.) It's also important to note that the biggest cut to Jefferson's original draft was his fierce, moving denunciation of slavery, which he called an "assemblage of horrors."

What remained in the JeffDec, however, was considered at the time to be such a "workaday" document that it was all but forgotten for decades. (So much for the "mystery" behind why the MecDec didn't get more attention at the time. Turns out that after the War of Independence, no one in America had any interest in talking about any kind of declarations for quite some time.) One theory proposed by Maier is that as a new nation with a lot on its mind—mainly the whole democracy-experiment thing—it wasn't until after the War of 1812 that we were finally ready to exhale and reflect on the Revolution. When we did, it mostly consisted of canonizing the Founding Fathers, something that Adams considered corrupt and distasteful, and that Jefferson loved and embraced. To Adams, the JeffDec had been little more than a decorative "Theatrical Show." Jefferson, he lamented, had just been shrewd enough to run "away with all the stage effect of that: all the Glory of it." In the end, though, the recasting of the JeffDec from a routine document into a sacred text came down to the work of one man: Abraham Lincoln. Very early in his political career, using language laced with religious overtones, Lincoln promoted the idea that the JeffDec, and not the Constitution, was the very foundation of our republic and even the "immortal emblem of Humanity." This culminated, obviously, in 1863 with the Gettysburg Address, wherein Lincoln's interpretation of the JeffDec and its themes of Liberty, Equality, and Freedom transformed it from a simple break-up letter to the King into the sacred scripture it is today.

It's no fun at all adding proper context to something that has been so deeply mythologized for so long and by such giants—it feels like blasphemy, to be honest, like I'm going to get a visit from the angry ghost of my JeffDec-loving sixth-grade teacher, Ms. Palazollo. But the more framework and perspective you add to the creation of the JeffDec, the more likely it seems that the MecDec and other documents had to be in the mix somehow.

Adams, for one, certainly thought so.

"For [Jefferson] has copied the spirit, the sense, and the expression of it verbatim, into his Declaration of the 4th of July, 1776."

According to Ellis's work on the JeffDec, when he was tabbed for the job, Jefferson was not even all that interested in the national scene or writing about it. His heart and mind were still back in his home state of Virginia where, until as late as mid-May, he had been helping with the state's constitution. Jefferson seemed petrified by the very thought of joining in on even the most necessary arguments and debates in Congress. So much so that Adams once recalled, "During the whole time I sat with [Jefferson] in Congress, I never heard him utter three sentences together." Jefferson was considered "utterly useless in situations that demanded the projection of a public presence." He had, however, distinguished himself as a writer among his peers in Philadelphia, and so Jefferson essentially got the Declaration gig because the top choices for the assignment were busy with far more important nation-building business. Adams called this the "Body, Soul, or Substance" of working toward independence, whereas Jefferson was much more suited for the "dress and ornament" part of drafting the Declaration. I know. I know. *What could possibly be more important than the Declaration of Independence?* Just about everything, it turns out. After all, the case for independence had already been won months earlier by the wildly popular *Common Sense.* On top of that we had already been at war for more than a year. And by June 1776 it was going poorly enough that there was a real possibility we might lose the entire revolution before even getting a chance to formally declare independence.

Outside of North Carolina, that is.

I know how shocking and disorienting this all is—to realize when it comes to the history surrounding Jefferson and the Declaration of Independence that, as Ruth Langmore said in *Ozark,* we all pretty much "don't know sh*t about f*ck." But in June 1776 the JeffDec was essentially a two-week rush job to complete what amounted to some overdue paperwork. It sounds crazy, but even Ellis confirms it was a "merely ornamental afterthought," especially to those charged with writing it. "It is the beginning of all genuine wisdom [on the topic of the JeffDec] to recognize that neither Jefferson nor any other of the participants foresaw the historical significance of what they were doing at the time," writes Ellis. "The golden haze around the Declaration had not yet formed. The sense of history we bring to the subject did not exist for those making it."

Given just days to complete the task and with no inkling anyone would care about a word of it, it's almost understandable why Jefferson may have felt so entitled to borrow so generously (and unapologetically) from so many outside sources. (Although, let's be honest, it has been fairly well-established that the guy had zero qualms about using the labor of others for his own pleasure and advancement.) "While it seems almost sacrilegious to suggest that the creative process that produced the Declaration was a cut-and-paste job," Ellis continues, "it strains credulity and common sense to the breaking point to believe that Jefferson did not have these [other documents] at his elbow and draw liberally from them when drafting the Declaration."

In fact, the scene that Ellis paints of the second-floor writing room at Market and Seventh is of Jefferson, quill in hand, blank page in front of him, with dozens of reference materials spread out across his desk and the entire room. To complete his "cut-and-paste job," Jefferson had his pick of "many similar documents at the time in which Americans advocated, explained, and justified Independence, the most painful decision of their collective lives," says Maier.

The documents likely included Jefferson's own work on the Virginia Constitution, John Locke's philosophy on government, the MecDec, which Maier mentions in her book, and the freshly minted words of Virginia's George Mason, which had been, not so coincidentally, published in the *Pennsylvania Gazette* the exact same week Jefferson started his own draft.

Mason's preamble might just ring a bell or two with some of the more serious history buffs among us. It states: "All men are created equally free and independent and have certain inherent and natural rights . . . among which are the enjoyment of life and liberty, with the means of acquiring and possessing property, and pursuing and obtaining happiness and safety."

If that sounds outrageously familiar, well, check out a few passages from the MecDec side by side with the JeffDec:

MecDec: . . . and to the inherent and inalienable rights of man.

JeffDec: . . . with certain unalienable Rights.

MecDec: . . . do hereby dissolve the political bands which have connected us to the mother country, and hereby absolve ourselves from all allegiance to the British Crown.

JeffDec: . . . they are absolved from all allegiance to the British Crown, and that all political connection between them and the State of Great Britain, is and ought to be totally dissolved.

MecDec: . . . do hereby declare ourselves a free and independent people; are, and of right ought to be, a sovereign and self-governing Association.

JeffDec: That these united Colonies are, and of Right ought to be Free and Independent States.

MecDec: . . . we solemnly pledge to each other our mutual cooperation, our lives, our fortunes, and our most sacred honor.

JeffDec: And for the support of this Declaration, with a firm reliance on the protection of Divine Providence, we mutually pledge to each other our Lives, our Fortunes, and our sacred Honor.

To Adams the resemblance was, shall we say, self-evident.

"Either these resolutions are a plagiarism from Mr. Jefferson's Declaration of Independence, or, Mr. Jefferson's Declaration of Independence is a plagiarism from those resolutions," Adams wrote. "I could as soon believe that the dozen flowers of the Hydrangea, now before my eyes, were the work of chance, as that the Mecklenburg resolutions and Mr. Jefferson's Declaration were not derived the one from the other."

Jefferson historian George Tucker, who published his two-volume *Life of Thomas Jefferson* in 1837, agreed that the MecDec and JeffDec were so similar it simply could not have been a coincidence. "Every one must be persuaded, at least all who have been minute observers of style, that one of these papers had borrowed from the other," Tucker concluded. "For they are identical, not in one instance, but in several, and not in single words only, but in phrases composed of many."

Perhaps even more disturbing, if that's possible, is that Jefferson was accused of plagiarism so often throughout his life that he had developed a standard boilerplate reply to this sort of thing. I used to think the most Jeffersonian thing ever was UVA's Rotunda and how he enjoyed such universal praise for "designing" what is basically a scaled-down carbon copy of Palladio's Roman Pantheon.

But I've changed my mind.

This right here, Jefferson's plagiarism-defense template, this is a level of pure, two-faced evil genius you almost have to respect.

In defense of his 1776 Declaration, Jefferson tried to claim that part of the assignment was *not* coming up with any wild new ideas or phrases and that the JeffDec was, he said, "neither aiming at originality of principle or sentiment, nor yet copied from any particular and previous writing." Instead, Jefferson added, his ideas came from "the harmonizing sentiments of the day, whether expressed in letters, printed essays, or in the elementary books of public right, as Aristotle, Cicero, Locke, Sidney, etc." That "etc." is my favorite part. The way Jefferson just kind of looks down at his nails and yada-yadas over the most important minds in human history? Uh-mazing.

Jefferson could have just stopped there. He really *should have* just stopped there. After all, his assignment was not to create something new with the JeffDec but to quickly synthesize the sentiments of the day. And he could argue that a lot of the language in question having to deal with inalienable rights and essential liberties had been pretty common in the colonies since as far back as the protests against the 1765 Stamp Act. There's also an argument to be made that the MecDec and JeffDec both borrowed from a pool of phrases regarding freedom and independence that were just part of the common lexicon at the time.

But, of course, Jefferson had to go a step further and claim that while his Declaration of Independence wasn't totally original, he absolutely, positively, did not borrow from any outside material whatsoever while writing it. Forgetting just for the moment that, uh, THOSE TWO THINGS CANNOT BOTH BE TRUE, this kind of audacious, boldfaced, IDGAF hypocrisy was, essentially, Jefferson's signature move. Kind of like how he warned the world in writing about the horrors of mixing races while simultaneously fathering six children during a decades-long relationship with a Black slave who was his dead wife's half-sister.

Jefferson's duplicitous nature had managed to turn even the JeffDec into just another piece of concealment architecture.

TJ used the exact same technique to deflect Adams's accusations regarding the MecDec. In early July 1819, the seventy-six-year-old Jefferson was still in relatively good health but under a ton of stress trying to resolve more than $40,000 in personal debt, all while racing to complete his beloved University of Virginia. Despite all this, just five days after the last MecDec letter from Adams, Jefferson penned a lengthy reply. It was classic TJ through and through: dizzying amounts of double-speak and misdirection presented through a velvety fog of beautifully crafted, statesmanlike prose. Even at this late stage of

Jefferson's life, he must have remained wary of Adams, who was neurotically jealous of his political success and especially his growing historic renown as the author of the Declaration of Independence. The gleeful "gotcha!" energy that oozed from Adams's MecDec letters could not have been hard to miss, either.

So instead of being defensive, Jefferson disarms Adams by thanking him for the information right away before cleverly undermining the seriousness of the entire ordeal by comparing it to a famous 1812 hoax of a volcano erupting in North Carolina.

Of course, those two sections only serve to soften and frame Jefferson's real response.

"You seem to think [the MecDec] genuine," he writes.

"I believe it spurious."

The rest of the reply is Jefferson, having done no research whatsoever, blindly nitpicking the publication, the timing, the strange secrecy of the document, the wishy-washy delegates from North Carolina, what he deemed as an overall lack of proof, and this so-called "McKnitt" guy who was behind the whole thing. "If the name McKnitt be real, and not a part of the fabrication, it needs a vindication by the production of such proof," Jefferson says. McKnitt was definitely real and such proof was indeed bountiful. Jefferson also knew better than anyone on the planet that there was no strange secrecy surrounding the MecDec. Remember: no one talked about his declaration, either, for almost four decades following the Revolution. For the time being, however, Jefferson said he was forced to remain "an unbeliever in the apocryphal gospel." Not entirely, though. Since a few lines earlier, in classic TJ form I might add, he had stated the exact opposite opinion, acknowledging that he could not say, positively, that the MecDec was a fabrication and that more evidence might just convince him it was legit. "I must not be understood as suggesting any doubtfulness in the State of North Carolina. No state was more fixed or forward," he concluded.

Your eyes are not deceiving you. Yes, Jefferson complimented North Carolina on its integrity and patriotism, and then he fully admitted a little more evidence might just change his mind on the MecDec, right before flipping the script and casually calling everyone in the state a bunch of liars, con artists, and heretics.

My first thought after reading this was: *Damn this guy's good*.

Adams was better, though.

Six days before Jefferson's reply, you'll recall, Adams had already written to the Reverend William Bentley suggesting that the MecDec was far superior to Thomas Paine's *Common Sense*, that Jefferson had "copied the spirit . . . of it *verbatim* into his Declaration of the 4th of July, 1776," and that the MecDec needed to be "more universally made known to the present and future generation." Publicly accusing Jefferson of plagiarism was no small matter. But Adams knew exactly what he was doing. Before Jefferson could weasel his way out of this mess or expertly cover it all up, Adams had locked the whole thing into the historical record with an unimpugnable second source.

This sentence is proof his plan worked.

Then, after hearing back from Jefferson, Adams proved he could be every bit as devious as his old political rival. In a letter to Monticello dated July 21, 1819, Adams informed Jefferson that he had convinced him the MecDec was fiction. Notice, though, that Adams, the former trial attorney, never says he himself believed the MecDec to be fake, only that Jefferson had convinced him of it. Now it was all on Jefferson. The rest of the letter is a similar master class of passive-aggressive soothing and taunting. Adams suggests that if the MecDec was unknown to someone of Jefferson's stature and intellect, then surely it must have been "unknown to all mankind." He then wonders what the possible motive could have been behind the MecDec story while coyly reminding Jefferson that because he took all the credit for being the sole author of the Declaration, he was on his own when it came to any charges of plagiarism. "What could be the Motive?" Adams asked. "Was it to bring a Charge of Plagiarism against the Congress, in 1776, or against you: the undoubted acknowledged draftsman of the Declaration of Independence?"

Just in case there was any doubt where Adams stood on the matter, a month later he wrote back to Reverend Bentley and opened his correspondence with "The plot thickens." Adams reported that he was blown away upon learning that one of the men vouching for the MecDec's authenticity was longtime North Carolina senator, and former speaker of the house, Nathaniel Macon. "The name of the Cato of North Carolina, the honest, hoary-headed, stern, determined republican, *Macon*, strikes me with great force," Adams exclaimed before providing Bentley with a detailed list of eight insights and theories on the MecDec.

"I know not whether I have written the tenth part of the reflections that have occurred to me," Adams confessed, "but I have written more than my eyes and nerves can well bear."

Those were Adams's last written words on the MecDec. He was, perhaps, waiting for a reply from Monticello. But it never appeared. Jefferson, The Monster, kept his remaining thoughts on the MecDec . . . concealed.

Which leaves me no choice.

I'll just have to go confront Thomas Jefferson myself.

ON TOP OF TJ's PRIVATE MOUNTAIN AT MONTICELLO, THE ONE THING you'd expect to be concealed is right there out in the open for everyone to see. Despite being clearly marked by a green and white *PRIVY VENT* sign, the first thing I see after exiting the shuttle bus is a handful of young tourists Winnie-the-Pooh-ing themselves deep into Jefferson's tunnel-shaped toilet vents. (There's a metaphor here, somewhere, but unlike these kids I'm not willing to dig too deep for it.) With forty-five minutes to kill before Thomas Jefferson is supposed to speak under a large tree on the southwest side of the grounds, I decide to escape the crowds milling about the mansion and venture down to Mulberry Row, where Jefferson housed his slaves. I've got the area to myself except for a family from Tokyo that I bonded with over a shared laugh at the privy spelunkers.

While UVA has recently done a lot to acknowledge and memorialize the school's deep connection to slavery, Monticello continues to move at a glacial pace when it comes to accurately updating Jefferson's story. For decades Sally Hemings's quarters were concealed under a bathroom installed for tourists. (Another metaphor, I suppose.) In 2014, though, a tiny, sparse wooden hut was reconstructed to give an example of what life was like on Mulberry Row, a spot one archeologist described as a "relatively shabby Main Street" at Monticello. Just inside the door of the structure there's a placard that reads *NOT SO BAD?* It's here to remind visitors that the relative "material comfort" of this horrific place does not lessen the severity and horror of enslavement. The sign has me frozen in the doorway for a long time in a WTF fog, trying to wrap my brain around the need for such a notice, when another example of Jefferson's architectural genius presents itself. As I look up from this exact vantage point on Mulberry Row, Jefferson's mansion up the hill just sort of magically disappears over the horizon, like some kind of optical illusion.

And, once again, the thought hits me: *damn, this guy's good.*

He's had a lot of help, though. On my way to Charlottesville, I finished Alexis Coe's great bio of George Washington. "We need to question and review *everything*—including presidential biographies," Coe says. Especially the countless hagiographies of our founders, most of them produced by fawning older white authors Coe brilliantly labels The Thigh Men of Dad History for their odd tendency to wax so poetically about Washington's voluptuous haunches. These are the writers who develop massive man crushes on their subjects somewhere along the way and, Coe suggests, end up trading in their objectivity to serve as self-appointed guardians. Jefferson has a full harem of his own Thigh Men. And for centuries, with the kind of vigor you normally see in religious fanatics, they've successfully suppressed the full, unvarnished truth about their man. The Thigh Men of Monticello even dismissed substantial anecdotal proof about Sally Hemings and instead concluded there simply was no affair based on rigorous research that, as far as I can tell, amounted to *because we said so.* "Within the scholarly world, especially within the community of Jefferson specialists," Thigh Man Joseph Ellis exclaimed in 1998, "there seems to be a clear consensus that the story [of the affair with Sally Hemings] is almost certainly not true."

Whoops.

That wasn't the only thing these guys got completely wrong, though. The Thigh Men of Monticello also managed to breeze over Jefferson's repeated infatuations with married women. Most people tend to focus on Jefferson's affair with married Italian artist Maria Cosway, which produced Jefferson's infamous 1786 love letter "My Head and My Heart." Even more sleazy, though, is the well-documented case of Jefferson full-on stalking and sexually harassing his best friend John Walker's wife *for years*. In 1768, before leaving for a long expedition to the frontier, John Walker entrusted the safety and care of his wife, Betsy, and their newborn daughter to his longtime friend Thomas Jefferson. Big mistake. *Huge* mistake. Jefferson pounced on the vulnerable, isolated young mother and relentlessly pressured her, unsuccessfully, to have an affair. When his friend returned, and even after Jefferson himself was married, the harassment only increased, as did the extreme creepiness. In a statement given to newspapers—one that Jefferson was compelled to confirm or face a pistol duel to restore Betsy's honor—Walker wrote that on more than one occasion, Jefferson, the sociopath, snuck into Betsy's room late at night and tried to force himself on her.

"All this time," Walker wrote, "I believed him to be my best friend."

I bring this episode up now because this is usually where we hear about "presentism" and how it's unfair to judge Jefferson's eighteenth-century behavior by today's standards. It's typically the Thigh Men of Monticello's last resort, and it's not without merit, but Jefferson doesn't come off a whole lot better in context, either. Many people throughout Western civilization opposed slavery by this point. And most of Jefferson's contemporaries, including George Washington and Ben Franklin, were able to evolve their thinking and free their slaves.

An older Washington said the thought of continuing to treat humans like "cattle in the market" disgusted him. And please remind me, during what era of human history was it cool to terrorize your best friend's wife? As Gordon-Reed put it, "Most Americans probably do not want anything to have been wrong with Thomas Jefferson. . . . [But] the only alternative is to face the unpalatable thought that there may have, indeed, been something wrong with him." If you require context for that conclusion, well, Martha Washington also found Jefferson's company to be "uniquely unpleasant." She considered "the election of Mr. Jefferson as one of the most detestable of mankind, as the greatest misfortune our country has ever experienced." The main reason Adams was so excited (and slightly obsessed) about his discovery of the MecDec, after all, was that he had always suspected Jefferson was a fraud, and the MecDec was his proof.

That's what I'm after as I make my way up from Mulberry Row to a group of wooden benches under a giant maple tree on Monticello's flower-lined west lawn. (TJ picked a breathtaking spot for his home, I'll give him that.) The weather changes frequently up here, though, and the sky has turned an ominous indigo as we wait for Jefferson to appear, or, more accurately, his stand-in, the much-acclaimed historical actor Bill Barker. Almost as unsettling as the storm clouds, though, are the legions of Jefferson followers gathering up for our chat. I call them T-Shirt Patriots because most of them are sporting some variation of less-than-clever, slightly obnoxious slogan-heavy apparel that seems to refer to the causes they think Jefferson championed—smaller government, states' rights, less taxes.

On the shuttle bus the guy across from me had on a shirt with portraits of Jefferson, Washington, and Franklin under the title: Right Wing Extremists. In the past few hours I've also come across a few Don't Tread on Me logos and witnessed the American flag festooned on grimy socks, camo shorts, and a bedazzled handbag. A guy sitting in the front row waiting for the talk from Jefferson/Barker is sporting a shirt covered in cartoon firearms that says One Gun, Two Gun, Red Gun, Blue Gun, which, I'm sure he knows, is actually from a book on acceptance by the dangerous revolutionary, and kids book author, Dr. Seuss. On a bench behind me a mom in a *Friends* hat is sitting next to a guy camouflaging his man boobs with a Faith/Family/Flag/Freedom shirt.

Nearby there's also an older man walking his white cockapoo around the grounds in an Amoroso baby stroller. From a distance it looks like this guy might be wearing a shirt featuring Jefferson's quote about the Tree of Liberty being refreshed by the Blood of Tyrants, which would complete my T-Shirt Patriot bingo card.

Alas, I'm wrong. It's just Old Navy.

Moments later, Barker strolls up, hands clasped behind his back, and introduces himself as our humble and obedient servant, Thomas Jefferson. He's so good at this it makes you wish Jefferson were more like Barker, not vice-versa. Resplendent in a pilgrim-style buckle hat, leather boots, knee breeches, and full-length linen long coat, from the get-go it's pretty clear just how much he enjoys making the T-Shirt Patriots squirm, making a show of reminding them that he is a man of science, a leading advocate for freedom of religion, and a strong believer in the idea that *what* America is—and *who*

America is—grows, expands, and improves with each more diverse generation. This makes me wonder what the T-shirt Patriots would think about TJ's aggressive sexual proclivities, his extravagant tastes for fancy furniture, clothing, and imported wine, his massive personal debt, his less-than-brave behavior during the war, or his take on Christianity, which he called "the most perverted system that ever shone on man."

With the T-Shirt Patriots rendered sufficiently speechless for the moment, I start TJ off with a softball.

"Did you really write the entire Declaration in just a week?" I ask.

"In fact I did not, young man," Jefferson replies. "I completed my rough draft in just three days."

"And were you . . . the first to consider it?" I blurt out, moving in for the kill before Jefferson can pick someone else to call on.

"Independence, I mean."

Jefferson cocks his head and squints at me as if trying to read my mind, or signal security.

"As a representative of Virginia, why yes, yes I was first," he replies.

I can sense my body coiling in anticipation, but before I can scream "LIAR!" Jefferson raises his finger, politely asking for a moment.

Standing there, with his chin in his hand and that index finger tapping his mouth as if to scold it, TJ says, "Well, no wait, I believe I've just caught myself in a fib . . . and as I've said many times, a man who lies once will lie often . . . Virginia, as I said, was in fact not the first to declare independence from Britain."

Oh my god, I think, *I did it*. TJ's about to come clean.

As my mind races—*He's gonna say MecDec . . . He's gonna say MecDec*—I'm picturing the street I'm going to get named after me back in Charlotte and the huge parade they'll throw in my honor when, out of nowhere, Jefferson rudely interrupts my daydream.

"Rhode Island was first," he says, his words landing like a gut punch to my soul.

"My dear friends, I stand corrected; it was Rhode Island that was first among us to declare independence."

As I stand there paralyzed with my mouth hanging open—now suffering from a severe case of RhoDec Face, I guess—TJ quickly moves on to another question before the whole spiel is cut short by a sudden downpour.

Distraught, I decide to skip the shuttle and descend Jefferson's mountain on foot. At the beginning, the path parallels Mulberry Row and then winds down toward Jefferson's cemetery, where I get enough of a break in the storm to confirm on my phone that Rhode Island was not, in fact, first to freedom. The Hope state declared independence on May 4, 1776, which is amazing, but still almost a full, safe, comfortable, and relatively risk-free year after our true Founding Fathers in Charlotte took action.

In this moment I'm more convinced than ever that when it comes to formally recognizing the group that bravely blazed our collective path toward freedom, being first matters. Being first to freedom matters a lot. And with this there can be no question:

The MecDec was first.

And TJ was wrong.

Again.

As I continue down toward his gravesite, I realize there's really no need for any kind of reprisal against Jefferson. The folks at Monticello have taken care of that quite nicely. Suffering from bouts of self-doubt and melancholy (and a guilty conscience) near the end of his life, Jefferson left very strict instructions for his grave marker to be a plain, coarse-stone obelisk that was to identify him as author of the Declaration of Independence and the Statute of Virginia for Religious Freedom, as well as the father of the University of Virginia, and "not a word more." The stone sits in a picturesque tree- and clover-filled family plot framed by a tall, ornate English-looking black wrought iron fence. The base of Jefferson's obelisk is supposed to serve as a memorial to Jefferson's daughter Martha, but it has been covered in coins and other detritus, like a toy compass, that people discarded through the fence on the way past.

A little less than half a mile farther down the mountain, inside the lobby of the visitor center and before you see or learn anything about Jefferson and his declaration, there is an incredible art installation by Maxine Helfman.

The piece is called *Forefathers* and it features the twelve US presidents who owned slaves. The small photographic portraits in gold leaf frames cover the walls, and until you stop and take a closer look, you don't realize that part of each president's face has been torn away and replaced by a portrait of a contemporary Black American.

The mood is considerably lighter next door at the expansive and crowded gift shop. There are Jefferson bobbleheads, Jefferson socks, framed Canons of Conduct that lack all manner of self-awareness, several books on the Hemings family and, for a mere eighty-nine dollars, you can own a blouse-y replica of something called Jefferson's Everyday Shirt. But the most popular things in the store seem to be the coffee cups, t-shirts, and tote bags featuring the gawd-awful pun "Life, Liberty and the Pursuit of Happiness (Hour)."

At this point of my quest I'd give anything to ask the author of those once important, immortal words what he thinks of them now being reduced to hacky coffee cup puns.

But then I remember that's impossible.

George Mason has been dead for centuries.

Nine

A Damned Hornet's Nest of Rebellion (Everywhere but the NBA)

The Battle of Charlotte begins in less than twenty minutes, and with our troops currently amassed along the corn dog stand, I'm not loving our chances. After the MecDec, this Revolutionary War battle was probably Charlotte's greatest contribution to the country's cause of independence and freedom. As one of today's reenactment narrators explains to me later, with the sulfur-y aroma of faux musket fire still lingering in the air, "this was *the* pivotal battle of the Southern Campaign because for the first time, even though he outnumbered us by, like, two thousand troops, the great Cornwallis went in the opposite direction that he wanted to go."

Charlotte's courageous, some might say miraculous, efforts in the battle being reenacted today were part of a long domino chain of events that led to British General Charles Cornwallis's ultimate surrender at Yorktown, the end of the Revolutionary War, and the birth of our nation. Which means you could make a serious argument that the American Revolution was won in the South, and by the South. It sounds a little nuts, I know, especially considering, well, every high school history textbook ever produced. Obviously, there were a few (hundred) other factors at play. And, yes, the war ended with Cornwallis's back to the Chesapeake (and the French Navy) and a third of his army in tatters. But the question no one ever bothers to ask is who drove him there in such a state? And the answer, at least partly, is the same force that created the MecDec. "On October 19, 1781, Cornwallis surrendered," say historians Jeffrey Denman and John Walsh. "And the war in the South, which has become the unknown American Revolution in the history books, had proved itself to be the deciding theatre of battle. The Carolinas were the proving ground of American resolve."

They had no choice, really. Starting in Charleston, then moving to Camden and Charlotte, Cornwallis's plan was to slice through the Carolinas. And he wanted to do it with such ferocity that so many fence-sitting colonists would join his ranks along the way, he'd have a colossal, unstoppable army by the time he turned north. The significance of the Southern Campaign of the Revolutionary War has been largely lost, or ignored, by most historians, which, by this point, we should all know means absolutely nothing. In fact, it's quite easy to connect the dots and understand the larger importance of today's battle. If the South and the Carolinas were a critical stage in the war and Britain's strategy in this theater was to persuade Southerners to switch sides and rally in support of the Crown, imagine, for a second, just how important the MecDec was as a revolutionary symbol and a rallying cry.

Today's reenactment, the Battle of Charlotte, would be the physical manifestation of that document.

"[The MecDec] had a general influence on the people of this county to unite them in the cause of liberty and the country . . . and [the MecDec] had considerable effect in harmonizing the people in two or three adjoining counties," said General George Graham, Joseph's older brother. "That same unanimity and patriotism continued unimpaired to the close of the war."

Nearly all the participants in the creation of the MecDec (and I'm guessing anyone who read or heard about it across the region) backed that 1775 declaration with fidelity and sacrifice to America in the war. The leaders in Charlotte didn't just demand freedom in writing, take their bows for their eloquent, powerful prose, and then, when the true test of their patriotism arrived, cower and flee to some mountaintop mansion (. . . in Virginia, just outside of Charlottesville, if you're catching my drift). No, in fact, most of the MecDec crew picked up their rifles almost as soon as they put down their pens inside the Charlotte courthouse. Patriot blood was shed, and many patriot lives were lost, on the very same courthouse steps where the MecDec was proclaimed.

That sacrifice means something in the greater context of this topic.

At least, it should.

On top of that, later, when called upon to document and defend the MecDec, these same men, sons of the American Revolution, high-level commanders of the Southern Theater, and war heroes beyond reproach—men like Thomas Polk, Robert Irwin, William Lee Davidson, Joseph Graham, and William Davie, just to name a few—would be charged with vouching for the declaration's authenticity. None more than Davie. Raised as an orphan on the Carolina frontier, Davie somehow managed to graduate from Princeton and become a lawyer in Salisbury, only to immediately set it all aside to serve in the cavalry when the revolution began. Seriously wounded in 1779, he had retired from military service but returned to fight when Cornwallis set his sights on Charlotte. By war's end he would be a general and, later, the governor of North Carolina. The "Father" of the University of North Carolina, Davie was also appointed by John Adams as a special envoy to France. And if what they say is true—that combat doesn't build character, it *reveals* it—then it's important to know how the MecDec men behaved in battle compared to contemporaries like, say, oh I don't know . . . someone like Thomas Jefferson.

This is why, on the glorious opening weekend of the college football season, instead of vegging out in front of the TV consuming my body weight in nachos, I'm here wandering around Rural Hill, a 265-acre historic site and nature preserve outside of Charlotte that's mostly known for something called the Amazing Maize Maze, which, I think, is where they charge you twenty dollars to get lost in a cornfield. Originally, Rural Hill was the estate and plantation of MecDec Signer Major John Davidson. He was the cousin of General William Lee Davidson, who fought in the battle being staged today. And Davidson College, a.k.a. NBA superstar Steph Curry's alma mater, is named in honor of William Lee. Rural Hill also provided the lumber for the original construction of the school, which just happens to be my current next-door neighbor. And by that, I mean that I live so close to campus I occasionally have to fish Natty Light empties out of my front yard bushes.

There's a lot of MecDec history to explore here at Rural Hill as well. As a verified cemetery connoisseur, the first thing I notice upon arrival is the

Davidson family's lovely burial ground, framed by an artisanal multicolored stonewall and featuring two bronze tomb markers and one marble marker signifying that Major John was, indeed, "A Signer of the Mecklenburg Declaration of Independence May 20th 1775." Next to Major John's tomb there's also a granite step from East Trade Street used by Cornwallis during his (very) brief occupation of Charlotte. Given what happened when Cornwallis tried to take on the MecDecers, the placement of a Cornwallis artifact inside a cemetery seems perfectly apropos.

Even after exploring the cemetery and the ruins of Major John's mansion, which burned down in 1886, I've still got more than an hour to kill before the battle begins. Lucky for me, there isn't a richer canvas on earth for the art of people-watching than one of these Revolutionary reenactment carnivals.

For starters, nearly everyone here is in authentic era outfits, decked out in tri-cornered hats, knee britches, bonnets, and Revolutionary-style big buckle shoes, giving the grounds the look and feel of a *Hamilton* cosplay convention. The first person I approach is a local militiaman in a puffy shirt who, between mouthfuls of corn dog and Mountain Dew, informs me that the patriot encampment is in a meadow on the north side of the property. Yes, these fantastic, lovely weirdos camp here for several days, using cloth tents and cooking methods from the time period. And it's easy to see why: the natural beauty at Rural Hill is stunning, and every last participant is beyond friendly and engaging. No one seems to have their phone out, either, and the longer I'm here the more I feel the restorative effects of this event's slow, quiet, communal old-school vibe. It's like that rare, euphoric feeling you get at concerts—one of the last places on earth where you know everyone around you fully loves the exact same thing.

"If you get to the pigs," the militia guy mumbles at me, "you've gone too far."

It takes me a moment (I'm distracted by the smell of corn dogs), but I soon realize that by "pigs" he means the British troops.

And just like that, my immersion into this world is complete.

Strolling on the path toward the meadow, I pass a blacksmith, a fiddler, and then the clicking sounds of a sewing wheel that's part of a sewing circle being led by a dead ringer for actor Leslie Jordan. There's also a deafening cannon demonstration that makes it look like we're laying siege to the Maize Maze, which is cool by me. The audience is full of what can only be described as groupies who giggle and swoon every time the weapon shakes the ground and the militia captain warns us to open our mouths just a bit to protect our eardrums and internal organs from the pressure created by the massive, impending explosion.

During the work week this dude is probably an assistant manager at Hertz.

But here at Rural Hill, he is the Cannon King.

At the tree line next to the cannons is a British battalion led by a commander decked out in the checkered red socks and matching beret of the Royal Highland Regiment. While our soldiers are stuffing themselves with deep-fried carnival treats, the enemy is drilling in preparation for battle. The second the snazzy captain notices me eavesdropping, though, he starts laying into his charges in a heavy, Benny Hill–style British accent. So, my money's still on the MecDecers.

Moments later, the town crier announces that, preceding the battle, there will be a reading of the MecDec by Sir Robert Ryals. This is truly an unexpected and special treat for MecDec nerds like me who know that Ryals is *the* voice of the MecDec. His thunderous renditions are the stuff of legend. And as soon as Ryals (in full costume, save for the modern reading glasses) steps out onto the porch of Major John's cabin, overlooking the battle grounds, a crowd begins to gather. When he dramatically removes the MecDec from his leather saddlebag and unfurls it, there is an audible gasp from the sewing circle, the blacksmith halts his hammer, and spectators lined up in front of the porch all place their right hands over their hearts.

"RESOLVED!" Ryals roars, his voice echoing across the valley, "That whosoever directly or indirectly abets, or in any way, form or manner countenances the invasion of our rights, as attempted by the Parliament of Great Britain, is an enemy to this country, to America, and to the rights of man.

"RESOLVED! That we, the citizens of Mecklenburg County, do hereby dissolve the political bonds which have connected us with the mother country, and absolve ourselves from all allegiance to the British crown, abjuring all political connect . . ."

And right on cue, those cheeky bastards from the Royal Highland Regiment fire up the crowd into a real pre-battle lather by interrupting Ryals with cries of "Treason!" and "God save the Queen!"

It's fine. It's fine.

Today, Her Majesty and her troops will need all the help they can get.

THE MECDEC SIGNERS WERE FOUNDING FATHERS TO AN ENTIRE NATION, but they were also father figures to one Joseph Graham. Thanks, in large part, to a 450-page memoir/archive compiled by his grandson, there's a vivid and detailed oral history of nearly every aspect of Graham's extraordinary and heroic life, including a portrait that reveals he was a dead ringer for Sting. (Unlike Cornwallis, who looked more like Jon Lovitz in a white wig.) Much of Graham's book was intended to be part of an extensive, scholarly history of North Carolina that never made it to publication. Because of this work, though, we know that Graham was four years old and living in Berks County, Pennsylvania, when his father died, forcing the family to relocate to Mecklenburg where they were taken in for a time by their Scots-Irish relatives. We also know that at fifteen Graham was a college student in Charlotte when he witnessed the MecDec's creation. He was "distinguished among his fellow students for talents, industry, and the most manly and conciliating deportment" and a frequent patron of Pat Jack's Tavern, where he loved Captain Jack's peach brandy. We also know that Graham's life was changed forever after witnessing, firsthand, the creation, oration, and celebration of the MecDec. Three years after hearing Thomas Polk read the MecDec from the Charlotte courthouse steps, Graham enlisted in the 4th North Carolina Regiment.

After several months of what sounds like mostly marching, waiting, and suffering in the swampy Carolina conditions, in the spring of 1780 a disillusioned Graham was discharged with a three-year exemption from military service. When he returned home, however, the circumstances were so alarming that Graham had no choice but to, once again, take up arms in defense of his beloved Charlotte.

Graham was plowing his mother's fields when word reached him about the horrors of Buford's Massacre. He left the plow right where it stood and raced back into town, where he saw his college had been turned into a field hospital, the wooden floors now soaked crimson with the blood of wounded American soldiers who had managed to flee from Cornwallis's bloody wrath in South Carolina.

They were the lucky ones.

England's Southern strategy was practically unstoppable at this point. Within the first eighteen months, the Brits had destroyed three colonial armies, taken Charleston and Savannah, and killed or wounded seven thousand American troops. In May 1780, retreating after the surrender of Charleston, American troops were overrun by the British cavalry of Colonel Banastre Tarleton, an utterly ruthless chap who so reveled in his own dastardliness he was given not one but two nicknames: Bloody Ban and Ban the Butcher. (Why not just Ban the Bloody Butcher, though, right?) Perhaps overcompensating for having to wear a silly helmet with a giant plume of feathers on top, Tarleton was said to have seduced his future wife on a bet and counted a royal courtesan among his many mistresses, along with her daughter. His mounted troops were known as dragoons, which is a pretty cool name, I have to admit. It's like a cross between dragon and goon, or a thuggish lizard, which in Tarleton's case fits perfectly.

Outside of Charleston, when American Colonel Abraham Buford finally raised the white flag of surrender, asking for mercy, someone seems to have fired one last shot at Ban the Bloody Butcher's horse. Trapped under his horse and thinking him dead (the British Colonel, not the horse), Tarleton's Raiders retaliated with what field surgeon Robert Brownfield described as "indiscriminate carnage never surpassed by the most ruthless atrocities of the most barbarous savages." Buford's Massacre, or Tarleton's Quarter, if you prefer, soon became a rallying cry on the front lines across the Carolinas.

For a long time in South Carolina, even after the arrival of Major General Horatio Gates, "indiscriminate carnage" was the best our troops could hope for. Gates had been a bona fide American hero credited (some say, by himself) with winning the Battle of Saratoga, New York, which helped turn the tide of the war in the North. It was such an important W that, for a little while at least, Gates was considered as a possible replacement for George Washington. There was just one tiny problem: Gates wasn't really all that strong of a field commander. And he was an even worse cook.

After his success at Saratoga, Gates was transferred to command the Southern Theater, which put him on a collision course with the mighty Cornwallis at the critical supply post of Camden. About eighty miles south of Charlotte, Camden would go down as one of the worst defeats in the history of the American military and the instant, ignominious end to Gates's command, to say nothing of his reputation. This was quite an accomplishment in the FUBAR Southern Theater where, after a hard-fought victory at Hanging Rock, the patriots found a large store of rum, got hammered, and forgot to take any prisoners. Those guys were downright professional compared to Gates, though. On the night before the decisive, disastrous battle, Gates fed his half-starved troops a bad mixture of molasses and cornmeal that (*Encyclopedia Britannica* confirms) crippled the Continental Army with volcanic diarrhea.

It was Gates, though, who ultimately came down with the worst case of the runs.

After a string of epic strategic blunders, Gates couldn't even get the retreat right. Fleeing Camden, the exhausted, emaciated Americans were easily tracked down twenty-two miles to the north by the British cavalry. In the middle of this secondary skirmish, Gates took off on his horse and galloped sixty-some miles into North Carolina without looking back. If he had, Gates would have seen the near total annihilation of the Southern Continental Army (and, perhaps, our hopes of independence). His abysmal cooking and cowardice left two thousand dead or wounded soldiers and nearly all of his supplies in enemy hands. As a disgusted Graham recalled in his book, Gates was still so spooked when he got to Charlotte that he didn't even bother getting off his horse. "He did not dismount," Graham wrote. One of his aides, instead, ran in to tell Thomas Polk what had happened and of the fury marching their way. Gates and the rest of the surviving officers and soldiers from Camden then scurried through Charlotte toward the safety of Salisbury.

With Cornwallis looming, Polk wrote to Gates twice begging for military support. In between the lines he was also clearly encouraging Gates to locate his backbone. "We hope for relief from you as soon as possible," Polk pleaded. "But I am afraid we are ruined if they come on."

Gates never even bothered with a reply.

The dream of independence seemed all but lost. The entire Southern Continental Army had practically been vaporized. Without it there was no way of slowing down the British campaign across the Carolinas and into the hearts and minds of all the lingering Loyalists in the South. And now, with a freshly restocked Cornwallis and a bloodthirsty Tarleton just a day's march from Charlotte, Polk, Irwin, Davie, Davidson, Graham, and the other local leaders had a decision to make. Once again, they were on their own. And with thousands of local militia captured or dead after Charleston and Camden, manpower in Charlotte was nearly nonexistent. As was any kind of fortification in such a small, rural town. Without even stopping, Gates and his men had taken one look at Charlotte and decided it wouldn't hold off Cornwallis for more than an hour.

Meanwhile, Cornwallis was now ordering all perfidious inhabitants to be imprisoned and punished "with the greatest rigor" and all rebel militiamen "put to death." In other words, pretty much the entire population of Charlotte. Since authoring the MecDec, the locals had not exactly made a secret of where they stood with regard to independence. To the contrary, at this point in the Revolution they were in what you might call full-blown *f*ck-around-and-find-out* mode. When the Mecklenburg militia got word of Loyalist lawyers John Dunn and Benjamin Booth mouthing off inside a Salisbury tavern, a posse of about thirty Charlotte patriots stormed north, snatched the Tory sons-of-bitches from their barstools, and galloped them back to the Mecklenburg Committee of Safety for trial. They were immediately found guilty, of course (I mean, Dunn's dog was named Tory for god's sake), and summarily banished to Florida, which honestly seems a little excessive.

But now, as Cornwallis marched toward Charlotte with a force that outnumbered them fifteen to one, some of the same town elders suggested that under the circumstances, continued resistance might be, well, insane. After all, when Thomas Jefferson was faced with roughly the same situation, he didn't hesitate for a second.

He bailed.

Actually, it was far worse than that. As Virginia's governor, Jefferson utterly failed to prepare the state's military forces. Then he abandoned the capitol altogether for the safety of his mountaintop estate, thereby leaving Virginia leaderless and under attack for eight long days. Remarkably, Jefferson fled yet again, this time from Monticello on a stallion called Caractacus. (The fact that he fled on a horse named after a British chieftain who bravely battled against the Roman invasion of England is just the perfect tribute to TJ's legendary faintheartedness.) Still, Caractacus only made it into the safety of the forest a few minutes ahead of British troops who had wanted to capture Jefferson as a forty-third birthday present for King George III. (I got a barbecue grill.)

Scouring Monticello, a British officer found Martin Hemings, one of Jefferson's slaves who also happened to be his relative.

The British soldier cocked his pistol, pointed it at Hemings, and demanded to know where Jefferson was hiding.

"Fire away, then," Hemings bravely replied, proving that at Monticello at least, all men *weren't* created equal.

Thankfully, Hemings's life was spared.

In an almost unfathomable twist, Jefferson later circled back on his estate and learned of Hemings's extraordinary act of bravery. Jefferson absorbed all of this and then, shortly thereafter, sat down and continued writing all that crap in *Notes on the State of Virginia* about how inferior he believed Black people to be. The cowardly Jefferson was widely mocked for his proclivity to flee and even faced censure for his actions, or lack thereof. At a time when Abigail Adams melted down her family's pewter spoons to make musket balls for the Continental Army in Massachusetts, and when Charlotte's Jane Parks McDowell rode ten miles at night to get information about enemy movements to our troops, Jefferson's actual defense was that he was an intellect, not a soldier.

The thought simply never occurred to him that you could be both.

Like the men who created the MecDec.

Meanwhile, back in Charlotte, with the MecDec patriots hopelessly outnumbered by Cornwallis, Graham says that when the suggestion of surrendering was brought up, it was "indignantly repelled, by a great majority" of local battle veterans. A group that certainly included Polk and Davidson, who had seen far worse in places like Valley Forge. Led by MecDec Signer and future General Robert Irwin, this group of local, veteran soldiers in Charlotte then commenced with what can only be described as a Revolutionary *Rudy*-type speech. "[We have] seen the British run like sheep and many of them bite the dust," they explained. "They were by no means invincible [and] under suitable commanders and proper arrangements they would at any time risk a conflict with them, man to man." The veterans then assured the troops "that their cause was just and they confided that Providence would ultimately give them success, notwithstanding the present unfavorable appearances."

Although it had been several years since the signing of the MecDec, the speech made it clear that the spirit and resolve in our country's cradle of independence was stronger than ever.

No matter the odds, the sons of Charlotte would stand and fight.

All they needed was a plan.

And a ton of luck.

From my vantage point atop the battlefield bleachers at Rural Hill I realize that, just like Graham 240-some years ago, I, too, am the first local to spot the approaching, green-jacketed British dragoons. They look pretty badass, to be honest, and suddenly I understand why even the fearless Graham tried to keep them at a "respectful distance." It's not exactly the same, I know, since there's a steady stream of airplanes overhead from the nearby Charlotte-Douglas International Airport, and one of the dragoons here keeps using "y'all" in his field commands. Overall, though, this battle scene really does help you to imagine what Graham must have experienced in the predawn hours of September 26, 1780, when, patrolling two miles south of town, he stumbled upon the entire British Army advancing toward

Charlotte. It must have been something: the earth trembling and Graham and his brother-in-law watching from the bushes in breathless awe, their hearts pounding through their chests, as row after impossible row of wagons, horses, artillery, and soldiers marched by.

Believing he had seen Cornwallis, Graham's brother-in-law raised his rifle, wanting to take a shot at the general and seize a chance at glory. Graham ordered him to cease fire. Giving away the element of surprise would endanger the troops back in Charlotte. And when his sister's husband hesitated, in a whispered scream Graham threatened to "cut him down in his tracks." (The in-law complied, but the two men had beef over this episode for the next thirty years.)

For the plan to work, the British needed to be allowed to reach their destination just up the hill in the middle of Charlotte, a city that has had the exact same layout for the last 255 years. The center of town is marked by where Trade Street, running east and west, intersects with Tryon Street, which runs north toward Salisbury and south toward Camden. Riding back into town from his predawn scouting exhibition, due to the gradual incline heading back into Charlotte, neither Graham nor the British would have been able to see the elevated courthouse standing in the middle of the Trade and Tryon intersection until they were practically right on top of it. (There used to be a bronze commemorative Battle of Charlotte manhole cover right in the middle of this intersection until someone at the DOT decided that having curious pedestrians standing in the middle of traffic reading about history was probably not a great idea.) The Charlotte courthouse had been built, by Polk, on ten-foot-high brick pillars with a three-foot-high rock wall running between the columns. It was constructed this way to create an open-air market and trading post, which, coincidentally, also doubled as an exceptional hidden bunker with a perfect sightline straight down Tryon.

Tryon Street's topography and the courthouse design were Charlotte's first two bits of what you might call incredibly fortunate, strategic good luck. The mosquitoes deserve their fair share of credit too. In the sandy, swampy conditions of Camden, Tarleton had come down with a bout of yellow fever, and rather than wait a few days for him to recover, the impatient

Cornwallis handed his command to an overeager underling named George Hanger whose military savvy was rivaled only by the likes of Horatio Gates and, maybe, George Custer.

Meanwhile, Davie, Davidson, and Graham had somehow managed to cobble together 150 soldiers, militia volunteers, and cavalrymen. In all aspects, Mecklenburg's contribution to the cause for independence was unprecedented, as was that of the Scots-Irish. By one calculation, although Mecklenburg contained just 3 percent of North Carolina's population, it contributed 25 percent of the colony's troops. (One possible motivator? The oldest trick in the book, printed up in pamphlets across the county, which read: *The young ladies of the best families of Mecklenburg County, North Carolina . . . will not receive the address of any young gentlemen except the brave volunteers who served and assisted in subduing the loyalist insurgents. The ladies being of the opinion, that such persons as stay loitering at home, when the important calls of the country demand their military services, must certainly be destitute of that nobleness of sentiment, that brave, manly spirit which would qualify them to be defenders and guardians of the fair sex.*)

That day in Charlotte, the majority of these soon-to-no-longer-be-single men were stationed, in three stacked lines, under the courthouse at Trade and Tryon. The rest of the men flanked that structure and hid behind houses, barns, and trees farther down on either side of South Tryon, using the guerilla warfare tactics the British found so utterly undignified.

The entire plan would hinge on the British lead party being overconfident and just cheeky enough to attempt a charge up Tryon toward the courthouse.

Hanger tried it three times.

Crouched under the courthouse, the MecDec militia must not have believed their own eyes.

Hanger advanced at full gallop to within fifty yards of the militiamen, unaware he was outflanked and unable from his low vantage point on South Tryon to see the American troops amassed under the Charlotte courthouse.

From the flank, watching the oblivious Brits parade right into range, Davie then roared:

"FIRE!"

"Our first line moved up to the stone wall and fired," Graham confirms. And the hot lead musket balls "fell with such effect among the cavalry that they retreated with great precipitation."

(At this point in the reenactment, I could hear the distant crackle of musket fire as a stampede of retreating dragoons thundered by like apparitions through thick blueish gunpowder smoke. And with the ground shaking under my feet I scribbled into my notebook: *God help me . . . this is so f*cking cool!*)

The Americans fought in line formation so that after the first row of soldiers discharged their weapons, they could step back and begin the cumbersome chore of reloading while the line behind them moved up into their spots and fired. In the chaos and smoke, a hopeful Hanger mistook the technique for a retreat and, instead, "rushed up to the courthouse and received the full fire from the companies placed on the cross streets." For a second time, battlefield accounts confirm that Hanger "immediately wheeled and retreated down the street . . . in the utmost confusion, and in the presence of the whole British army."

When Hanger was repulsed for a third time, a perturbed Cornwallis stomped up Tryon and delivered what was either a brilliant commentary on the British psyche or the worst halftime speech of all time.

"Legion," he yelled, "remember you have everything to lose, but nothing to gain!"

Now, with the full force of the British Army headed their way, the Americans began a tactical withdrawal north toward Sugaw Creek Church through the thick backwoods that they all knew so well. Although they were in full retreat, the ride probably felt more like a victory parade. The enemy "must have sustained the greatest damage in Charlotte," wrote Graham, who concluded that "the small damage sustained in proportion to the risk appeared providential." Years later in his memoirs, a redcoat officer was still astounded at the miraculous turn of events in Charlotte. "The whole of the British army," he wrote, "was actually kept at bay, for some minutes, by a few mounted Americans."

As if overcome by road rage, the embarrassed Brits chased Graham and his troops north for several miles. "The British, chagrined to see their laurels snatched from their army by this detachment of Militia, loudly charged the Legion with pusillanimity," states Davie. One of the more captivating passages in Graham's memoir is one in which he recalls Hanger's dragoons opening fire in the dense woods with such force that it shredded the trees and filled the air with confetti from the tree bark and twigs exploding all around them. Graham says the show of force caused more panic in his men than anything he had ever seen. For good reason. When the enraged Brits did catch George Locker, the sixteen-year-old son of a general, he was "literally cut to pieces, in a most barbarous manner. The barrel of his rifle, with which he endeavored to shelter himself from their sabers, was cut in many places."

This was the gruesome way in which most men died in the Revolutionary War—in close quarters, slowly, by bayonet plunge, not bullet holes.

And that would have been Graham's fate as well, if not for a single silver buckle on his shirt collar.

His grandson picks it up from here in the woods near Sugaw Creek Church:

> As Captain Graham was engaged in a hand-to-hand fight, his horse backed under a limb of a tree which knocked him off. He received three bullets in the thigh, one saber thrust in the side, one cut on the back of the neck and four upon the forehead. And from one of these some of his brains exuded. The cut on the back of the neck must have been given as he fell or fought on foot. It cut a heavy silver buckle which he wore on his stock entirely in two; but for the buckle it would have severed his head from his body.

(I didn't think the low-key brilliant phrase "some of his brains exuded" could possibly be improved upon until I saw a completely unironic footnote below this passage that noted, *Some years afterwards an old lady acquaintance asked Graham if he thought he had as much sense as before losing a portion of his brains. He replied that he had not perceived any difference.*)

Collecting their wounded after the Sugaw Creek skirmish, a British soldier came across a prostrate Graham bleeding out in the grass. The men locked eyes. With every labored breath, more blood (and brains) exuded from Graham's body.

The soldier raised his gun and prepared to execute the American hero, who was all of twenty-one.

"Put up your pistol," Hanger yelled, "save your ammunition; he has had enough."

To the contrary.

Bleeding from nine wounds, somehow Graham managed to drag himself to a nearby spring to "slake his thirst and bathe his wounds." At twilight, with death and darkness creeping in, he was rescued by Susan Alexander, a young Scots-Irish parishioner of Sugaw Creek Church, who had come to the spring for water. (In one version of this story, Susan was looking for a lost cow, not in need of water. In another, it was actually a female slave who saved Graham. And in yet another, a young Andrew Jackson himself was living with the Alexander family at the time and was forever moved by Graham's valor.) In the official version, though, Susan and her mother carried Graham back to their house where they dressed his wounds and "hung hanks of hackled flax around the bedstead to conceal him." Graham's clothes were so caked in dry blood that he looked like he was wearing a British redcoat's uniform.

For the rest of the night he lay there so still that several times when the women checked on Graham, they felt certain he had passed on.

He survived the night, though, and the next morning, after he was seen by a nosy British officer's wife who had come to the Alexanders' house looking for milk, Graham was evacuated to his mother's home four miles away where he convalesced for almost three months before returning to his command in December. In the meantime, one of Graham's charges went back into the woods and located the other half of the buckle that saved his life. A blacksmith in Charlotte rejoined the pieces, and once the venerated Graham started wearing the good luck charm in place of a cravat or necktie, the rest of the men in Charlotte followed suit, and that style remained in vogue for half a century. After the war, Graham's children honored Alexander—the woman who saved his life and possibly the nation's—by referring to her as Aunt Susie. (Aunt Susie also received a Revolutionary War pension for her bravery.)

While Graham recovered, Cornwallis attempted to occupy Charlotte, snatching Polk's home as his headquarters. The locals, though, had not exactly warmed up to the King's army as Cornwallis and British strategists had predicted. According to the state records of North Carolina, most Charlotteans either burned or packed up anything that could be of use to the enemy and abandoned their homes and farms rather than suffer occupation by British forces. "His Lordship Cornwallis soon discovered that he was in an enemy's country," the report states. "He was without provisions, without forage, without friends, without intelligence, his communication with Camden cut off and his dispatches intercepted."

Other than that, Cornwallis was absolutely thriving in MecDec country.

The feisty inhabitants of Charlotte had managed to get so far under the General's pasty skin that Cornwallis went to Pat Jack's Tavern looking for Captain Jack and a bit of revenge. When he couldn't find Jack, Cornwallis ordered his troops to drag Captain Jack's aging, infirm father out of his feather bed and into the street before burning the bar and the Jack family home to the ground. Later, Cornwallis is said to have done the same to the Charlotte law offices of MecDec Signer Waightstill Avery. Brevard's papers were also believed to have been destroyed by Cornwallis. These were no random war crimes. "This evidence of displeasure was visited upon only a few of those whom Cornwallis considered leading offenders," author Samuel Ashe wrote in 1905 in the *Biographical History of North Carolina from Colonial Times to the Present*. A general as cunning and ruthless as Cornwallis understood the suppressive symbolism of arriving in hostile territory and sending a message by immediately terrorizing the town's most famous patriot and its most outspoken revolutionary voice. On the flip side, Cornwallis notably left Duncan Ochiltree's house completely undisturbed. The local merchant is said to have been one of the original MecDec Signers. During the war, however, Ochiltree "turned coat" to make a quick buck supplying the British Army. Ochiltree was able to barely escape Charlotte with his life. Forever after, though, his name was stricken from the MecDec records.

By targeting Captain Jack and others, Cornwallis was simply trying to intimidate the remaining MecDecers into compliance. This being Charlotte, it had the opposite effect. Jack's beloved father died a short time later, which only inspired the locals to increase their guerilla-style attacks on the British. The women of Charlotte developed a signaling system to alert militia when the Brits were foraging nearby. And after decades of hunting small prey in the thick woods, the locals were such good shots with long rifles that they made exceptional snipers. No sooner had Cornwallis posted a sentinel, he found the poor guy full of holes. The redcoats tried posting signs that said, "This is murder, we will retaliate!" But each subsequent sentinel usually had to take his post next to the fresh graves of his predecessors.

Completely cut off from the rest of the British Army and harassed at every turn, a few weeks in the hometown of the MecDec sapped the fighting spirit of even the sadistic Tarleton. "The foraging parties were every day harassed by the inhabitants," he wrote. "They continued their hostilities with unwearied perseverance. It was evident, and it had been frequently mentioned to the King's officers, that the counties of Mecklenburg and Rowan were more hostile to England than any others in America." Cornwallis agreed, with one caveat: "This County of Mecklenburg is the most rebellious and inveterate that I have met with in this country—not excepting any part of the Jerseys."

Think about this for a second: Two of the most feared military men in history both considered the MecDecers to be among the scariest enemies they had ever faced. That's some real gangster sh*t right there. Seriously.

In early October 1780, a British detachment of about five hundred men was sent to scavenge on the McIntyre farm outside of Charlotte, just a few miles southeast of Rural Hill. As the carefree Brits laughed and messed around while stuffing their wagons with stolen corn and livestock, about a dozen colonial militiamen, including Graham's older brother George, watched from the woods, sighting their rifles on the enemy and itching for the right moment to strike. The McIntyre farm had several beehives and, as legend has it, when the bumbling Brits tipped over a hive, the bees attacked first and then, in the chaos, the Americans finished the job. Standing in the doorway of the farm's log cabin, a British captain chortling at the scene was the first to get it, sniped from "150 steps distant" by sharpshooter Captain James Thompson. In all, eight redcoats were killed and another dozen wounded. Although they held a forty-to-one advantage, the panicked Brits assumed they were outnumbered and retreated. (Yet again.) With all those patriot bullets lodged in the structure's wood planks, the McIntyre farmhouse stood for centuries as a monument to the MecDec militia—until 1960, that is, when in typical Charlotte fashion, they tore it down (probably to make room for a gated golf community).

The famous skirmish known to this day as the Battle of the Bees was the last straw for Cornwallis. Afterward is when he is supposed to have famously referred to Charlotte as a "damned hornet's nest of rebellion," although Graham believed the nickname first came from Tarleton. After Cornwallis retreated from Charlotte, he camped south of town at Robert Wilson's home near Steele Creek. Wilson had been taken prisoner in Charleston, and Cornwallis promised to free him if his wife and children joined the royal standard. "I would take these boys," Mrs. Wilson snapped back, pointing to her four small children, "and would myself enlist under Sumter's standard and show my husband and sons how to fight; and, if necessary, how to die for their country."

Hearing this, Tarleton quipped to Cornwallis, "Ah, General, I think you have got into a hornet's nest."

Thus, our town's cool nickname of the Hornet's Nest was born.

References to hornet's nests are everywhere in this city: the badge worn by the Charlotte police is in the shape of a hornet's nest; the basketball teams from Davidson College and Charlotte compete for a Hornet's Nest trophy that truly looks like a giant brass turd; there's a Hornets Nest elementary school, Hornet's Nest beer, and Hornet's Nest Park; and you can't throw a Frisbee in this place without hitting a historic marker decorated with a hornet's nest that warns: *LET US ALONE.* And then there's the Charlotte Hornets, our perpetually sad NBA franchise, which is run by Michael Jordan but has only ever truly rebelled against two things—logic and success.

Anyway, in the autumn of 1780, after the original hornet's nest incident, the dominos began to fall for Cornwallis in rapid succession. A few days later, the Americans' stunning, momentous victory at Kings Mountain, South Carolina, wiped out a force of a thousand Loyalists and exposed Cornwallis's southwestern flank. Powered by local militias, the shocking successes in South Carolina and Charlotte (and, later, at Guilford Courthouse in North Carolina) left England's Southern strategy in ruins. "A glorious affair," a homesick Polk gloated after word from Kings Mountain reached Charlotte.

"In a few days doubt not but we will be [back] in Charlotte & I will take possession of my house & his Lordship Cornwallis shall take to the woods."

The great British general had no choice.

On October 14, 1780, Cornwallis retreated from Charlotte for the fourth, and final, time.

Cornwallis was in such a rush to get out of the Hornet's Nest that he left behind several wagonloads of supplies. At this point, provisions were the least of his worries. The rout at Kings Mountain and the retreat from Charlotte were essentially the beginning of the end for Cornwallis and the Brits. And, once again, America's fortunes had turned right here in the land of the MecDec. Marking the occasion even further, later that same day, George Washington finally canned Gates and officially named Nathanael Greene as the new commander in chief of America's Southern forces. (Greene took command on December 3, 1780, in Charlotte, in a house next to Polk's.)

By March 1781, Greene had reorganized his army and perfected the art of smaller hit-and-run clashes with strategic retreats that utilized the thick Carolina backcountry for cover and relied heavily on the surveying expertise of one John McKnitt Alexander. "Alexander, though his age would have excused him from such exposure, accompanied Greene as a pilot," wrote Draper.

"By his zeal in the cause, and his intimate knowledge, as an old surveyor of the topography, roads, and people of the country, Alexander was able to afford valuable assistance as counselor to the American General." Greene was so grateful for the help that he named one of his encampments Camp Mc-Knitt Alexander. With England growing low on cash and patience, Greene understood—perhaps by watching the success of the guerilla tactics used by the militias in Charlotte and Kings Mountain—that we didn't necessarily have to defeat the British. We just had to sting, frustrate, and outlast them.

And no one on earth had proven more adept at annoying the ever-loving crap out of the Brits than the Scots-Irish MecDecers in Charlotte.

After recovering from his wounds at the Battle of Charlotte, Graham continued to be one of Cornwallis's biggest tormentors, leading more than fifteen skirmishes and wreaking havoc every time the British tried to cross the Catawba or the Yadkin rivers near Charlotte. It would be hard to sum up Graham's service better than the eloquent testimony offered many years later during his war pension hearing:

> Never was he known to shrink from any toil, however painful, or quail before any dangers, however threatening, or to avoid any privations or sacrifices which might promote his country's cause. To secure her liberties he spent many toilsome days and sleepless nights, for her his body was covered with wounds; and for her he endured fatigue, sickness, and suffering without a murmur; to her welfare he consecrated his time, treasure, and influence during a long, unblemished life. It was not by empty words or arrogant pretentions, but by self-denying and long-continued actions that he proved himself devoted to the welfare of his country.

Other than his pension hearing, the only time Graham ever elaborated on his military service was to specify that he was wounded in Charlotte while defending "the ground first consecrated by the Declaration of American Independence."

After the war Graham went on to serve in the North Carolina state senate from 1788 to 1792, leading the way on the adoption of the United States Constitution. He became quite wealthy as the owner of an iron foundry he named Vesuvius Furnace. According to his papers, Graham also served as a doctor, of sorts, sewing wounds and setting broken bones. As the town's justice of the peace, Graham loved officiating wedding ceremonies, especially the ones that served his favorite peach brandy afterward. In his later years, Graham ate a steady diet of the Scots-Irish staple of mush and milk. And in a testament to just how much he was beloved and respected, when dignitaries like the governor of North Carolina would pay him a visit, they'd eat it too.

In 1814 Graham was called back into service one last time to lead the combined brigades of North and South Carolina in a brief war against the Creek Nation. Even after his final retirement in 1834, at seventy-five, his grandson recalled that at social occasions, the General, as everyone called him, "would challenge some of the young men for combat with hickory canes instead of swords. He would give them permission to strike him—if they could. [Each] antagonist would endeavor in good earnest to do so, but soon found his cane knocked out of his hand and received a sound tap on the head [from the General]."

Cornwallis certainly knew the feeling.

In the spring of 1781, the British general was run ragged dealing with sniping attacks by Graham and Davidson while chasing Greene back through North Carolina. (This time, Cornwallis went the long way around Charlotte.) The Continental Army's plan was to delay Cornwallis as long as possible to allow Greene time to fully prepare for battle. Leading an attack to disrupt the British crossing at Cowan's Ford near Charlotte, Davidson was shot from his horse and killed instantly, the bullet hitting him just below his left nipple. Although it extracted a heavy toll, the plan to delay the British worked to perfection. At one point a frustrated Cornwallis torched his own supply wagons hoping to move faster to catch Greene for a large-scale showdown, which he finally got at Guilford Courthouse in North Carolina. (Thus, playing right into Greene's hands.) Cornwallis enjoyed the battlefield "victory" he so desperately craved, but it cost him a quarter of his men. "Another such victory would ruin the British army," quipped a member of the British House of Commons. Indeed, the irreparable damage suffered at the hands of the original Charlotte Hornets and the rest of the Carolina insurgents forced Cornwallis to withdraw to Wilmington—and, later, to Yorktown.

That plan went about as well as his original assault on Charlotte, though.

I should know.

I saw the whole thing myself.

IN MY VERSION OF THE BATTLE OF CHARLOTTE, THOUGH, CORNWALLIS gets a curtain call and a standing ovation.

"We sure hope y'all enjoyed the battle," the narrator says as my fellow Graham stans and I climb down from the bleachers with our heart rates and hearing slowly returning to normal. "Please stick around, grab a beer or something to eat. The band starts at six, and remember there's another cannon demonstration at three, followed by a colonial-era sewing class, and then, at four, you definitely don't want to miss the field surgery."

Come again? The what-ery?

Did he just say . . . *surgery*?

Good lord, I think, heading back to the corn dog truck.

Haven't the MecDecers sliced up Cornwallis enough already?

TEN

AN EPIC BURN

ELEVEN YEARS AFTER CORNWALLIS FLED CHARLOTTE, GEORGE WASHington paraded back into town as the president of a free and independent nation. In the spring of 1791, with the not-so-United States still little more than a tenuous political experiment, Washington took off on his famed Southern Tour, traveling what must have been an exhausting 1,900 miles, round trip, from Philadelphia to Georgia to explore and unite a wobbly nation struggling to survive its infancy. While Washington's cabinet bickered about the framework of our new country in Philadelphia, the president's plan was to journey south along the coast to Savannah, Georgia, and then turn inland to visit Augusta, Columbia, and Charlotte on his return north.

Much like the country, Washington's Southern Tour got off to an inauspicious start. On April 7, 1791, just ten miles south of Philadelphia, Washington's entire entourage nearly drowned. During what should have been a routine ferry crossing of the Occoquan, the president's horses got spooked and, still attached to the carriages, started cannonballing, one by one, into the drink. After safely dragging himself to shore, a presumably soaking wet Washington wrote in his extensive trip diary: "Providentially, indeed, miraculously . . . no damage was sustained." Which is why, to this day, you can hardly venture ten miles in the southeast without bumping into a plaque, marker, stone, tavern stool, bed, or even a menu commemorating the tiniest details of Washington's famous, nearly tragic trip. Starting with a cafe on the shores of the Occoquan where the menu wonders "Did Washington Drip Here?"

Historian Archibald Henderson wrote extensively about Washington's tour in 1923. A math professor at the University of North Carolina and an amazing tennis player to boot, according to his contemporaries, Henderson was "the leading Southern intellectual of his age." While researching Washington's Southern Tour, Henderson discovered that the president developed a habit of stopping unannounced at private homes along the route for rest and refreshment, often right before many of his numerous, and tedious, large-scale public appearances. When Washington did this early one morning during his time in North Carolina, Henderson says, "At the door, in answer to his knock, appeared the rosy-cheeked, bright-eyed Betsy Brandon of some twelve summers." Betsy explained to the kind, soft-spoken stranger in her doorway that she was upset about missing her chance to see the president. The man at the door proposed a bargain: if she would give him a cup of coffee and a bite to eat, he would arrange for her to meet the famous General Washington. Betsy quickly prepared the snack and immediately afterward demanded that the man keep his part of the deal.

A pleased Washington wiped his face, sat up, and straightened his shirt and jacket.

"General Washington is now before you," he laughed as Betsy nearly fainted.

Washington had that effect on a lot of Carolinians during his tour.

In his 1855 autobiography, Carolina native Dr. Charles Caldwell, a distinguished faculty member at Penn and the head of the medical department at Transylvania University in Kentucky, recounted the days he spent in 1791 as Washington's escort from the North Carolina border to his appearance in Charlotte. (It was then reprinted, in its entirety, in Henderson's book.) As a young man Caldwell had worked for weeks to memorize his official greeting for the president, which, of course, he immediately forgot as soon as he caught a glimpse of Washington atop Prescott, his magnificent (and beloved) white parade horse. "An awe came over me, such as I had never before experienced," confessed Caldwell, making him the first official Thigh Man of Dad History. "And its effect on me was as deeply mortifying as it was unprecedented."

I get the feeling that the awkward silence was so bad between these two as they rode north toward Charlotte, Washington just finally blurted out, "Pray, sir, have you lived long in this part of the country?" in an effort to break the ice.

"Ever since my childhood, sir," Caldwell responded.

"During the late war, if my information be correct, the inhabitants were true to the cause of the country, and brave in its defense," Washington said.

"Your information *is* correct, sir," said Caldwell. "They were, almost to a man, true-hearted Whigs and patriots, and as gallant soldiers as ever drew swords or pointed rifles in behalf of freedom. . . . It was in a small town, through which we shall pass, that Lord Cornwallis lay encamped, when he swore that he had never before been in such a damned nest of Whigs—for that he could not, in the surrounding country, procure a chicken or a pig for his table, or a gallon of oats for his horse, but by purchasing it with the blood of his soldiers who went in quest of it."

"Pray, what is the name of that town?" Washington inquired.

"Charlotte, sir," came the response, "the county town of Mecklenburg, and the place where independence was declared about a year before its declaration by Congress; and *my father* was one of the Whigs who were concerned in the glorious transaction. We shall arrive at Charlotte tomorrow morning where you will be enthusiastically received . . . by the most respectable inhabitants of the country; a large portion of whom served in the revolutionary war—several of them, I believe, as officers and privates under your own command."

Caldwell writes that Washington then "at length inquired of me whether he might expect to meet at Charlotte any of the leading members of the convention which prepared and passed the Mecklenburg Declaration of Independence."

And then something truly miraculous occurred.

Washington actually smiled.

Well, it was either that or what sounds more like the first-ever documented case of MecDec Face.

"The General was evidently pleased with my narrative," Caldwell wrote. "And so diverted by the increased freedom and ease of my manner (for I was now perfectly myself), that though he did not actually smile (for he rarely smiled), he seemed, at times, as I fancied, more inclined to a little merriment than to maintain unchanged his habitually grave and dignified aspect."

After three grueling months on dusty, bumpy dirt roads and more pomp and circumstance than any man should have to endure in ten lifetimes, once Washington's carriage turned back north he became even more cantankerous as he struggled to conceal his joy about the prospect of finally returning home. Although North Carolina was the third-largest state at the time, and Mecklenburg had played a key role in the Revolution, Washington famously referred to Charlotte as a "very trifling place," and that's usually where the topic of his visit ends for most polite and proud locals.

Which is too bad because Washington's reception here, at the Cradle of Independence, was anything but trifling.

Henderson recalls that Polk, the Alexanders, and a group of esteemed local leaders, most of them associated in some way with the MecDec, greeted Washington on the outskirts of town. That reunion certainly could not have been trivial. After their leading role in the Revolution, many of the MecDec Signers had gone on to serve at the highest levels of the military, government, industry, education, and religion. More importantly, back during the war, Polk and his local charges served Washington with the utmost bravery, beginning at Valley Forge and in Philadelphia, protecting the Liberty Bell, and continuing through all the key stages of the Southern Campaign. In fact, it was Polk who single-handedly kept Greene's army supplied, McKnitt who kept it one step ahead of Cornwallis, and Irwin, Davie, and Graham who kept it stocked with fervent Scots-Irish warriors rallying around the MecDec's clarion call for freedom.

Years later, many of these same soldiers included references to the MecDec in the sworn testimonies they submitted with their Revolutionary War pension applications. Starting with Graham who wrote that he was *present in Charlotte on the 20th day of May 1775 when the Committee of the County of Mecklenburg made their celebrated Declaration of Independence of the British Crown upwards of a year before the Congress of the United States did at*

Philadelphia. For the critical purpose of establishing the timing and authentication of their service, many rank-and-file soldiers, like private William Culberson Sr., also used the MecDec as their key reference point. *The first service [Culberson] performed was as a private in a company of Captain Oliver Wiley in the County of Mecklenburg North Carolina in the year 1775 or early in the year 1776 just as the Patriots of Mecklenburg had declared themselves independent of the British Government.*

Washington, Polk, and the rest of the greeting party then rode through the streets of Charlotte to thunderous applause from the locals until they passed through Independence Square and the courthouse made famous by the MecDec and the Battle of Charlotte. "From the steps of the courthouse over there, sir, I had the honor of reading what we Mecklenburgers regard as the first overt assertion of freedom from British rule promulgated on this continent," Henderson imagined Polk saying at the time. "The people were so enthusiastic that they threw up their hats in all directions and some of them fell on the roof of the courthouse."

Washington notes in his own extensive diary that just across the street from the famous courthouse, Polk had set up a picnic-style dinner reception in the front yard of his white, Tudor-style cottage home. Henderson suggests that while eating and drinking in the front yard of what had once briefly been Cornwallis's headquarters, our true Founding Fathers and their president surely raised a glass or two of whiskey while reminiscing about the MecDec, the Battle of Charlotte, the Battle of the Bees, and Greene running Cornwallis ragged across the Carolinas.

Now, I'm not suggesting for a second that our first president partied like a true Scots-Irish MecDecer that night, but when a groggy Washington finally rolled out of Charlotte's two-story Cook's Inn at a leisurely 7 a.m. the next morning (three hours behind his normal schedule), he completely forgot his box of wig powder. "On this occasion the President, after making his toilet, neglected to replace the box in his valise," wrote local nineteenth-century historian Dr. George Graham. "It became the property of Mrs. Cook, who amused herself with powdering the heads of girls and young ladies who rushed to the inn after the departure of the great hero to hear the news, remarking to each one as she applied the puff: 'Now you can always remember that you have had the distinction of having your hair powdered from General Washington's box.'"

It wouldn't be the last time a president lost his head over the MecDec. Washington was the first of five sitting US presidents who would make a special trip to Charlotte to pay homage and celebrate the MecDec in person.

Not bad for such a trifling place.

Charlotte wouldn't stay that way for much longer, though. On a Sunday morning in 1799, about twenty-five miles east of Charlotte, a boy named Conrad Reed skipped church to go fishing in Little Meadow Creek. Waiting for a nibble, Conrad noticed a shiny, metallic rock protruding from the water. He picked it up and carried the seventeen-pound rock home where, for the next three years, the Reed family used it as a doorstop. When a jeweler in Fayetteville finally identified it as gold (and bought it for just $3.50 from the unknowing Reed family), Conrad's nugget became the earliest authenticated discovery of gold in the United States. When other nuggets, some as large as twenty-eight pounds, were found nearby, the first gold rush was on—to Charlotte, of all places. Soon there were more than fifty gold mining companies in the region, and a US Mint in Charlotte, where, until 1829, North Carolina was the only state producing gold for the nation's coin supply.

Besides gold boulders, Charlotte now had a college, several new iron foundries, a network of Presbyterian churches, and some of the most respected and powerful political leaders in the region, if not the country. At the same time, Charlotte was gaining even more luster as the country's first, true Cradle of Independence as word of the MecDec continued to spread. Newspapers across the state were running stories referencing the MecDec, and it seemed like every patriotic toast in the region included a mention of Charlotte being first to freedom, like the one recorded on April 14, 1801: "To the citizens of Mecklenburg, being the first in their declaration of Independence, may they ever be the first in resisting usurpation by defending their civil rights."

At the dawn of the new century, Charlotte was truly enjoying its own little golden moment in the spotlight as the young country's epicenter of precious metals and patriotism.

Then, in a flash, it was all reduced to ashes.

THE FIRE MUST HAVE BEEN VISIBLE FOR MILES. ON APRIL 6, 1800, A PORtion of John McKnitt Alexander's beloved Alexandriana burned to the ground, along with a substantial amount of the MecDec paperwork. Sadly, this wasn't all that rare of an event at the time. In fact, in 1770 fire destroyed Thomas Jefferson's childhood home at Shadwell along with all of his books and papers. Luckily, without much fuss, historians were able to recreate this important phase of Jefferson's life by relying on myriad other sources, anecdotal and otherwise. Not to Monday-morning quarterback McKnitt two and a half centuries after the fact, but maybe his brother Hezekiah's Rock House, which is still standing to this day and impervious to fire (because it's made of, you know, *ROCKS*), might have been a wiser choice for storing the country's first declaration of independence.

Although the Alexandriana fire would forever cast some amount of doubt on the MecDec's authenticity, it's pretty clear that McKnitt himself wasn't all that alarmed that the original copy of the MecDec had been destroyed. Most of the structures at Alexandriana were not touched by the flames and, thankfully, neither were his extensive Rough Notes from the May 20th Convention, a document that fully detailed the events of May 20 in Charlotte, as well as the content and scope of the MecDec. The truth is McKnitt really dodged a bullet because his surviving Rough Notes by themselves were a full, detailed, and authenticated account of the MecDec. And throughout North Carolina at the time, McKnitt had a reputation that was "proverbial for his scrupulous accuracy in recollecting and detailing events." So if his MecDec Rough Notes had been all that was salvaged from the fire, they would have been more than enough documentation.

But there was more. A lot more.

And this is where the MecDec takes a complicated but fascinating turn.

Another full record of the events from the May 20th Convention, along with a "true copy" of the original MecDec, was later discovered by McKnitt's son at Alexandriana rolled up with a bunch of other Revolutionary War–era papers and pamphlets in an area of the estate that had not been damaged by the fire. Because this copy is unsigned and undated, it is often mysteriously referred to as the Copy in an Unknown Hand even though it's fairly obvious that it is one of the numerous copies of the MecDec made between 1787 and

1794 by Thomas Polk's oldest son, William, a man once honored with the title of Raleigh's Most Illustrious Citizen.

Besides the surviving documents, McKnitt must have also been reassured by the fact that the MecDec had become common knowledge pretty much all over North Carolina. It had been discussed, written about, and witnessed by the most powerful and respected men in the region, if not the country (or the world, for that matter), including England's Josiah Martin, George Washington, Ben Franklin, North Carolina Governor Montford Stokes, Waightstill Avery, the state's first attorney general, and several highly decorated war heroes, including Generals Davie and Graham, Colonel William Polk, and the Reverend Humphrey Hunter. "The combined testimony of all these individuals," wrote Stokes, "prove the existence of the Mecklenburg Declaration, and all the circumstances connected with it, as fully and clearly as any fact can be shown by human testimony."

If history truly belongs to the eyewitnesses, then McKnitt was correct: he had no reason to be worried.

Just in case, though, distinguished men of Charlotte, including Hunter, John Davidson, and Reverend Hezekiah Balch, began etching the details of the MecDec onto their gravestones. They left behind a marble tapestry across the region that serves almost like ancient cave drawings to ensure the story will never disappear or be threatened by fire ever again. Anyone who has ever flown into Charlotte, in fact, has likely passed over Hunter's white marble tombstone and would-be billboard, located in the Steele Creek Presbyterian Church Cemetery a mile south of the middle runway.

SACRED to the memory of the Reverend Humphrey Hunter . . . one of those who early promoted the cause of freedom in Mecklenburg County May 20th, 1775, and subsequently bore an active part in securing the Independence of his Country.

After serving valiantly in the Revolutionary War, Hunter dedicated the rest of his life to education, history, and God. Imagine a man like this placing a lie on his tombstone for all eternity. For Hunter and McKnitt it was just a different time, I guess. A time when the MecDec men simply couldn't fathom a world where the honor and witness of all these distinguished patriots wouldn't be enough proof for the historiography.

"I've learned in twenty years of writing history books that because there is no extant, contemporaneous documentary proof of something, it doesn't mean it didn't happen," says Andrew Roberts, one of Britain's most prevalent military historians and a biographer of Churchill, Napoleon, and King George III. "Fires that destroy crucial documents are incredibly common throughout history and oral history can sometimes be more visceral and honest than written history anyhow. Of course, the Mecklenburgers (years later) could not remember, verbatim, precisely what they declared so bravely in 1775, but that doesn't in any way undermine the likelihood of their having called for independence a year earlier than the Revolutionaries in Philadelphia. If twenty-six North Carolinians say that something took place, my inclination is to believe them."

At the time, though, there were countless original copies of the MecDec still in circulation. Captain Jack had taken at least four MecDec copies to Philadelphia. In a 1775 letter to King George III, seeking to add urgency to his request for more troops, Josiah Martin, the state's former royal governor, had referenced the "treasonous" documents in Mecklenburg as well as a specific edition of the *Cape Fear Mercury* newspaper that included the MecDec. Syfert, Wheeler, and other historians believe in August 1775, a copy was sent to Samuel Johnson, the moderator of the Provincial Congress in Hillsboro who officially presented it to that body. Graham and Hunter were also said to have been given copies. Brevard's brother said there were rough drafts of the MecDec in Ephraim's room at Queen's College. Governor Stokes would also later testify that in 1787 he had seen a copy of the MecDec in the possession of Dr. Hugh Williamson, who was writing a history of North Carolina. In addition, historian Francois-Xavier Martin included what is widely believed to be a pre-1800 copy of the MecDec in his book *The History of North Carolina from the Earliest Period*. Author Alexander Garden had also acquired a copy of the MecDec, which he published in *Anecdotes of the American Revolution*.

All of that, however, was nothing compared to the multitude of MecDec copies cranked out by William Polk. According to V. V. McNitt's seminal

1960 work on the documentary evidence surrounding the MecDec, other than McKnitt Alexander himself, William Polk was the only other person known to have made copies of the original MecDec.

And he made a lot.

William was a commissioned officer in the Continental Army in May 1775 when he was in Charlotte and witnessed the MecDec's creation, which he later testified to at length in the North Carolina governor's report. William served for the entire war, including a lengthy winter hospital stay at Valley Forge after a musket ball shattered his jaw during the Battle of Germantown on October 4, 1777. After his service William lived and worked as a surveyor general in what is now Nashville, Tennessee. In 1786 he moved back to Mecklenburg and sought to represent his native county in the House of Commons. And what better way to reintroduce himself and provide his patriotic bona fides to the locals than to share copies of his father's MecDec, which he himself had witnessed and then fought so tirelessly to defend? We know that William sent the copy to Dr. Hugh Williamson that Stokes witnessed in 1787, and then he also later sent copies to William Davidson and North Carolina judge A. D. Murphy. It was politically savvy, sure, but it must have also been a painstaking labor of love for William, who wanted to ensure that his father's leading role in our quest for independence wasn't lost to time.

If it wasn't for William, that may have been the MecDec's fate. Instead, one of the critical surviving documents from the Alexandriana fire of 1800 is a copy of the MecDec almost certainly created by the hand of William Polk. In his MecDec book *Chain of Error*, McNitt spends almost four pages documenting in detail why it could have only been William who made that copy. (Yes, just to utterly confuse everyone, V. V. McNitt, the preeminent scholar on the MecDec documents, has a last name almost identical to McKnitt Alexander, one of the central characters in this saga. They are not related. If it helps, I always think of the author as "Mc-Nitt" and the Alexander as "Mc-Knight.") Anyway, in analyzing the authorship of this surviving copy of the MecDec, McNitt's evidence includes a long list of similarities in the content, corrections, and handwriting, all the way down to the "slightly florid" capital letters, as well as the identical reproduction of the family name Polk. At the beginning of his analysis, the cautious former newspaper editor McNitt uses words like "probably" and "inconclusive," but even now, two centuries later, when you hold up examples of William's handwriting next to the MecDec document that survived the Alexandriana fire, there's nothing even remotely "inconclusive" about it.

William Polk wrote them both.

Years before the fire he must have left the extra copy with the official MecDec Secretary McKnitt Alexander, who then, for safekeeping, rolled it up with his Rough Notes from the May 20 meeting and stored it, thankfully, in a far-less flammable part of Alexandriana. All of this was confirmed by McKnitt's son, Dr. Joseph Alexander, who authenticated the surviving document as a "true copy" of the MecDec. "The entire sheet is most probably a copy taken long since from the original for some person . . . and never sent on," Dr. Alexander explained.

A few months after the Alexandriana fire, using his memory along with the surviving Rough Notes and William Polk's "true copy" of the original MecDec, McKnitt made a full copy of the records and documents from May 20, 1775, and dispatched them to his friend and confidant General William Davie for curation. (These papers would become known as the "Davie Copy" of the MecDec.) The two men had served together during the Revolution, and in 1800, as a war hero, a member of the Constitutional Convention of 1787, the former governor of North Carolina, and a founder of the University of North Carolina, Davie was easily the most revered man in the state. According to historians William Henry Foote and Draper, even though McKnitt mourned "the loss of the original copy of the Mecklenburg Declaration of Independence . . . he consoled himself by saying that he had himself given a copy to General Davie some time before, which he knew to be correct."

"The document is safe," McKnitt declared.

Draper states this firsthand account is "unquestionably reliable" and comes from lifelong McKnitt confidant and North Carolina judge Duncan Cameron, who also served as the president of the State Bank from 1829–1849. Judge Cameron is just one of many highly respected eyewitnesses to the MecDec that make up a mountain of anecdotal and corroborating proof. To review: both the Rough Notes from the actual 1775 meeting and the "Polk Copy" of the MecDec from the 1780s had survived the Alexandriana fire. On top of that, the official MecDec secretary had provided the most respected authority in the state with a full, sworn copy of the MecDec records that a judge confirmed was "certainly correct." The wordings of these documents were all practically identical and, later, closely matched the sworn testimony of more than a dozen eyewitnesses from May 20, 1775, in Charlotte.

As far as McKnitt was concerned, the historical record had been upheld.

And it stayed that way.

For about seventeen years.

McKnitt Alexander died on July 17, 1817, and was buried at Hopewell Cemetery next to his wife and near General William Lee Davidson and three MecDec Signers. He was eighty-four.

With his passing, nearly all the men who had gathered on that historic day inside the Charlotte courthouse in May 1775 were gone. And the Mec-Dec might've faded into oblivion right along with them if it hadn't been for a notorious Virginia politician and powerbroker named William Wirt.

The same year McKnitt passed away, President James Monroe named Wirt, a lawyer and Virginia aristocrat, the ninth attorney general of the United States. Wirt had risen to national prominence in 1807 when Jefferson tabbed him to prosecute Aaron Burr (unsuccessfully) for treason. Wirt then served as AG from 1817–1829. After leaving that post he was placed on the presidential ticket of the Anti-Masonic Party even though Wirt, himself a Freemason, steadfastly refused to say anything derogatory about Masons. Predictably, Wirt finished behind Andrew Jackson and Henry Clay but managed to win Vermont—where my guess is they *really* hate secret societies.

Orphaned at eight and raised by his aunt and uncle, Wirt attended classical schools and fancied himself a writer and amateur historian. (Imagine that.) In 1817, at the height of his political power, he published *Sketches of the Life and Character of Patrick Henry*. There was just one little hitch with

Wirt's hagiography of his hero and beloved fellow Virginian: Henry had been dead for eighteen years, and Wirt had never seen or spoken to him. In the preface of the book, Wirt freely admits with a cocky shrug that he "knew nothing of Henry, personally" and that he was "compelled to rely wholly on the information of others." By "others" Wirt means a few of Henry's best friends and fellow Virginia aristocrat Thomas Jefferson, that straight-shooting paragon of truth and integrity, who for all intents and purposes became Wirt's coauthor. "Mr. Jefferson . . . not only favored the author with a very full communication in the first instance," Wirt wrote. "But [he] assisted him, subsequently and repeatedly, with his able counsel, in reconciling apparent contradictions, and clearing away difficulties of fact."

No kidding. An actual footnote in the book just says: *This is affirmed by Thomas Jefferson. The incident, therefore, becomes authentic history.* That's not how this works, of course. And by the end of the project, Wirt and TJ had taken so many liberties and fabricated so much material that Jefferson himself shelved *Sketches* under "fiction."

Even Henry's famous "Give me liberty, or give me death!" line from March 1775 may have been invented by Wirt.

That's right, no actual documentation, original or otherwise, exists to confirm the veracity of one of the most important and iconic rallying cries in American history. Instead, it is said to have come from a speech by Henry that, thirty-three years after the fact, Wirt was able to "reconstruct" purely from the "recollections" of Jefferson and others.

The peculiar workings of historical scholarship are enough to give anyone a permanent case of MecDec Face. Consider how, in some instances when no concrete proof exists, anecdotal evidence and eyewitness recollections are considered perfectly sufficient. When you get right down to it, this is how it works: if the eyewitness accounts support the popular version—or the version preferred by the author, the historiography, or the patriarchy—then they are judged to be reliable. If they don't (like, say, in the case of Sally Hemings or the MecDec), well, then they are deemed to be the unreliable, biased ramblings of confused imbeciles. You won't see a better (or worse) example of this selective use of evidentiary criteria than with the MecDec. Historians are perfectly willing to rely on the vivid eyewitness accounts of

Hunter and General Joseph Graham when it comes to the Revolutionary War battles in Camden and Charlotte. Yet when it comes to corroborating the MecDec's creation just a few years earlier, suddenly Hunter and Graham are no longer considered reliable witnesses.

With all this stuff, whether it's Paul Revere, Patrick Henry, Thomas Jefferson, the Declaration of Independence, the Southern Campaign of the Revolutionary War, or the MecDec, the unvarnished truth is often no match for human nature and, frankly, four million years of evolution. Even though there are hundreds of important and interesting details surrounding the American Revolution, most of us only have the bandwidth to process and retain a handful of those key facts. And, as one historian and sociologist explained to me, once our brains are "full" of things like the Boston Tea Party and Valley Forge, subconsciously, we don't even bother trying to retain lore like the MecDec, no matter how critical it might be. Stuffed to the brim, our brains just wave those details off, like dessert after a big meal. Which is exactly what happened to me with that sociologist. After our initial back-and-forth, I inquired by email what this all might say about the current state of the American intellect, that our brains have room for every last Rob Base lyric from "It Takes Two" but we can't find space for the first, true Declaration of Independence. And I never heard from the guy again. (You might say I was . . . *out of sight.*)

Well, it turns out our brains have been hardwired to conserve energy and oxygen by stubbornly refusing to change our minds about things we have already come to believe, especially things that are tied to emotions like, say, cool facts about the American Revolution that, for most of us, were our first childhood forays into history. Instead, without even being cognizant of it, our biased brains seek out and overemphasize evidence that supports our already-held beliefs while disregarding anything that might possibly contradict them and force us to relearn something.

Forget MecDec Face. This is MecDec Brain.

But all the history books say Jefferson was a saint and a sage. The Declaration of Independence could not have been a "workaday" document. Come on, I've never heard of Cornwallis fighting in the Carolinas. All that MecDec evidence can't be real, it just can't. So what happens when someone like Wirt recreates a speech and an iconic proclamation practically out of thin air from a moment in history when he was exactly three years old? Well, of course, that badass quote that we all love so much is going to be immediately and fully accepted into the scholarly canon on the Revolution for all eternity—and good luck trying to change anyone's mind.

Incredibly, though, that doozy was just the beginning of Wirt's overreach. Within the context of telling—or should I say inventing—Henry's story, Wirt and Jefferson also presented, as fact, an exaggeration of Virginia's role in the Revolution that was absurdly biased and misleading. Not to mention unnecessary. I mean, no one has ever questioned Virginia's critical role in the Revolution. This was just a gluttonous grab for even more prestige by privileged men. Along with recasting the JeffDec as some kind of sacred American scripture, *Sketches* became part of a larger power grab by Virginia and other states to horde as much credit for American independence as possible.

In Wirt's book and elsewhere, what you see happening during the first quarter of the nineteenth century is a kind of massive rebranding of our Revolution story that tends to downplay any leadership outside of Philadelphia, New York, or Boston, along with any battle without Washington in charge and any sacrifice made south of the James River. The Boston Tea Party. Paul Revere. Bunker Hill. Valley Forge. It has been drilled into our collective consciousness that those are the only things that mattered. As if Cornwallis decided on a whim in the middle of the war to kick back and recharge with his army on the coast at Wilmington and Yorktown for a spell. As if he wasn't, in fact, driven to the brink by the bravery and sacrifice of thousands of mostly Scots-Irish soldiers, leaders, and *authors* who fueled the success of the Southern Campaign and the Revolutionary War as a whole.

Instead, Wirt asserts that "the American revolution is universally admitted to have begun in the upper circles of society [because] it turned on principles too remote and abstruse for vulgar apprehension or consideration."

Poor people were too dumb to understand and appreciate freedom?

Wirt was just getting warmed up.

"Had it depended on the unenlightened mass of the community . . . no doubt can be entertained at this day, that the [Stamp] tax imposed by parliament would have been paid without question." Sure, this goes roughly 100 percent against the known facts, but I'm willing to ignore it because it leads to Wirt's perfect turd of a conclusion: "And since the upper circle of society did not take its impulse from the people, the only remaining inquiry is who gave the revolutionary impulse to that circle itself? It was unquestionable Patrick Henry. This is affirmed by Mr. Jefferson."

You don't say?

Wirt managed to top that, however, by then claiming that Henry, Virginia, and the colonial upper class deserved all the credit for the American Revolution.

"There was no colony which resisted, with more firmness and constancy, the pretensions of the British parliament, than that of Virginia," Wirt wrote. "The impulse thus given by Virginia, was caught by the other colonies."

As you might expect, Wirt's book sparked heated arguments (everywhere outside of Virginia) about proper recognition regarding the American Revolution. The debates eventually made it all the way to Congress in 1818, where "the claim was made that North Carolina made the earliest movement [toward independence]." This headline-making dispute on the House floor inspired William Davidson, the representative from Mecklenburg, and North Carolina Senator Nathaniel Macon, the former Speaker of the House, to solicit information from their constituents back home on, among other things, the Mecklenburg Declaration of Independence.

The goal was to set the record straight, once and for all, on who was really first to freedom.

In Charlotte at the time, that kind of historic request would have only gone to one person: McKnitt's son, Dr. Joseph Alexander. A Princeton grad and renaissance man, Joseph was described by a contemporary as having "early developed indications of not only genius and talents, but the highest attributes of intellect, sound judgement and profound thinking."

Using McKnitt's Rough Notes along with the Polk Copy of the MecDec, Joseph immediately sent the entire documented story of the Mecklenburg

Declaration of Independence to Congress with a note: "The foregoing is a true copy of the papers on the above subject, left in my hands by John McKnitt Alexander, deceased." A delighted Davidson shared the historic papers with Macon, who, in turn, immediately forwarded them to the largest newspapers in North Carolina, the *Raleigh Register* and the *North Carolina Gazette*.

On April 30, 1819, the *Raleigh Register* printed the entire bombshell.

It is not probably known to many of our readers, that the citizens of Mecklenburg County, in this State, made a Declaration of Independence more than a year before Congress made theirs. The following Document on the subject has lately come to the hands of the Editor from unquestionable authority, and is published that it may go down to posterity.

In the spring of 1775, the leading characters of Mecklenburg county, stimulated by that enthusiastic patriotism which elevates the mind above considerations of individual aggrandizement, and scorning to shelter themselves from the impending storm by submission to lawless power, &c. &c. held several detached meetings, in each of which the individual sentiments were, "that the cause of Boston was the cause of all; that their destinies were indissolubly connected with those of their Eastern fellow-citizens—and that they must either submit to all the impositions which an unprincipled, and to them an unrepresented, Parliament might impose—or support their brethren who were doomed to sustain the first shock of that power, which, if successful there, would ultimately overwhelm all in the common calamity." Conformably to these principles, Colonel T. Polk, through solicitation, issued an order to each Captain's company in the county of Mecklenburg, (then comprising the present county of Cabarrus,) directing each militia company to elect two persons, and delegate to them ample power to devise ways and means to aid and assist their suffering brethren in Boston, and also generally to adopt measures to extricate themselves from the impending storm, and to secure unimpaired their inalienable rights, privileges, and liberties, from the dominant grasp of British imposition and tyranny.

In conformity to said order, on the 19th of May, 1775, the said delegation met in Charlotte, vested with unlimited powers; at which time official news, by express, arrived of the battle of Lexington on that day of the preceding month. Every delegate felt the value and importance of the prize, and the awful and solemn crisis which had arrived—every bosom swelled with indignation at the malice, inveteracy, and insatiable revenge, developed in the late attack at Lexington. The universal sentiment was: let us not flatter ourselves that popular harangues, or resolves; that popular vapor will avert the storm, or vanquish our common enemy—let us deliberate—let us calculate the issue—the probable result; and then let us act with energy, as brethren leagued to preserve our property—our lives—and what is still more endearing, the liberties of America. *Abraham Alexander* was then elected Chairman, and *John M'Knitt Alexander*, Clerk. After a free and full discussion of the various objects for which the delegation had been convened, it was unanimously ordained—

1. *Resolved*, That whoever directly or indirectly abetted, or in any way, form or manner, countenanced the unchartered and dangerous invasion of our rights, as claimed by Great Britain, is an enemy to this country—to America—and to the inherent and inalienable rights of man.

2. *Resolved*, That we the citizens of Mecklenburg county, do hereby dissolve the political bands which have connected us to the Mother Country, and hereby absolve ourselves from all allegiance to the British Crown, and abjure all political connection, contract, or association, with that nation, who have wantonly trampled on our rights and liberties—and inhumanly shed the innocent blood of American patriots at Lexington.

3. *Resolved*, That we do hereby declare ourselves a free and independent people, are, and of right ought to be, a sovereign and self-governing Association, under the control of no power other than that of our God and the General Government of the Congress; to the maintenance of which independence, we solemnly pledge to each other, our mutual co-operation, our lives, our fortunes, and our most sacred honor.

4. *Resolved*, That as we now acknowledge the existence and control of no law or legal officer, civil or military, within this country, we do hereby ordain and adopt, as a rule of life, all, each and every of our former laws, wherein, nevertheless, the Crown of Great Britain never can be considered as holding rights, privileges, immunities, or authority therein.

5. *Resolved*, That it is also further decreed, that all, each and every military officer in this county, is hereby reinstated to his former command and authority, he acting conformably to these regulations. And that every member present of this delegation shall henceforth be a civil officer, viz. a Justice of the Peace, in the character of a '*Committee-man*,' to issue process, hear and determine all matters of controversy, according to said adopted laws, and to preserve peace, and union, and harmony, in said county,—and to use every exertion to spread the love of country and fire of freedom throughout America, until a more general and organized government be established in this province.

A number of bye laws were also added, merely to protect the association from confusion, and to regulate their general conduct as citizens. After sitting in the Court House all night, neither sleepy, hungry, nor fatigued, and after discussing every paragraph, they were all passed, sanctioned, and decreed, unanimously, about 2 o'clock, A. M. May 20. In a few days, a deputation of said delegation convened, when Capt. *James Jack*, of Charlotte, was deputed as express to the Congress at Philadelphia, with a copy of said Resolves and Proceedings, together with a letter addressed to our three representatives there, viz. *Richard Caswell, William Hooper and Joseph Hughes*—under express injunction, personally, and through the State representation, to use all possible means to have said proceedings sanctioned and approved by the General Congress. On the return of Captain Jack, the delegation learned that their proceedings were individually approved by the Members of Congress, but that it was deemed premature to lay them before the House. A joint letter from said three members of Congress was also received, complimentary of the zeal in the common cause, and recommending perseverance, order and energy.

Two months later, Adams and Jefferson began their infamous correspondence on the MecDec. Jefferson famously declared that he believed the document "spurious." And that's all it took. His reputation may be nearly beyond repair today, but in 1819 Jefferson was like a living god, so highly and universally regarded that one word from the sage's mouth could end any discussion or debate.

And that's exactly what happened:

"Jefferson had become increasingly proud of being the author of the Declaration of Independence," says author Gordon S. Wood. "Thus he was not at all happy when he learned from Adams in 1819 that an earlier declaration of independence had anticipated his famous document." Adds Draper: "Mr. Jefferson . . . was not disposed to share in any degree the immortality with which [the Declaration of Independence] had crowned him, with a comparatively obscure citizen of North Carolina."

It didn't matter that there were authentic meeting notes from May 20 and true matching copies of the MecDec itself, as well as countless eyewitness testimony. From the beginning, McKnitt and the Alexanders had also offered to make the MecDec documents "subject to the inspection of any one desirous to examine them." No one ever took them up on their offer. Instead, Jefferson, the man we're supposed to believe was a great, tirelessly curious, and fair-minded intellect, simply deemed the MecDec bogus out of hand with no investigation whatsoever, and his army of sycophants stepped right in to defend his honor. Not by proving Jefferson correct or innocent, of course, but by attempting to dismiss and diminish the MecDec and Charlotte's Founding Fathers.

More than anything, though, it was Jefferson's patronizing tone that really set off the MecDecers. With no actual research or evidence to base his response on, Jefferson resorted to name-calling. I'm guessing the religious undertones of him dubbing the MecDec an "apocryphal gospel" did not sit well with the devout Presbyterians who had founded Charlotte. And once Jefferson coupled that insult with an offhanded comment comparing the MecDec to a previous hoax about a North Carolina volcano erupting in 1812, there was no turning back. The feud was on. Nearly everyone in Mecklenburg knew of a loved one who, inspired by the spirit of the MecDec, made the ultimate sacrifice on the battlefield for our country. And then here comes Jefferson up in Virginia, practically a deserter during the war, cracking jokes and comparing the MecDec to a fake volcano, ignoring the striking similarities between the two documents, and, in the case of Wirt, writing about how the war was inspired by the "upper circles of society" because the "unenlightened masses" were too dimwitted to understand taxation without representation.

In the end, though, Jefferson and his stans made one fatal miscalculation: Don't pick a fight with a region full of devout Scots-Irish patriots.

The responses from the incensed North Carolinians were so epic and colorful that it would be impossible for me to narrow down my favorites. Writing in the *National Intelligencer*, a distant Alexander descendant named Joseph Wallis called all the MecDec deniers up north a bunch of "liars and slanderers" before politely offering—in the most Scots-Irish way ever—to supply "personal satisfaction" to anyone from Virginia man enough to question the MecDec to his face.

Wallis's threat to kick some Jeffersonian ass ended up being one of the more restrained responses to what Joseph Alexander called "Mr. Jefferson's denial of this, our birthright."

Preaching at Hopewell Presbyterian Church, one of Charlotte's (and Craighead's) original Seven Sisters and the final resting place of several Mec-Dec Signers, the Reverend Doctor M. Winslow Alexander called the Mec-Dec "the proceedings of our fathers, of our relatives, of our fellow citizens; every individual of whom has descended to the silent tomb."

As you read his sermon in the *Catawba Journal*, you can practically hear the church rafters rattling with the reverend doctor's thunderous oration aimed directly at Thomas Jefferson.

"Who would not glory in such ancestors?" Alexander roars. "Who would not emulate such virtue? Who would not sanction such principles? These are their living deeds of patriotism, which misfortune cannot now tarnish, and which the malignant breath of envy durst not now assail to blast."

But of all the retorts, nothing can compare to the way that legendary North Carolinian bon vivant Joseph Seawell Jones put the Jeffersonians on full blast for all eternity.

Of all the fantastic, truly insane tangents that have popped up along the way on this adventure, one of the most wonderfully weird wormholes I found was the story of Seawell Jones. Nicknamed "Shocco" after the Carolina creek he grew up on, Seawell Jones was described by classmates at the

University of North Carolina as "swarthy, tall, long-haired, and wild-eyed." That wasn't the half of it.

After receiving eighty dollars from his father to cover his entire college education, once he arrived in Chapel Hill, Shocco struggled mightily to attend class and, especially, required chapel. Administrators could forgive the first, but not the latter. And when his nemesis, renowned UNC math professor James Phillips, calculated Shocco's church absences (seventy-six), our hero didn't have a prayer and was summarily excommunicated from campus. (The Phillips family, as we'll later learn, was just getting started tormenting the MecDecers.) Meanwhile, like any normal college dropout, Shocco responded to the setback by promptly enrolling at Harvard Law School. From there Shocco claims to have killed a man in a duel, left at least one debutante at the altar, talked his way into a Harvard law degree, swindled the state bank of Mississippi out of a fortune, lived deep in the woods for a while as a hermit, and, as an author, archivist, and national media darling, built a following larger than the Queen herself.

And it all appears to be true.

Except the part about the duel—Shocco faked that with pig's blood.

"The time has been," recalled one newspaper profile, "when the sayings and doings of this singular personage were chronicled with as much avidity as is displayed by the Court Journal in the narration of the British Queen." That notoriety allowed Shocco access to "Van Buren, Jackson, both Adamses, Calhoun, Clay, Randolph, and every man who had figured on the world's stage for the thirty years past, and he had anecdotes to tell of each."

Somehow, in the middle of all this, Shocco also managed to write and publish *A Defense of the Revolutionary History of the State of North Carolina from the Aspersions of Mr. Jefferson*. In addition to all his other talents and eccentricities, Shocco was actually kind of an amazing writer. I mean, he even got a book blurb from Supreme Court Justice Joseph Story, who called the work "a triumphant refutation of Jefferson's misrepresentations."

After damning Jefferson as a "heathen god," a "zealous idolater," and, for good measure, a "radical autocrat," Shocco concluded that "the reasons, upon which Mr. Jefferson doubts the Mecklenburg Declaration are shallow, and the language, with which he chooses to express his suspicions, are indicative of a jealous and malignant spirit . . . A more flagrant instance of violation of truth cannot be found in the annals of cabalistic literature."

As for Wirt's claim that, apparently, the entire revolution was conceived, inspired, planned, funded, fought, and won all within the borders of Virginia?

Yeah . . . Shocco wasn't having that either.

"Whilst the Sage of Monticello was pondering on the various projects of reconciliation with the mother country, and never, for once, looking beyond *'that desirable end'*; while Virginia and even Massachusetts were continually avowing allegiance to the Throne; and North Carolina herself, through the medium of her Congress, was declaring that independence was not her object, the people of Mecklenburg, with the sagacity of an honest and injured race, untutored in the craft and cunning of politics, recoiled at once on the power that oppressed them, and dissolved forever the unhallowed union of British domination and American allegiance. A junto of politicians would have recommended forbearance, and pointed to some future and more propitious period for action; but in the simplicity of their hearts they appealed to the law of nature indelibly stamped upon the human bosom that when power becomes tyranny, resistance is a duty and the God of battles must decide. . . . For my own part, I am willing, thus publicly, to lament dominant influence of the Virginia Republican party over the state of North Carolina. I do look upon it as the most fatal stroke ever aimed at the dignity and honor of my own country, and I would willingly lay the first stone of a Chinese wall to divide forever the physical and intellectual resources of the two states."

Ultimately, the final say in the matter would belong to the North Carolina General Assembly and Governor Montford Stokes. In 1829 they created and empowered a select committee of scholars to investigate the Mecklenburg Declaration of Independence. The committee traveled across North Carolina and as far as Georgia and Tennessee collecting documents, interviewing witnesses, and gathering sworn testimony from Captain Jack himself, Graham, William Polk, and Major John Davidson, among others. Dr. Joseph Alexander also provided the committee with "all the papers in my possession," which would have included his dad's Rough Notes along with the Davie and Polk copies of the MecDec.

After two years, the committee published its findings in an overwhelming thirty-two-page, fifteen-thousand-word report that includes thirteen sworn eyewitness statements from many highly decorated veterans of the Revolution, including Valley Forge survivor William Polk. In the report's preface, a candid Governor Stokes asks: "Need it be inquired, in any portion of this Union, if *he* will be believed?" In other words: *Is the sworn testimony of a dozen war heroes good enough for Virginia?* Stokes was on to something, because the true genius and power of the NC Report turned out to be the eyewitness testimonies. After the report was published, no one could disparage the MecDec without also doing the same to the character and honor of a dozen war heroes, attorneys, professors, and priests. Whatever argument there was at the time about the MecDec's authenticity was pretty much over by the end of the preface, anyway. In a footnote, Stokes confirms that in 1793—seven years before the fire at Alexandriana destroyed the original—he had seen the Williamson Copy of the MecDec and had spoken to Williamson about the document while visiting the historian in Fayetteville.

One of the very first research requests I made on the MecDec was to the head librarian at the Presbyterian Heritage Center in Montreat, North Carolina. While she was flipping through one of the Center's old archived books for information on the Reverend Alexander Craighead, what appeared to be an original copy of the NC Governor's Report on the MecDec, discolored and brittle, fell out from between the pages where it had been preserved for the past 190 years like a pressed flower.

Maybe it was dumb luck. But I, of course, took it as a sign.

And so I sat down right then and there and read the entire pamphlet, cover to cover, in one sitting, starting with this amazing opening statement:

The first claim of Independence evinces such high sentiments of valor and patriotism, that we cannot, and ought not, lightly to esteem the honor of having made it. The fact of the Declaration should be announced, its language should be published and perpetuated, and the names of the gallant representatives of Mecklenburg, with whom it originated, should be preserved from an oblivion, which . . . would as much dishonor us, as injure them. . . . To them, at least, belongs the proud distinction of having first given language to the thought; and it should be known, and, fortunately, it can still be conclusively established, that the Revolution received its first impulse towards Independence . . . in North Carolina. The Committee are aware that this assertion has elsewhere been received with doubt, and at times met with denial; and it is, therefore, believed to be more strongly incumbent upon the House to usher to the world the Mecklenburg Declaration, accompanied with such testimonials of its genuineness, as shall silence incredulity, and with such care for its general diffusion, as shall forever secure it from being forgotten. . . . Whatever the brilliant achievements of other States may have been, let it never be forgotten, that at a period of darkness and oppression, without concert with others, without assurances of support from any quarter, a few gallant North Carolinians, all fear of consequences lost in a sense of their country's wrongs, relying, under Heaven, solely upon themselves, nobly dared to assert, and resolved to maintain, that independence, of which, whoever might have thought, none had then spoken; and thus earned for themselves, and for their fellow-citizens of North Carolina, the honor of giving birth to the first Declaration of Independence.

When the full report was officially released in 1831, a triumphant Governor Stokes declared: "More satisfactory evidence, drawn from more reputable sources, Mr. Jefferson, if alive, could not, and would not require. It is not hazarding too much to say, that there is no one event of the Revolution which has been, or can be more fully or clearly authenticated."

This statement was aimed directly at Wirt and his cohorts up in Virginia. At the time, though, Wirt was likely too busy to respond while figuring out how, exactly, to run for president as a confirmed Freemason on an Anti-Masonic ticket.

Just two years later, Wirt died from complications due to a severe cold. It gets weirder.

With the MecDec, it always does.

Wirt was buried in a large, ornate marble crypt in Washington, D.C.'s Congressional Cemetery, where he rested in peace for 140 years until the 1970s when a random grave robber seems to have, well, stolen his skull. From there, Wirt's detached melon somehow ended up in the macabre memorabilia collection of Robert L. White, an eccentric cleaning supply salesman from Maryland. The *Washington Post* says White achieved "minor celebrity" in the 1990s for his large collection of Kennedy items and other oddities, like a seltzer bottle autographed by two-thirds of the Three Stooges and dozens of shrunken heads and skulls.

All of which he exhibited, naturally, "in a makeshift museum in his mother's basement."

When White died in 2003, an appraiser cataloging his collection discovered Wirt's skull in an old tin box inscribed in gold block letters with "Hon. Wm. Wirt." The appraiser handed it off to a local councilman who rang up the cemetery and asked, "You guys missing William Wirt's head?" Then, under one of the greatest newspaper headlines of all time—More Bodies Than Heads—*The Post* explained how a forensic anthropologist from the Smithsonian climbed down into the Wirt tomb and, after a quick head count (sorry), was able to return the skull to its proper owner inside the family's ransacked crypt.

Anyhow, Wirt's deadly case of the sniffles spared him from having to endure the humiliation of the 1831 NC Governor's Report. Overflowing with page upon page of irrefutable evidence, the report quickly had even the staunchest Jeffersonians reconsidering their stance on the MecDec. "Everyone must be persuaded, at least all who have been minute observers of style, that one of these papers has borrowed from the other," wrote George Tucker, noted historian, University of Virginia professor, and author of the two-volume biography *Life of Thomas Jefferson*. "For they are identical, not in one instance, but in several, and not in single words only, but in phrases composed of many. . . . We cannot suppose it to be the result of accident."

Wanting to settle the question once and for all before the publication of his second volume on Jefferson, Tucker solicited help from US officials in England.

That seemingly innocuous request triggered an international conspiracy that would reach the highest levels of the US government and eventually ensnare a US ambassador, a senator, a corrupt university professor, and a renowned Beltway charlatan.

It would also inspire the greatest text message exchange of my life.

Anything going on tomorrow? *I asked my wife.*
Nope. Y?
Think I might fly to London.
MecDec?
Yep.
FF Miles?
Yep.
Cheerio.

Eleven

The Cocked-up Trail of Dispatch 34 and US Ambassador Stevenson, the Dodgiest of Wankers

THE FOUR-THOUSAND-MILE COMMUTE IS PROBABLY THE EASIEST PART of gaining access to the British National Archives. For starters, there are the typically mind-numbing bureaucratic hoops that must be cleared. Upon arrival you must also avoid, as best you can, the local London obstacles, which in my case includes the latest batch of Fuller's Honey Dew Ale being generously poured at The Hereford Arms across the street from my South Kensington hotel. There's also a treasure map of Tube transfers required to reach the archive compound just outside the city. Lucky for me, the morning after my arrival, my hotel doorman agrees to help me decipher the Underground, but first he wants to know exactly what on earth brought me here on such short notice and so utterly unprepared. "It's very likely," I coolly explain, "that your National Archives contain proof of either America's original declaration of independence, or a pretty substantial conspiracy to cover it all up—you know, crime-of-the-century type stuff." After this, and for the rest of my visit, every time the doorman tips his enormous black felt top hat at me, he adds "Indiana!" or sometimes "Cheers, Indiana!" which is either a reference to the state of Indiana and my Midwestern tourist-y vibes, or, as I choose to believe, my swashbuckling Indiana Jones treasure-hunting historian charm.

Located on the Thames, in the Borough of Richmond just west of the city, the National Archives are bordered by the renowned Royal Botanical Garden. The immaculate three-hundred-acre Kew Gardens, as they're known, are a tempting distraction of lush, exotic botanicals as far as the eye can see. For those Yanks strong enough to resist the siren song of the Gardens, the path to the Archives only gets more intimidating. A sign in front of the building's glass and steel atrium entrance reminds visitors from the States that this is sacred ground. In November 1942, a battalion of American topographers secretly moved in here. Using aerial photographs of the coast of northern France, they produced millions of the detailed maps our soldiers relied upon during the D-Day landings in Normandy.

Today, the building is divided into two massive wings. To the east, a brighter, more contemporary and welcoming academic-style structure for government archivists, researchers, and educators. And to the west, my daunting destination: something that more closely resembles a six-story cement spaceship docked for repairs.

After a security screening and a triple check on IDs and paperwork, I'm issued an official visitor's pass and escorted past the cafeteria for my final challenge before being granted access to the Archives: the most gloriously nerdy locker room on earth. Along with scrubbing your hands like a surgeon, you're also required to stow all your belongings in the gym class–style lockers provided. (The only personal luxury allowed inside is one eraserless pencil.) Near the front door of this parallel universe version of the Star Wars cantina, there's an ink board reminding researchers to use the available oxo-degradable plastic bags, and that today's lunch special is carrot soup and pickle and cheddar toasties. There's also a Lost and Found that contains an international assortment of pharmacy-style reader glasses, flip-flops, and an inhaler. The final amazing perk of being an international researcher is the fresh stack of out-of-circulation books the Archives regularly gives away to any good home. Today's offerings include such gems as a hardbound municipal yearbook from 1977 (which does not contain one Mr. David Bowie—I checked), Crockford's Clerical Directory from 2004–2005, and a coffee table–style photo book called, quite simply, *Gunfire*, an exploration of the ammo England used to defeat Germany. I immediately make a mental note to grab this page-turner later for my doorman, but it gets claimed exactly eleven seconds after hitting the shelf.

Waiting with me in here for the Archives to officially open are, among others, a lovely grandma researching her family history, a Black graduate student from London, and a skinny, chatty chap who looks like he walked right off the *Harry Potter* set. Along with sharing some tips about navigating the Archives (including: stay away from the carrot soup), this guy casually lets it slip that he's after some ancient scrolls and writs from around, oh, 1150. I might be new here, but I'm pretty sure this guy's trash-talking me and, by comparison, my practically brand-new 1775 correspondence between Josiah Martin, North Carolina's last royal governor, and the Earl of Dartmouth, the British secretary of state for the colonies.

As a quick reminder, in June 1771, North Carolina's original governor, William Tryon, was "promoted" out of the South to become governor of New York. Syfert and others believe that even though Tryon had many faults, at least he was decisive and pragmatic. So naturally, when it came time to name his replacement just as the colonies were careening toward open rebellion, KG3 picked Tryon's exact opposite: the whiney, entitled, puffy-pink-cheeked Martin, who once complained that "death was preferable" to his family's estate in the Caribbean. Instead, Martin got North Carolina, where one of his first interactions with the MecDecers was delivering the double-cross decree from the King denying them the charter for Queen's College and reinstating the despised Marriage and Vestry Acts.

These were, essentially, the final acts that pushed the Princeton men gathering at the Freedom Spring in Alexandriana to begin formulating the MecDec. Things devolved rather quickly from there, obviously, and by the summer of 1775, after taking the dramatic step of dissolving the North Carolina General Assembly, Martin sent a series of frantic notes to the Crown requesting troops to squash the impending rebellion on the North Carolina frontier. Martin sent so many panicky letters in such a short amount of time that the poor record-keepers in England started labeling them as Dispatch 1, Dispatch 2, and so on, just to keep track. In a time long before "read receipts," Martin occasionally wrote letters just to confirm the letters he had already sent. (So much for his father's hopes that in America Joey might be cured of "his two vices, that of women and extravagance." At this point, I'm starting to get the distinct feeling that England wasn't exactly sending its best and brightest to oversee the New World.)

Several times in his nonstop string of letter bombs a thoroughly shook Martin mentions the "treasonous" MecDec and the "Traitorous Conspiracies" being circulated by the *Cape Fear Mercury*, a paper published throughout the Revolution in Wilmington, North Carolina. (Charlotte wouldn't get its first newspaper for another half century.)

On June 30, 1775, in a letter to Dartmouth, Martin lays it all out:

The Resolves of the Committee of Mecklenburgh which Your Lordship will find in the enclosed News Paper, surpass all the horrid and treasonable publications that the inflammatory spirits of this continent have yet produced; and Your Lordship may depend, its authors and abettors will not escape my due notice, whenever my hands are sufficiently strengthened to attempt the recovery of the lost authority of government. A copy of these resolves I am informed were sent off by express to the Congress at Philadelphia, as soon as they were passed in the Committee.

In a single paragraph Martin manages to confirm almost everything about the MecDec. But it's those three words in the opening sentence that would create an international MecDec mystery for the next 248 years and counting. "The Resolves of the Committee of Mecklenburgh, which your Lordship will find in the *enclosed News Paper . . .*"

In order to bolster his umpteenth request for military backup in North Carolina, Martin went full Revolutionary Karen, actually enclosing for the British secretary of state published proof of the MecDecers formally "dissolving" their ties to England reprinted in an edition of the *Cape Fear Mercury* most likely on June 23, 1775, or somewhere near that date. Five weeks later, Martin would repeat his request in even more detail:

Whereas I have also seen a most infamous publication in the Cape Fear Mercury importing to be resolves of a set of people stiling themselves a

Committee for the County of Mecklenburg most traitorously declaring the entire dissolution of the Laws Government and Constitution of this country and setting up a system of rule and regulation repugnant to the Laws and subversive of His Majesty's Government.

For as much as he hated North Carolina and the MecDec, it's beautifully ironic that Martin would contribute so much to its authentication and preservation. Because, in this second letter, by mentioning two distinct documents created in Mecklenburg—one that specifically "dissolved" the connection to England and another that set up a new system of rules and regulations to govern by—Martin confirms the sequential tale of the MecDec and the Mecklenburg Resolves.

As with all other royal correspondence, Martin's letter, and the all-important "enclosed News Paper" containing the MecDec, was then recorded and preserved. During the process it was labeled Dispatch 34 by the British Public Records Office in London, which eventually became the British National Archives.

And that's where Dispatch 34 sat, undisturbed, for the next six decades.

UNTIL JUNE 1837, THAT IS, WHEN TUCKER, THE UVA PROFESSOR AND *LIFE of Jefferson* author, began to get cold feet about dismissing the MecDec and Jefferson's possible plagiarism. Later in life, Tucker developed into a prolific, talented writer and a respected sociologist, but he always remained, quite literally, a gambler at heart. Even in his own autobiography, there are several references to Tucker's gambling addiction and massive gambling debts, which, at one point, led to a lottery scam that ended with him serving jail time. After his release from prison, naturally, Tucker was elected to the House of Representatives, where he served Virginia for six years until 1824. On top of a crippling fear of public speaking, Tucker confessed that he was never able to overcome his "livelier ambition to be a great chess player than to be a distinguished member of Congress." Jobless at fifty, he was rescued by Jefferson who, just before his death, offered Tucker a teaching position at the University of Virginia where Tucker could get paid to lecture occasionally while continuing to work on his dream of becoming a successful science-fiction novelist.

Based on his initial theories regarding the MecDec, though, Tucker had already accomplished that goal. His first lame argument was a common trope that would be repeated ad nauseum: those hicks in Charlotte were too backward to contemplate being "free and independent," forgetting, for a moment, that many of the MecDecers were Princeton grads and, thus, just as educated and (if you ask any Princeton grad) of far greater intellect than their critics. Next, Tucker tried to suggest that, okay, even if the MecDec was real, it probably had little impact because Charlotte was so close to the frontier, forgetting, for one more moment, that Captain Jack had delivered the document straight away to the halls of Congress.

Much closer to the actual truth is that in Tucker's voluminous bio of the president, he had gone all-in, risking his reputation, livelihood, and legacy on defending his financial savior, Jefferson.

And like any true gambler, Tucker knew a bad beat when he saw one.

The publication of the NC Governor's Report was just the beginning. In 1837, the opening of the US Mint in Charlotte was a clear sign that the town was booming in population and influence. With the site of the original courthouse just down the street from the Mint, the MecDec remained at both the literal and figurative heart of the city. A few years later the prestigious Davidson College, located north of town, also honored (and codified) the MecDec with its school motto: *Alenda Lux Ubi Orta Libertas* (Let Learning Be Cherished Where Liberty Has Arisen.) Soon, the irrefutable Moravian diaries and the countless sworn testimonies in war pension applications would also come to light.

Sensing his luck running out, Tucker began looking for ways to hedge his bet. Hoping for a Hail Mary of exculpatory evidence, Tucker reached out to his longtime friend and former political crony Andrew Stevenson, the former Speaker of the House, who had just arrived in London as the new United States Minister to the United Kingdom. Tucker's plan was simple: get Stevenson to use his political clout to gain access to the British Archives, locate Dispatch 34 and the enclosed copy of the *Cape Fear Mercury* containing the MecDec, and then clear Jefferson of plagiarism charges by sharing with the world what Tucker believed would be an inferior and dissimilar Mecklenburg Declaration.

I only managed to decipher this plot thanks to the keen instincts I've developed over many years as an investigative magazine writer and reporter.

Well, that and Tucker put the entire scheme in writing.

In a letter to Stevenson in June 1837, Tucker wrote:

You will perceive that in the 2nd volume I have been at some pains to defend Mr. Jefferson from what appeared to be the preposterous charge of plagiarism from the "Mecklenburg Declaration of Independence," and in doing this I have supposed that that paper affords intrinsic evidence that the only two resolves (therein) in which there is any similarity to Mr. Jefferson's Declaration have been subsequently interloped. For the purpose of sustaining or refuting this supposition I have in vain sought in North Carolina for a copy of the Cape Fear Mercury (of the date of July 1775) in which these Mecklenburg resolves were published. Now as they are particularly noticed by Gov. (Josiah) Martin, the Royal Governor of that State, in his Proclamation of the 8th of August 1775, I have thought it probable that in his dispatches to his Government, he sent a copy of the newspaper containing the treasonable publications to which he adverts, and consequently that these newspapers may still be found in the State Paper Office of Great Britain. If so, a reference to them would show us this far famed "Declaration of Independence," in its original form, and the precise extent of the resemblance (if any at all, which I don't believe) to Mr. Jefferson's draught. An application from you to make the inquiry would, I am confident, . . . meet with ready attention—and you would render an essential service to the memory of Mr. Jefferson, and to a part of American history that always must be peculiarly interesting, if you could succeed in obtaining the information.

So now, here I am on a wet and bone-chillingly cold spring day in London, inside this gloriously weird locker room at the British National Archives, thinking about carrot soup and World War II ammunition, about to follow a 185-year-old, four-thousand-mile trail of breadcrumbs left by

Tucker and Stevenson to discover what I hope will be Dispatch 34 and the MecDec. While it's true I'm not the first MecDec treasure hunter to go looking for Dispatch 34, incredibly, I do appear to be the first who was willing to cross the ocean for it. I'm well aware that all the research on Dispatch 34 leads to the same conclusion: it's a longshot, at best. But that's what all the experts and old-timers said about the Freedom Spring too.

With just a single day of allotted archive time, I make my way out of the locker room and up the stairs to the reading room, where I'm subjected to yet another ID and security check before I can access the air-locked sliding glass doors that make a *sheeeff-fooosh* sound—exactly like the entrance to the bridge of the Star Trek *Enterprise*. Inside the glass airlock is the final frontier where an archivist is waiting with all my requested research items. A computer monitor near her desk lists all the items in my lengthy queue, although Archive policy only allows me to physically check out one folder at a time. I see right away that Josiah Martin's correspondence is more than halfway down the list. It's a bummer since I've been dreaming for days now about flipping open Dispatch 34, locating the MecDec, and then, I don't know, phoning the mayor of Charlotte and the Smithsonian before taking all my new locker room buddies back to The Hereford Arms for many, many Honey Dew Ales.

Instead, at the top of my queue is the Archives' sporadic collection of original editions of the *Cape Fear Mercury* from the same summer—in 1775—when Josiah Martin became such an avid subscriber.

"This one first, then?" asks the archivist.

"Sure, thanks," I say, as she places the oversized light blue cardboard folder in my hands.

With my mind focused so much on Dispatch 34, I guess I hadn't fully processed what might actually be inside the blue folder full of *Cape Fear Mercury* editions now in my possession. Some part of me must know, though, because all of a sudden, I can barely breathe, let alone speak or move; and I'm frozen in place right in front of the automatic airlock doors that comically keep opening and closing—*sheeeff-foosh . . . sheeff-foosh . . . sheeff-foosh*—as I stare at the binder like someone just handed me a folded ceremonial flag at a funeral.

The MecDec could be right here in my very hands.

Andrew Stevenson's biographer categorized him as "an ardent disciple and personal friend of Thomas Jefferson." Along with Tucker and Wirt, Stevenson was also a founding member of the original Virginia frat boy–style cabal known as the "Richmond Junto." It was the "central corresponding committee of the Republican [Democratic] party in Virginia—[a] powerful, controlling clique that exalted Jeffersonian principles in Old Dominion politics." So you don't have to dig too terribly deep into Stevenson's background to understand why he'd stop at nothing to protect the legacy of his pal Jefferson. A fellow William & Mary grad, Stevenson first distinguished himself on a national scale while presiding over the House of Representatives from 1827 to 1834 during a precarious period in American history. (Although you learn quickly with American history that it's all pretty precarious, and it remains so right up to this very day.) All the while during that seven-year stretch, though, Stevenson's critics accused him of extreme partisanship and reckless subservience to President Andrew Jackson. It was a charge Stevenson never bothered to argue. To the contrary. He was partisan to a fault and proud of it. So much so that at the end of his final term in Congress, when a colleague reading the standard resolution of thanks used the word "impartiality" to describe Stevenson, the entire House burst into laughter.

Stevenson had originally been nominated for the London post in 1834. While serving as Speaker, however, he had organized the House in a way so closely aligned with President Jackson's wishes that the Senate deemed the London gig a form of *quid pro quo* and denied his confirmation. The stubborn "Old Hickory" simply waited two years and renominated Stevenson, who was easily confirmed the second time around. Upon his arrival in London, Stevenson and his wife, Sally Coles (a cousin of Dolly Madison), were the toast of the town. Equipped with wavy strawberry-blonde hair, an impossibly long nose, and a kind of Philip Seymour Hoffman in *The Talented Mr. Ripley* air about him, Stevenson fit right in with the old-school English aristocrats.

It wasn't long, however, until he began to find the "social whirl in London strenuous and tiresome." In his letters back home to Virginia, Stevenson compared the "oppressive," endless dinner parties and nonstop soirees to . . . to . . . I can't even type it. "I presume you all think a Minister's life is one of leisure and ease," Stevenson wrote. "Far from it. It is one of labor, care, and vexation, I may almost say slavery. . . . The continued round of dinners (public and private), parties, soirees, and what not, to which we are doomed to go are enough to break one down . . . it is a great bore. I find it oppressive, tho' get along as well as I can."

Although it was fairly standard political gamesmanship at the time, Stevenson's rivals back in the States immediately tried to have him recalled from London. They weren't the only ones. As a slave owner himself and the kind of staunch, lifelong defender of slavery who "heartily wished" all abolitionists "would go to Africa," Stevenson's presence and his utter lack of self-awareness didn't exactly sit well in the United Kingdom, which had abolished slavery several years before he arrived.

Delivering an address condemning slaveholding in the United States, Daniel O'Connell, the Irish leader in the House of Commons, accused Minister Stevenson of not just slave-owning but slave *breeding*, which was considered a far more heinous crime. "I believe their very Ambassador here is a slave-breeder, one of those beings who rear up slaves for the purpose of traffic," O'Connell shouted. "Is it possible that America would send here a man who traffics in blood, and who is a disgrace to human nature?" Stevenson responded by challenging O'Connell to a duel because, apparently, before arm wrestling or rock-paper-scissors were invented, men were not capable of any other form of conflict resolution except death by close-range lead projectiles. (Seriously, this is at least the fifteenth reference to pistol dueling I've come across within just this one tiny slice of American history.) Anyway, O'Connell prudently offered the bare minimum response needed to avoid death by gunfire, claiming to have been slightly misquoted while continuing to rail against America's role in the "abominable, most hideous, most criminal, most revolting practice" of slavery.

Stevenson remained unmoved. His biography notes that for the rest of his life he advocated for "the protection of slave property and property rights at any cost, even if it should mean disunion and war."

Perhaps feeling a bit isolated in England, when Tucker's letter arrived requesting help finding the MecDec, Stevenson jumped at the chance to assist a fellow member of the old Richmond Junto. Almost immediately after hearing from Tucker, Stevenson reached out to the British government. Initially, though, Stevenson had almost as much difficulty getting into the Archives as I did. The British Foreign Minister's reply was, basically, *not so fast, Yankee Doodle*: "If you will have the goodness to state the points upon which you desire to obtain information connected with proceedings which took place in North Carolina prior to the War of Independence, I will endeavor to procure for you the desired information."

Oozing with that famous Virginia haughtiness, Stevenson passive-aggressively replied: "The Declaration of Independence, as you are probably aware, was drawn by Thomas Jefferson of Virginia, and proclaimed on the Fourth of July, 1776. Since Mr. Jefferson's death, efforts have been made to fix on him the charges of plagiarism from certain resolutions adopted in the State of North Carolina. It is supposed that a newspaper called the Cape Fear Mercury of July 1775 which contained these resolutions, was transmitted by Governor Martin to the British government in his dispatch of that period. The friends of Mr. Jefferson believe the charge [of plagiarism] to be unfounded, and my object is to obtain a copy of these resolutions as they were originally adopted and published, and ascertain the extent of the resemblance, if any at all, to the Declaration of Independence."

A few weeks later, Stevenson would get his answer.

FOLLOWING IN STEVENSON'S ARCHIVAL FOOTSTEPS (METAPHORICALLY, AT least), I exit the airlock and navigate back to my assigned desk where I gently open the first folder full of yellowed, crumbling editions of the *Cape Fear Mercury*. My mind is truly racing as I leaf through the papers to confirm the time frame. After a few pages—July 5, 1775; July 28, 1775; August 7, 1775; August 11, 1775; September 3, 1775—it's clear we're right in the sweet spot for the MecDec.

After such a promising start and an entire morning spent on the first folder, however, it becomes painfully clear that all of the Archive's "enclosed" newspapers are from every Martin dispatch imaginable—except Dispatch

34. Folder after folder, and hour after hour, goes by. After every near miss my initial giddiness at being so tantalizingly close to the MecDec is replaced by the agonizing sensation of having an impossible itch just millimeters out of my reach. After several hours and hundreds of documents, the only truly exciting discovery I've made at the British Archives is that pickle and cheddar toasties are actually quite good.

I eventually look up from my desk and realize the entire day has just flown by. The reading room is now practically empty. What little sky I can see through the narrow bunker-style windows has turned inky when the archivist gives me the telltale librarian look that lets me know, in Premier League parlance, I'm into extra time. With the few minutes I have left I decide to take one more crack at the big blue folder with the *Cape Fear Mercury* editions.

This time, though, when I get to the end, preparing to return the folder to the airlock, I reach my hand under and flip the entire thing over so that the front cover is now facing down.

That's when I see it.

Stapled to the back is a small index card with a few scribbled lines of what look like filing notes from the staff. Drained, discouraged, and trying to calculate how many Goyard bags I'll need to bring home to make this wasted transatlantic excursion up to Kim and the girls, the card barely registers as I head back into the airlock, defeated.

"All done?"

"All done," I mutter, handing back the blue folder.

"How did you do?" asks the filing clerk.

"Close," I shrug. "I think I got close."

And then, just as she's turning away to return the folder to the dark recesses of the Archives, perhaps for good, without thinking I blurt: "Hey, sorry, does that card there on the back mean anything?"

When she flips the folder over, her head rears back in the tiniest, most imperceptible way.

And my nerdy little heart skips a beat.

"It's a code directing to another file, letters probably, too rare for regular access," she says, tearing the card off and handing it to me. Then, directing me toward the other side of the room with a nod and an optimistic smile, she says, "Type it into the terminal. See what comes up. But be quick about it, closin' soon."

Based on my locker room experience this morning, I think it's safe to say that no one, perhaps in the entire history of the British National Archives, has ever moved as fast across the building. In a flash I'm at the computer desk, leaning over the top of the chair to punch in the code without wasting time by sitting down. The internet here operates like it was installed by George VI, so it takes what feels like an eternity to process my request.

But when the page does finally refresh, there it is, beaming in front of me with all the majesty of the Crown Jewels:

Dispatch 34.

Having pretty much memorized the contents of Josiah Martin's 1775 letter, and not knowing exactly how long I have before security runs me out of here, I move with purpose to the end of the document, searching for the payoff: the infamous "enclosed News Paper" containing the MecDec.

"Come on," I whisper, trying to will it into existence. "Come on come *ooonnn*."

But the file is empty.

After all this time, and after coming all this way, the *Cape Fear Mercury* that's supposed to be attached to Martin's Dispatch 34 is simply nowhere to be found.

What remains in its place, though, turns out to be far more shocking.

On the backside of the final page of Dispatch 34, written in thin pencil and nearly obscured by the yellowing paper and ink bleeding through from the previous page, there's a faint two-line communique left by a nineteenth-century archivist.

A Printed Paper taken out for by Mr. Turner for Mr. Stevenson, August 15th 1837.

Stevenson, that red-headed son of a gun. He found it.

He actually found the MecDec.

Then he got rid of it.

Later, I would learn from his biographer, "On August 15, 1837, Stevenson, it is asserted, obtained through [the Archives] a newspaper which Governor

Martin had enclosed with his dispatch to the Earl of Dartmouth on June 30, 1775, and which most probably contained the resolutions adopted by the Mecklenburg patriots. What Stevenson did with the newspaper, if it actually came into his hands, remains an enigma."

Not really.

There's absolutely nothing mysterious, enigmatic, or "asserted" at all about this illicit chain of events. The note from the archivist confirms that the newspaper in question was found and then "taken out" for Stevenson. This was verified yet again after Stevenson's death in 1857 when family members said that although they couldn't locate the missing *Cape Fear Mercury*, "dispatches and other memoranda among the deceased minister's papers indicated that the copy had once been in his possession."

So based on these facts, the clear motive revealed in Tucker's letter, and Stevenson's acknowledged devotion to Jefferson, there's only one way this could have possibly gone down.

If there had been a mistake or a miscommunication and Martin's enclosed *Cape Fear Mercury* had simply not contained the MecDec, or if it was only a reprint of the Resolves, Stevenson would have certainly dropped a note to update his buddy Tucker. A record of which would have found its way into Stevenson's extensive and thoroughly cataloged personal papers. Instead, "His reply to Tucker's inquiry—if there was one—has eluded discovery," says Stevenson's biographer. Furthermore, given Tucker's well-stated plan, once Stevenson found the MecDec we know that if it helped prove, in any way, that Jefferson wasn't indeed a plagiarist, Stevenson, Tucker, and the rest of the Richmond Junto would have been shouting from the rooftops about their discovery, and the proof of Jefferson's boundless virtue, while papering the streets with copies of the fraudulent MecDec.

But that never happened.

Instead, once Stevenson found the *Cape Fear Mercury*, it was never seen again and he never spoke or wrote of it again.

So here's what happened. In 1837, at the height of the national MecDec debate, after finding Dispatch 34 and extracting the "enclosed News Paper," the most logical explanation (really the *only* explanation) for Stevenson reacting the way he did, is that what he found in the British Archives turned out to be Jefferson and the Richmond Junto's worst nightmare: an authentic copy of the Mecklenburg Declaration of Independence and definitive proof of America's first, true Declaration of Independence.

And as soon as Stevenson realized what he had, he freakin' got rid of it.

"Many students have asked themselves the question: What has become of the true copy of The Cape Fear Mercury, which for many years remained in the archives of the British government?" wondered the *Charlotte Observer* on the 130th anniversary of the MecDec. "Minister Stevenson, while in England in the late '30s of the last century, borrowed the copy and it was never returned. Where it is now or what became of it are questions that cannot be answered. It is believed to have been destroyed almost immediately after it was secured. Minister Stevenson never alluded to it, and it was not found among his papers when he died, so far as has been recorded.

"Its whereabouts have remained a mystery to this day."

STEVENSON LASTED ANOTHER FEW YEARS IN LONDON, AND WHEN HIS AMbassadorship came to a close he landed in the same cushy place where, it seems, anyone who had ever done the Jeffersonians a favor ended up—the University of Virginia. But the questions about his direct role in the mysterious disappearance of such a key piece of historical evidence followed him there and hounded Stevenson for the rest of his life, and beyond.

In June of 1848 President James Polk, the grandnephew of Thomas Polk, was still writing letters to Navy Secretary George Bancroft asking for help locating "The Declaration of Independence by the people of Mecklenburg on the 20th of May, 1775 . . . [which] more than probable . . . may be found among the archives of the British Government."

In 1909, under the headline "America's Greatest Historic Controversy," the first line of a front-page editorial by the *Charlotte News* said: "The seeming utter disappearance from the face of the earth of the Cape Fear Mercury is responsible for the greatest historical controversy of modern times in America."

And finally, in another front-page story in 1875, the *New York Herald* asked Stevenson directly: "WHERE IS IT?"

"It has slipped out of sight," the paper wrote. "It has disappeared from its appropriate corner in the British Record Office, and no eyes seem sharp enough to say where it now rests . . . (perhaps) in the forgotten rubbish of some garret, whether reduced to ashes and scattered years since in some unremembered conflagration, or whether carefully treasured by some sly gatherer of the secrets of the past. . . . In this view, the honor of the Stevenson family is implicated in the loss of this very precious document."

In an effort to track down that document, a *Herald* reporter traveled to Covington, Kentucky, to confront Stevenson's son, Senator John White Stevenson, who was also the former governor of Kentucky. Afterward, the paper published a transcript of the interaction:

"I have my father's papers," Stevenson said, directly, once the object of my visit was stated.

"And may I inquire their condition?"

"Contrarily to what you may have been informed, they have not remained unopened since their return from London."

"They have been examined then?"

"Yes," replied the senator. "They are all in accurate order, and the contents of every box is known. Indeed, they were all methodically copied and bound under the directions of my father during his life."

"You say, sir, that the contents of the boxes are known?"

"Yes, sir."

"Can you, then, give me any information of the paper noted at the (British Archives), as withdrawn by the consent or under the responsibility of your father—the report of the Royal Governor of North Carolina on the transactions of May 31, 1775?"

"That document," said the senator, "is not among my father's papers. . . . But in its stead is a memorandum which states that though the paper was withdrawn under the sanction of my father it was not withdrawn for his use, but for the use of another person whose name is there given."

"And you remember that name of course?"

"No; I have forgotten it."

WE KNOW NOW THAT SENATOR STEVENSON WAS COVERING UP FOR HIS FA-
ther and George Tucker, who made the original request for Dispatch 34.
We also know that Ambassador Stevenson abused his power and destroyed
public records, and that by doing so he robbed the world of a chance to
solve one of the great mysteries in American history. The real damage would
come later, though, when without the documentary proof of the *Cape Fear
Mercury*, the MecDec remained eternally vulnerable to doubters, academic
frauds, hoaxes, and hucksters, especially one guy in particular who, in 1905,
became known throughout the Carolinas as the MecDec's Flim Flam Man.

On July 1, 1905, Stevenson, Dispatch 34, and the *Cape Fear Mercury*
were back in the national news once again when a story by Dr. S. Millington
Miller appeared in *Collier's* magazine under the headline "The True Cradle
of American Liberty." The story claimed that Miller had made the discovery
of a lifetime: Governor Martin's infamous *Cape Fear Mercury* from June
1775 that included, as long suspected, a full reprint of the Mecklenburg
Declaration of Independence.

For one brief, glorious moment, at least, the patriots in Charlotte were
able to finally, and fully, claim their rightful title as the first, true Founding
Fathers of American independence.

In the bombshell story, Dr. Miller explained that he had purchased from
a collector several thousand pages of Ambassador Stevenson's official correspondence. While going through the collection, Miller was reading a letter
Stevenson had sent to B. B. Thatcher in Brighton, when, miraculously, the
long-lost edition of the *Mercury* just fell out into his trembling hands.

Right away, though, there were some serious red flags in Miller's story.
For starters, the Thatcher letter is from February 17, 1837, when it was long
believed that the first-known inquiry about the *Mercury* hadn't reached Stevenson until June or even July of 1837. In most of 1775 the *Mercury* only
published on Fridays. The date on Miller's newspaper—June 3, 1775—was
actually a Saturday. Not only did Miller's *Mercury* use the wrong tense and

209

multiple fonts, there also appeared to be visible lines where the paper had been cropped. A detail that was backed up quite convincingly by a Massachusetts librarian who came forward to say that Miller had paid him for reproductions of an old edition of the *Cape Fear Mercury*.

The incident was quickly labeled "The Cape Fear Hoax." Still holding out a glimmer of hope, though, a committee from Charlotte reached out to Miller for explanation. He responded that the discrepancies were all just "hysterical rubbish" from "inheritors of Jefferson's vindictive desire to annihilate all the evidence of May 19th and 20th" and that he already had twenty offers of up to $50,000 [$2 million today] to buy his copy of the *Mercury*. Before selling his discovery for "a king's ransom," Miller agreed to meet with the Charlotte reps on December 30, 1905, at a hotel in Baltimore. After grilling Miller for hours, the Charlotte group proposed that the document be independently verified by Worthington Ford, the head of manuscripts at the Library of Congress.

Miller agreed.

Informed that Ford could be there in less than an hour to begin the authentication process, Miller suddenly remembered urgent business across town that required his immediate attention.

The committee offered Miller the full $5,000 at their disposal just to stay put.

Miller refused but promised to meet with Ford and the document experts at the Library of Congress at a later date.

By then, though, word had already begun trickling back into Charlotte about Miller's rep as the Flim Flam Man and how he had been banned from bookstores and libraries up and down the eastern seaboard. It seems that expensive and rare books had a strange habit of going missing whenever Miller showed up, even in the middle of summer, in his distinct, bulky wool overcoat. The first person to thwart Miller's book scam was a bright, young librarian in Chapel Hill by the name of Louis R. Wilson. For the damage inflicted upon his reputation (and pocketbook), Miller threatened to cover the brave bibliophile in "blood and bruises." Wilson never flinched, and he went on to a long, illustrious career at the University of North Carolina, where today, the Mecklenburg Papers and the entire Southern Historical Collection are all safely stored inside the school's Louis R. Wilson Library.

Miller only dared to show his face in the South one more time. Early in 1916 in Savannah, Georgia, a local librarian and MecDec fan recognized the telltale bulky overcoat and accosted Miller for being "a fraud and a literary faker." Enraged, the librarian then "swung his mighty left, landing the open palm squarely upon [Miller's] left cheek," the local paper reported. "Dr. Miller beat a hasty retreat and was followed out on the street as far as the Georgia State Savings Bank corner. It was there [the librarian] advised Dr. Miller to take the first train out of town."

After torturing MecDecers for years, it took a heroic librarian to finally, and properly, shush up the Flim Flam Man.

Too bad those same librarian superpowers, and especially that "mighty left," didn't work on vindictive math professors.

TWELVE

UNC's Old Fatty the Fabulist

THE ANTI-MECDEC SCREED PUBLISHED ANONYMOUSLY IN 1853 BY AN obscure University of North Carolina math professor, Dr. Charles Phillips, was so blatantly fraudulent, but infuriatingly effective, that in 2011 a superior court judge in Charlotte, Chase Saunders, was still advocating for posthumous disciplinary action to be taken against Phillips for extreme academic misconduct. Now, that's what you call a grudge. Yet even the Mec-Decers don't seem to despise Phillips nearly as much as his own students once did. According to a nineteenth-century remembrance published by his own university, Phillips, the "archpriest" of MecDec deniers, was often called "Old Fatty" behind his back by UNC students "on account of his tendency to corpulence."

The insight into his cruel nickname is actually one of the lighter moments in the less-than-glorifying eulogies for Phillips. In recollections after his death, his sister described him as "not a little inclined to be overbearing" and utterly devoid of "deference, amiability, insight." Piling on, Old Fatty's brother-in-law added how "in social conversations in those days [Phillips] often appeared to be impatient of contradiction, or even of difference of opinion from him on the part of his intimates." For most of his adult life Phillips was sickly, obese, and in chronic pain from pneumonia and recurring bouts of rheumatic gout. And the suffering seems evident in his grimacing portrait, his eyes barely visible hidden behind dark circles and under a heavy brow.

Further cursed with a style as a writer and a speaker that was "never polished or elegant"—again, these are his friends talking—Phillips was never able to escape the enormous shadow of his legendary father, Dr. James Phillips, a beloved professor at North Carolina. The rather brutal (and, truthfully, kind of sad) description of Charles goes on like this for thirty-two tortuous pages. And while the remembrance includes a long section on Charles's love of solitary ice-skating, it is telling that never once does it mention his infamous association with the MecDec. Instead, the most profound thing anyone shares in the entire piece—"A better, nobler, braver man I have never known"—is from the school's chancellor, but it's in reference to Charles's iconic father.

The elder Phillips was a titan of the math department at Carolina who, coincidentally, went by "Old John Bull" or "Old Johnnie" in honor of his English heritage and love of all things British. (He was the professor, you'll remember, who ran our dear nutty friend Shocco Jones off campus for skipping pretty much every single mandatory church service.) A force on campus, Old John Bull died while lecturing in 1867 with a copy of *Pierce's Plane and Solid Geometry* still in his grasp. Today in Chapel Hill the strange fortress-like Phillips Hall, which is sometimes referred to by students as "the Southern Hogwarts," is named in honor of Old John Bull and his family.

While the elder Phillips was such a fixture on campus, Charles was raised and educated by his very strict mother who "had in full measure the Puritan notion that it was half a sin to be amused." Novel reading was forbidden. Household games were also frowned upon. And cards? "Not to be thought of," said a family member. After almost dying in college from a bout of pneumonia, Charles graduated in 1841 with what seems like the sole intent of not following in his father's footsteps. However, after trying (and failing) at med school and an initial attempt at the seminary (perhaps due to health issues that made it difficult to preach), Charles took a job as a tutor in Chapel Hill in 1844 and toiled there for nine long years before finally being elected as a professor in the new school of civil engineering.

In 1852 Charles was also working as the secretary of the university's Historical Society. Around this time UNC President Dr. David Swain, who had coauthored the 1831 NC Governor's Report on the MecDec, brought the full collection of Mecklenburg Papers to Chapel Hill for what he deemed "critical examination." Part of this collection was, of course, the Davie Copy, the document McKnitt Alexander had famously produced from (mostly) the "journals and records of said [MecDec] Committee" in the immediate aftermath of the Alexandriana fire. In the years since, the importance of the Davie Copy had grown significantly. The Williamson Copy of the MecDec, the one witnessed by Governor Stokes, had burned in the "Great Fire" of New York City. And with the corroborating evidence of Dispatch 34 having mysteriously disappeared in London, the Davie Copy was now the single most important piece of MecDec evidence.

When Phillips realized that as secretary of the UNC Historical Society he alone had access to such a rare and critical piece of historical evidence, Old Fatty decided this was finally his chance to make a mark on the world with an explosive magazine piece he would title "May, 1775."

As the Northern-born son of John Bull, a proud Englishman and Episcopalian, young Charles must have felt terribly out of place in North Carolina. (I'm just guessing here, but I don't think his mother offered much in the way of comfort.) Phillips was such a snobby Anglophile-wannabe that he insisted on using the Old English spellings for words such as "labours" and "flavours." Based on his other writings, religious bigotry may have been driving some of Phillips's rancor for the MecDec. He believed "no true gentleman" could have wanted to secede from the Crown. Thus, he found the very idea of the MecDec and a movement toward independence among a bunch of Scots-Irish Presbyterians on the Carolina frontier to be absolutely "distasteful."

In the 1850s, at a time when tensions in America were escalating toward civil war—a conflict that would decimate his beloved UNC for more than a decade at the height of his career—Phillips likely saw an academic attack on the patriots in Charlotte as a way to even the score with all of his perceived adversaries in one fell swoop. More than anything, I suspect, when he sat down to invent "May, 1775," Phillips accidentally tapped into the growing pre–Civil War sentiment that if the South should actually dare to secede, by default, it would also have to surrender any and all historic claims to "true" patriotism, starting with Charlotte's incredible distinction of being First in Freedom.

"Anti-Southern animus was high," confirms Syfert, and "bias against the South played a role in the case against the Mecklenburg Declaration."

You can see this hostility in the subtext when the younger Phillips and other supposed nineteenth-century academics repeatedly dismiss the Mec-Dec based on nothing more than their instinct that, as Phillips put it, people in the "backwoods of North Carolina were not apt to blow off steam about the inherent and inalienable rights of man. Jefferson brought that stuff from Paris." It's a deeply biased and easily refuted theory (as I've noted a few times already), and it's one I'm sure the alumni association at Princeton would take major issue with. But perhaps this is how powerful the overriding sentiment was (and is) that the traitorous South—and even the MecDec patriots—deserved to be punished, perhaps even eternally.

Because once you expose the purposeful errors, omitted evidence, and slanderous post-publication propaganda, there's absolutely nothing new or relevant in Phillips's 1853 article. In fact, there really would be no reason at all to even mention Phillips, except for the fact that Old Fatty the Fabulist somehow managed to influence MecDec skeptics for generations to come.

"The powerful impact of Phillips's article is all the more mystifying given how vapid, shallow, and unoriginal it is," says Syfert. "Nonetheless, Phillips gave an intellectual foundation to what would become a cult of denial."

An even greater mystery, in my mind, is how anyone was ever able to wade through Phillips's mind-numbingly pretentious prose in the first place. (No wonder he wouldn't put his name on it.) Published anonymously in the *North Carolina University Magazine*, "May, 1775" runs for ten pages, half of which are dedicated to the reprinting of the MecDec materials everyone had already seen, along with something at the very beginning that can best be described as the essay word count stretching technique I myself employed as an undergrad when I hadn't bothered to learn the deeper facts or read any of the source materials, either.

Now, remember, this is the work of the definitive source and patron saint of MecDec deniers:

The soul of man has its seasons as well as his soil. There has been a winter of deadness, whose storms disturbed only a desolation. This was succeeded by the time of sowing the seeds of truth and righteousness. Now seems to be the month of May, wherein what has been sown is promising abundant harvests, and what is yet needed may still find time for development and maturity. There will be a season of repose wherein all trees and plants are steadily growing for the harvest—and then the end shall come—when the great white throne shall be set, the angels be sent forth to separate the tares from the wheat, and all, according to their works, shall receive unerring praise or blame. In the physical world it is well to observe the various relations of the seasons . . .

Phillips goes on like this for *several hundred words* before even bothering to mention the term Mecklenburg. I bravely read on, expecting, at some point, that Phillips would at least reach the absolute lowest acceptable standards of academic objectivity. It never happened. There is no mention of all the highly distinguished eyewitnesses in the NC Governor's Report, the multiple surviving documents, or the mountain of corroborating evidence.

Instead, when he does finally get around to the point of his article, this is what turns out to be Phillips's big explosive MecDec revelation:

McKnitt Alexander and his son probably made the whole thing up.

That's it.

That's Phillips's entire argument.

The theory is so deeply flawed, in fact, that to make it work Phillips had to alter, and then suppress, his sole source of evidence: the Davie Copy. And here's the craziest part: at a time in our country's history when people were looking for ways to punish the South, this flimsy and fraudulent theory seems to have caught on. At least initially.

There's a simple reason no one with access to the Davie Copy during the previous four decades had ever reached the same conclusion as Phillips. It's because the Davie Copy itself states, several times, right there on the parchment in black and white, the exact opposite of Phillips's conclusion.

Both McKnitt and his son, Dr. Joseph Alexander, went to great lengths to point out precisely which parts of the Davie Copy were from "journals and records" and which parts "tho fundamentally correct, may not literally correspond with the original records of the transactions." The Alexanders did

217

to be clear and transparent after the original MecDec records
d because, with so much corroborating evidence at their disposal,
n't have any need for sleight of hand. (I'd also point out that if
really trying to pull off a massive historical hoax that involves war hero governors, lawyers, professors, priests, and multiple US presidents, the
first thing you *don't* do is admit up front, right on the document itself, any
potential gaps in your records.)

The Alexanders had nothing to hide, and they were not the least bit subtle about this, either. In the "Davie Copy," when McKnitt wrote, "Thus far
from the Journals & records of Sd Committee," he underlined it and added
a breakpoint in the text for clarification. Just in case that wasn't enough,
McKnitt's son then drew the symbol of a tiny little hand (perhaps the world's
first emoji) also pointing to the phrase "Here the copy of the record ends."

I've got to hand it to Phillips, though. He found an ingenious way around
all the bothersome and well-documented evidence that flew directly in the
face of his ridiculous "May, 1775" theory.

He just ignored it.

Seriously.

Phillips simply left out of his analysis anything in the historical record that
challenged his headline-making condemnation of the MecDec as a fake. And
for decades Phillips got away with it because he held all the cards. Examination of the Davie Copy would have been the only way to expose the outlandish fraud of "May, 1775," but Phillips was the only one with access to the
receipts. And he knew it. "I have always believed that in dealing with what
I had in 1853," Phillips wrote, "I was in possession of the only originals then
in existence—all that were ever known at the time." It was as if Phillips had
found the tablets Moses brought down from the mountaintop, and then, after
squirreling them away, he claimed there were actually only nine commandments. And with the tablets hidden and no way to verify the actual number
of commandments, everyone was forced to trust Phillips (and free to covet as
much as they wanted, I suppose).

Emboldened by his advantage, Phillips went so far as to include a highly
altered Davie Copy in the text of his magazine article. In it, on top of deleting
the Alexanders' page notes about "journals," "records," and "transactions,"

Phillips also reinserted deleted words that bolstered his theory that the Mec-Dec was meaningless because McKnitt had written the entire thing from memory. Any cursory examination of the Davie Copy would have immediately exposed Phillips and ended his career in academia. But as secretary of the school's historical society, Phillips had been allowed to "borrow" the Davie Copy while researching his article. And Old Fatty was the last person to see it.

Then, wouldn't you know it, right after the publication of "May, 1775," the Davie Copy, a critical piece of evidence in one of the greatest historical controversies in American history, went missing for the next *sixty* years. It was finally uncovered in the early twentieth century by a history professor at the University of North Carolina who found it hidden away among the papers of a Phillips family member. But by then the damage had already been done.

While the Davie Copy remained hidden for six decades, in the interim the world—and generations of historians—had no choice but to trust the veracity of Phillips's conclusion that the MecDec was nothing more than a "Charlotte falsehood." On the surface, after all, Phillips was a respected professor at the second-largest university in the South and a member of a renowned academic family who was also working toward becoming an ordained minister. To the outside world Phillips appeared to be a pillar of science and faith, and there was simply no reason to doubt his stance on the MecDec.

Meanwhile, North Carolina didn't do itself any favors by choosing May 20, 1861, as the day it seceded from the Union. But afterward, egged on by Phillips and his fraud, the world at large seemed hell-bent on discrediting the MecDec and any proof of North Carolina's patriotic contribution to America's founding.

And Phillips's "May, 1775" was all the "proof" anyone needed.

Reporting on Phillips's findings, one Northern newspaper called the Mec-Dec "The Great Rebel Fraud. . . . [nothing more than] an attempt of the South to steal the glory of the nation."

By the time the country could entertain any thoughts beyond the Civil War, emancipation, and reconstruction, Phillips's fraud had fully metastasized into fact. Then it was repeated, time and again, by nearly every subsequent historian. You can sense author V. V. McNitt fuming when he writes in *Chain of Error* how so many respectable historians just "accepted as true the error of the 1853 magazine article which offered mistaken evidence that McKnitt Alexander admitted his record of the MecDec was written only from memory and might not be literally correct."

"McKnitt Alexander made no such admission," V. V. McNitt sternly reminded everyone.

After the Civil War, with the Davie Copy presumed lost or destroyed, Phillips must have assumed he was in the clear. But in 1875 the MecDec Centennial Celebration once again put the issue of America's first, true Declaration of Independence back on the national stage. At that point it became obvious that Phillips lacked the con artist's most important tool: a poker face.

With UNC still shuttered following the war, Phillips was teaching and studying at Davidson College just north of Charlotte. Being that close to the nonstop MecDec Centennial festivities while living on a campus with so many direct ties to the MecDec and the MecDec Founding Fathers, Phillips was reminded of his fraud on a daily, perhaps hourly, basis. Davidson College, after all, had been built by a MecDec Signer, was named in honor of a Revolutionary War hero, and had a motto that referenced the MecDec. A faculty member in 1858 had even gone so far as to suggest that the school officially celebrate May 20 instead of July 4.

(As an imposter, Phillips would have fit right in on the Davidson campus, though. Local legend says, I swear, that the man who designed the college's seal and motto, fellow nineteenth-century Davidson professor Peter Stuart Ney, may have actually been Napoleonic General Marshal Michel Ney. After somehow faking his own execution in 1815, Ney escaped from France to North Carolina where we're supposed to believe the legendary army commander mentioned in Tolstoy's *War and Peace* enjoyed a second career as a schoolteacher. Although, when Ney died in 1846 he is said to have uttered the deathbed confession: *I am Ney of France*.)

The freakin' MecDec . . . *amiright?*

There really is just no end to the stories within the stories of this story.

Meanwhile, as Phillips's own fear of being exposed continued to mount, Old Fatty's behavior became erratic, and his health took a nosedive. In advance of the MecDec Centennial, when historian Lyman Draper began looking into the hullabaloo, Phillips was "entirely unhelpful" in locating the Davie Copy. Instead, Phillips sent Draper a series of letters totaling fifteen thousand words—an unholy punishment for anyone who has slogged through "May, 1775." After bragging about becoming famous abroad (and infamous in America) for his work on the MecDec, Phillips coyly claimed to have no earthly idea about the whereabouts of the Davie Copy.

"It's clear," V. V. McNitt writes, "that Phillips was somewhat nervous about the Davie Copy, which he possibly might hope would not appear again."

Next, an increasingly desperate Phillips told Draper that Dr. Swain, the former governor of North Carolina and president of UNC, supported his findings in "May, 1775." This was just another blatant Phillips fabrication, though. The truth is that Phillips had begged and pressured Swain to cosign his findings, but Swain refused.

Instead, Swain offered what he called a Special Verdict on the MecDec before his death in 1868:

The documentary evidence in my possession satisfies me that there was a meeting of the citizens of Mecklenburg, at Charlotte, on the 19th and 20th of May, 1775, and that resolutions in relation to independence were discussed and adopted. I entertain no doubt that the record of the proceedings of the Mecklenburg Committee was burned in the home of John McKnitt Alexander, in the month of April, 1800, and that the Davie paper contains what Gen. Graham, Co. Wm. Polk, and other gentlemen of high character, whose certificates appear in the State pamphlet, believed to be a true narrative of the transactions of those two days.

With that scam no longer available, Phillips took the extraordinarily desperate step of sending anonymous letters to the editor of the *New York Evening Post* and other national newspapers. In them, he denounced the centennial celebration of the MecDec and supported the assumptions in "May,

1775" by quoting—get this—his own dishonest work at length without ever revealing that he was the anonymous author of both.

Finally, Phillips began an even more despicable behind-the-scenes campaign of character assassination against the MecDecers. The results of which were, to some, far more damaging than "May, 1775" or the phony letters to the editor. Egged on by Phillips's outlandish attacks, subsequent historians escalated what had been honest confusion and healthy debate regarding the MecDec story into something far more sinister. As devastating as it was, the 1800 fire at Alexandriana only destroyed one physical copy of the MecDec. Phillips's gaslighting campaign against everything, and everyone, associated with the MecDec would prove to be far more disastrous.

Writing to Draper and other contemporary historians, Phillips accused Dr. Joseph Alexander of suppressing the truth and being a godless "Infidel"; he called Adam Brevard, the son of MecDec author Ephraim Brevard, a drunk; he alluded to McKnitt Alexander as possibly being a "forger"; he mocked Captain James Jack; and he said that William Polk "did not care a bawbee" about the truth. It doesn't take a trained psychologist to see that Phillips was falsely lashing out at others for the very things he knew himself to be guilty of. The remarks were so vile, though, that a colleague at UNC once speculated that should they become public, they would probably cost Phillips his professorship.

Once again, though, Phillips's MecDec slander found an eager audience, especially in, of all places, academia. The result was a one-two knockout punch by heavyweight historians A. S. Salley and William Hoyt. In his book, Salley went so far as to parrot Phillips's private accusation that McKnitt and his son were guilty of "forgery," while Hoyt's tome *The Mecklenburg Declaration of Independence . . . Is Spurious* gave birth to the ridiculous theory that everyone in Charlotte had experienced a group hallucination and ended up confusing the make-believe MecDec with the Resolves. Even though there would be no earthly need for a whole new comprehensive set of government guidelines unless you had, you know, just declared yourself free and independent from the previous form of government you were under.

The work of Phillips, Salley, and Hoyt contains an almost irrational level of hostility toward the MecDec, which, to this day, seems to have influenced historians and casual observers far more than their laughably thin theories. This certainly played a big role in the mystery behind the MecDec's ongoing mystery. But it's easily explainable when put into context. At the time, Salley and Hoyt and other professional historians were trying to wrest control of American history from generations of amateurs and antiquarians. According to Dr. Jeff Webb at Huntington University, for a time this power struggle required an over-emphasis in history writing and scholarship on empiricism and evidentiary integrity. And because the original copy of the MecDec had been destroyed in a fire, that alone gave license to Salley, Hoyt, and others to go overboard in disqualifying the MecDec and deriding its supporters. These kinds of lazy, nasty, narrow-minded takes on the MecDec's validity were then allowed to solidify into the collective consciousness as the "truth" on the matter. So much so that it has muzzled nearly all discourse on the topic simply because anyone who dares to consider the mountain of corroborating evidence on the other side risks being dismissed out of hand as some kind of MecDec kook.

When, in the end, it was Salley, Hoyt, and Phillips who were exposed the true hucksters.

Especially Phillips, who eventually earned the recognition he'd been desperately craving all his life. It just wasn't the kind he had hoped for. Once the Davie Copy was located and Phillips's extraordinary fraud exposed, V. V. McNitt crowned him the "most effective propagandist in the history of American letters" and the official founder of the MecDec Cult of Denial.

Wracked by gout (and perhaps guilt), Phillips spent the final eleven years of his life as an invalid.

Meanwhile, by all accounts "May, 1775" and Phillips's odd obsession with destroying the MecDec had almost no effect on the 1875 centennial celebration of the country's first, true declaration of independence. Featured in a full page of national coverage in *Harper's Weekly* under the banner headline "A Big Day in a Small Town," the MecDec's centennial drew forty thousand patriots to Charlotte, where the streets were packed with parades, fireworks, and endless rows of American flags. The biggest MecDec party to date also featured a cock fight between birds representing North Carolina and South Carolina, a speech by future Vice President Adlai Ewing Stevenson, and, on the morning of May 20, a raucous reading of the Mecklenburg Declaration of Independence followed by a thunderous one-hundred-gun salute.

"The town is embowered in green trees, shrubbery, and flowers," *Harper's* reported, "and the residences are neat, and some very handsome, with pretty churches."

At this point the Founding Fathers of Charlotte and the patriots of North Carolina were done messing around with Old Fatty and his ilk. A few years later, North Carolina codified the MecDec for all time by adding the date—*MAY 20, 1775*—to the state flag and the state seal. In 1881, May 20 became a holiday in North Carolina. And in 1898, a massive marble obelisk commemorating the Mecklenburg Declaration of Independence, emblazoned with a bronze hornet's nest that warned "Let Us Alone," was erected in front of the courthouse.

At the beginning of the twentieth century, to continue to restore the legacy and luster of America's first, true Declaration of Independence, Charlotte turned to the single most powerful ally on the planet.

The president of the United States.

THIRTEEN

EXECUTIVE POWER

WILLIAM HOWARD TAFT LOVED POSSUMS. ROASTED, PREFERABLY, ON a bed of apples and yams. In January 1909, at a banquet in Atlanta, our twenty-seventh—and, at 350 pounds, our largest—president, Taft, once devoured an entire serving of his favorite beady-eyed marsupial so fast that a doctor seated at his table begged him to slow down. (As did the *New York Times*: "We earnestly beg Mr. Taft to stop with the possum.") The next day, though, the iron-gulleted Taft informed reporters, "I ate very heartily of it last night and it did not disturb in the slightest my digestion or my sleep." On a lavish White House diet that included a twelve-ounce steak for breakfast *every morning*, Taft's housekeeper guessed that the Commander in Beef's weight may have ballooned beyond four hundred pounds. And legend has it that the rotund Taft once wedged himself so tightly into the White House bathtub, six members of the Secret Service were required to extricate him. Taft was also an intellectual heavyweight, of course, later serving as the tenth Supreme Court Justice, but he yo-yo dieted through his entire presidency, and, for a short time, even cut back on his beloved sunrise steak. Nothing seemed to work. And by May 1909, when Taft made history by accepting an invitation from the North Carolina governor and Charlotte officials to celebrate MecDec Day on May 20 in person in Mecklenburg, the president's Secret Service detail came to Charlotte to double-check the safety and reliability of the town's . . . furniture.

els Taft had destroyed so many chairs (and possums) that part
  detail's job was ensuring the pres would have safe seating.
  te, that last-second task fell to Biddle University (later renamed
  n C. Smith University), where the faculty pooled its resources to pur-
  ase something sturdy enough to accommodate Taft's prodigious aft. The
students, meanwhile, delighted Taft with a rendition of the fight song from
his alma mater, Yale. Today, that massive seat, now known as "The President's Chair," sits in the corner of a conference room on the second floor of
the library at the center of Johnson C. Smith's campus. Taft's custom chair
looks like an outdoor Adirondack lounger designed for Andre the Giant.
This being Charlotte, though, no one's really sure if this is the actual chair,
a replica, or a repurposed rendition. The only thing denoting its special history is a thin white ribbon stretched across the armrests that, I guess, is
supposed to prevent people from having a seat (and feeling downright thin)
in Taft's sacred spot.

Taft earned that special recognition, though, by accepting the city's invitation to celebrate the MecDec. Taft may have simply been following in the
footsteps of a long line of presidential MecDec fans that included George
Washington, John Adams, Andrew Jackson, James Polk, and Teddy Roosevelt, but Taft's visit helped change everything. In 1909 the Davie Copy
was still believed to be lost, and UNC professor Charles Phillips had yet
to be exposed as an utter fraud. What's more, the "Cape Fear Hoax" or-
chestrated just a few years earlier by the Flim Flam Man, Dr. Millington
Miller, allowed critics of the MecDec to cast the declaration as little more
than a folktale, or even a punchline. So the visit, and the impending confirmation from Taft about the document's authenticity and proper place in
history, was absolutely critical in breaking the long cycle of misinformation
and sparking the MecDec's resurgence.

Although, a good deal of the credit belongs to Roosevelt and those
eternally journaling Moravians. In October 1905, on his own Tour of the
South, Roosevelt tentatively agreed to return on May 20 for MecDec Day.
(Teddy was of Scots-Irish descent, and the MecDecers' us-against-the-world
credo resonated deeply with him.) When a scheduling conflict kept Roosevelt from attending, the president dispatched US troops to Charlotte in

Even with the First Lady's absence and the worst deluge in more than twenty years (accompanied by "rotary motion of wind," which sounds an awful lot like a tornado to me) Trade Street in downtown Charlotte was packed with more than twenty thousand MecDec partygoers, er . . . supporters. "If the floods that have descended today could not dampen the ardor of Twentieth of May spirit," Governor Kitchin said, "you may know that that spirit is warmed by the eternal truth."

And, by a good deal of whiskey.

Reports from the day sounded like they were describing MecDec Mardi Gras. At Independence Square, the two most prominent signs were "Get Right with God" and "Near-Beer Saloon," and in classic Scots-Irish tradition a reporter noted that "the crowd appeared to have taken much more obedient notice of the second sign." After over-indulging during the first day of MecDec festivities, a "well-dressed" young man from South Carolina was arraigned before a Charlotte magistrate the morning of Taft's arrival.

"Do you subscribe to the authenticity of the Mecklenburg Declaration?" the judge asked.

"I do," replied the startled defendant.

The judge tapped his gavel. "Case dismissed," he said.

The young man was freed in time to see Taft make his grand ride from the train station to the Selwyn Hotel in an open landau led by four black horses. The route took Taft under the huge Roman-style triumphal arches that had been added across Trade and Tryon streets for the celebration. Fearing he'd get trapped by the huge crowds, Taft's carriage stopped only once, in front of Stonewall Jackson's home, so that the president could tip his hat to the Confederate general's widow, Mary Anna Jackson, who waved back from her window. Mary Anna Morrison Jackson was Charlotte royalty. She was the granddaughter of MecDec eyewitness and Revolutionary War hero General Joseph Graham and the daughter of Reverend Robert Hall Morrison, the first president of Davidson College. To this day, Mary Anna's 1915 funeral is the largest wake ever held in Charlotte. (The second biggest? Dr. Annie Alexander, McKnitt Alexander's great-granddaughter and North Carolina's first female physician.)

It may have just been smart politics on both sides, but Taft and Mary Anna seemed to genuinely hit it off, setting the tone for what would be a lovely and symbolic visit despite the horrible weather and the still-lingering animosity in the South—and *for* the South. The president's reception was held inside the glass-roofed lobby of the Selwyn, where crowds clapped after the sun peeked through the clouds for one brief moment. Undeterred, Taft shook hands for several hours with more than 1,000 Charlotteans, but none more important than the widow Jackson, who arrived dressed in a black gown festooned with her late husband's field medals.

Holding Taft's giant paw in her hands and beaming at the president through her spectacles, Mary Anna said, "It is a very great pleasure to welcome one whom we all regard as the great harmonizer of our hearts."

"It is a very great pleasure to meet you, Mrs. Jackson," Taft responded.

Later, Mary Anna told the press, "The president certainly is a fine-looking man. He will find a warm welcome in the hearts of the people of Charlotte, who are most hospitable to Northerners. They feel that President Taft is not only sympathetic toward the South but that he understands the South, its spirit, and its problems. Our only regret is that Mrs. Taft could not come."

The next day the pair sat together on a covered dais on South Tryon to watch the four-mile-long MecDec Day parade, which was, at the time, the biggest celebration in North Carolina history. When the historic downpour threatened to soak Mrs. Jackson's shoes, Taft reached over with either his walking cane or umbrella and elevated her feet above the water, earning the title of Sir Walter Raleigh in the next day's paper. Tensions were still so high in the South, though, that the sight of Taft aiding Mrs. Jackson and giving the MecDec "higher praise than it ever had before" was so unsettling for some, the Secret Service remained on high alert during the entire visit. "It is true that political divisions have continued in such a way as at some times to seem to perpetuate the lines which were made at the time of the [Civil] war," Taft admitted while in Charlotte. "But even those lines are rapidly disappearing. And it is the duty of all of us . . . to wipe out those lines as fast as we can." Just to be safe, though, the three-man Secret Service detail in Charlotte still carried eighteen-inch guns under their coats and physically forced anyone close to the president to remove their hands from their pockets.

Taft was having so much fun watching the parade he barely seemed to no-tice. He was enthralled by the "gigantic" hornet's nest decorating the parade stand. And he enthusiastically doffed his hat for a float featuring nine pos-sums labeled "The President's Cabinet," the first of several to highlight the commander in chief's favorite critter. (At the time, a toy company in Geor-gia was trying to get "Billy Possum" to catch on like the "Teddy Bear" had during Roosevelt's time in office. It didn't.) Every time Taft would chuckle, which was often, the ends of his distinctly long, bushy, white mustache would curl up toward his ears. Taft also paid special recognition to a float of the Revolutionary reverend himself, Alexander Craighead. Almost 150 years after Craighead's death the float reminded parade-goers that "it was perhaps more largely due to Rev. Alexander Craighead's preaching and influence that the immortal Mecklenburg Declaration was promulgated." This was followed by the "float of floats" featuring fourteen descendants of MecDec Signers all decked out in matching silk hats and Prince Albert coats.

Taft must have had that image of the Founding Fathers on his mind when he took to the stage for his speech that evening inside a downtown au-ditorium packed to the rafters. Resplendent in a three-piece suit with a high tuxedo collar, Taft began by apologizing for leaving his voice at his last stop in Virginia. Then, while speaking mostly off the cuff with "vigorous gesticu-lations," Taft wasted little time establishing where he stood on the MecDec:

> We are here to celebrate a declaration of independence. There are some un-regenerate persons (here there was a long break for laughter) who live in South Carolina (more laughter) and elsewhere that for various motives have cast doubt upon the claim. Now anybody that comes to Charlotte who is not willing to admit in the full the Declaration of Independence made in Mecklenburg, is in the position of a man of whom a lord justice of the Court of Appeals of Ireland once told me. I met him in Canada. He had a good deal of experience in courts and he was redolent with Irish stories. He said that he was holding court in the County of Tipperary and that a man came before him and a jury charged in the indictment with manslaughter, and that the evidence showed that the deceased had come to his death by a blow from a blackthorn stick in the hands of the defendant; but the evidence also

showed that the man who died had a "paper skull" as it is called in medical parlance—unduly thin.

The verdict brought in was that of "guilty of manslaughter" and his lordship called the man before him and asked him whether he had anything to say why the sentence of the court should not be pronounced upon him. The defendant, turning to his lordship said, "No, your lordship, I have nothing to say, but I would like to ask one question. I would like to ask, 'What the devil is a man with a head like that doing in Tipperary?'"

(Laughter.)

I would like to add in explanation of my position, what the devil is a man who does not believe in the Declaration of Mecklenburg doing in this presence?

(Laughter and applause.)

The claim is that more than 12 months before members of the Continental Congress declared that it was necessary to have a separate and independent government in this country, free from British control, that Declaration was made in the court house in this Town of Charlotte by a committee of the county, of whom there are now descendants living among you entitled to your respect and to your congratulation on such ancestry. . . . Now there are things in that Declaration that make me thrill with pride, that there was a community in this country, and I venture to say this was not the only community, but it seems to have been the one most charged with its sense of responsibility—which knew that self government was not a mere gift, but it was something when it is to be enjoyed must be enjoyed with a full sense of its responsibility, and with the idea that there is a duty imposed on everyone who enjoys it of seeing to it that it is carried on for the benefit of all.

The Scotch-Irishmen who lived in this community were hardheaded. They were willing to take upon themselves the risk of being strung up as traitors to Great Britain; they were willing to fight it out as they did so often thereafter in the Hornet's Nest.

(Cheers.)

. . . But all that time we were gathering experience, we were gathering a sense of responsibility as to our own communities so that when in '75 you declared your independence here, and in '76 we all declared our independence at Philadelphia, we were in a condition with men as great, as able, as full of the knowledge of statecraft as any nation in Europe or any nation that ever lived, to step into the ranks of nations and carry on a government worthy the consideration of the entire world.

Taft concluded his speech by promising to do everything he could as president to "wipe out the feeling that the central government at Washington was a government alien to the Southland." Immediately after his standing ovation he made good on that promise by traveling to Biddle University on the western outskirts of Charlotte to speak to nearly five hundred students and faculty at the historically Black college. "I do not wish to be oblivious of the troublous times through which you and your fathers and mothers have passed, or of the burdens, and possibly the cruelties which circumstances have made it necessary for you to bear," Taft told the Biddle students. "But I thank God that those things are passing away and the proper place for your eyes to be, for your hopes to be directed, for your thoughts to be pushed, is forward and not backward."

Taft's visit concluded with a small banquet at the Selwyn and then a trip back to the rail station where, to commemorate his historic visit and the "hardheaded" MecDecers, the president was presented with a silver paperweight bearing his likeness and the inscription *W. H. Taft, Charlotte N.C. May 20, 1775.*

Upon the president's departure the locals joked that Charlotte's population of possums seemed to suddenly come out of hiding, no longer in danger of ending up on the president's plate.

After the discovery of the Moravian *Beilage* and Taft's triumphant visit in 1909, the only truly endangered rodents left in Charlotte were MecDec deniers.

MEcDEC DAY IN 1916 BEGAN WITH PRESIDENT WOODROW WILSON STANDing outside his freshman dorm room at Davidson College. By then, the celebration had been a recognized holiday for nearly forty years in North

Carolina, so on this particular May 20, Davidson's pastoral campus of spacious quads, red-brick buildings, and shaded slant walks was nearly deserted when the presidential motorcade of several large gray Packard automobiles rolled up to Chambers Hall. Wilson was a Princeton grad and served the school as a professor and president. But he spent his first year of college at Davidson, located just a few hours north of where Wilson grew up in Augusta, Georgia. (Wilson's father was a Scots-Irish Presbyterian minister, so Davidson was a natural collegiate springboard for the future president.) And President Wilson must have had fond memories of his time in Mecklenburg—a "region very familiar to my heart," he said—because it sounds like all it took for city leaders to lure him to MecDec Day 1916 was the promise of a trip back to his old college stomping grounds.

The first Southern-born president elected since before the Civil War, Wilson rolled back into Davidson with little fanfare and was able to exit his special Packard car and stroll right into his old dorm practically unnoticed. Overcome with nostalgia while walking on the first floor of Chambers, the president stopped and knocked on his old dorm room door.

"This is President Wilson," he announced. "May I come in?"

"Why, yes, come in, for I am Christopher Columbus myself!" came the reply from a groggy, skeptical freshman named "Strawberry" Young.

When the door opened to reveal that it was, in fact, the real Woodrow Wilson standing there surrounded by Secret Service, legend has it that poor Strawberry got so flustered he turned and jumped out his dorm window and escaped across the quad in his pajamas.

While on campus Wilson also visited Davidson's Eumenean Literary Society Hall, where he bumped into "Skit" Schofield, described as a pudgy little eccentric fellow with a soda shop in town that was a popular student hangout. Skit yelled, "Hello, Tom!" (Woodrow is actually Wilson's middle name) and threw his arms around the president before Secret Service pounced on him. Somehow this laughable incident seems to have grown into a rumor that Wilson had been threatened or even assaulted in Charlotte, which the local press dismissed, correctly, as "apocryphal" gossip. Although downtown, when a large commemorative hornet's nest was given to Wilson's chief of staff for safekeeping, he looked "at the nest askance . . . whether he suspected it of harboring live hornets or of being the hiding place of a bomb is not known."

MecDec Day 1916 was later described as "pageantry without parallel in the history of Southern celebrations," but not everyone among the record throng of 100,000 MecDec supporters made it out of Charlotte unscathed.

Just like with Taft, MecDec Day 1916 had issues with severe weather, only this time instead of torrential downpours it was an early wave of Carolina's suffocating summer heat. (In the most Charlotte way ever, seven years after Taft visited, the town's leaders were *still* apologizing about the rain.) This time, under perfect cerulean skies, Wilson's day in Charlotte began with a celebration of its boom as a Southern textile and manufacturing hub. Charlotte's new Ford Motor Company plant put on a display of the fifty-one automobiles it had just built. And in one of the most famous photos in town history, which ran above the fold and across the entire front page of the next day's paper, Wilson, decked out in a Prince Albert–style top hat and tails, posed with hundreds of power brokers and dignitaries in front of the Southern Manufacturing Club on Trade Street.

Stealing the show, however, was little Mildred Greenleaf, who became something of a local celebrity after she snuck in at the last second and sat at the president's feet, proudly decked out in her Sunday finest with matching bonnet and shiny black Mary Jane shoes.

By midday, when it was time for Wilson to deliver his speech, First Lady Edith Wilson wrote that it had become a "boiling hot day; one of those sudden descents of summer that cause unexpected discomfort." Far more painful, according to the first lady's memoirs, was the interminable introduction given by the Charlotte mayor, which by some estimates ran close to an hour under the scorching Carolina sun. Charlotte may have been smitten with the First Lady—who was dressed in a midnight blue embroidered Georgette crepe and silk gown with a black lisera hat turned up on the left side by chinchilla ostrich feathers—but several decades later, Edith was still throwing massive amounts of shade at Charlotte's long-winded mayor:

> On and on he went—thirty, forty, fifty minutes—when suddenly members of the Marine Band (dressed in wool uniforms) began to succumb to the

heat. They dropped like flies, and the valiant little Boy Scouts tried to lift and carry them to some blessed shade. . . . Hardly had the band received first aid when women all around me began to faint, and the Scouts, with perspiration pouring down their boyish faces, came to tender their services. . . . At last he stopped, for lack of breath, I think, and sat down, looking more like a vanquished prize fighter than anything I can think of; for both cuffs had slipped their moorings, and one was open. His hair was standing on end, and the necktie had sought sanctuary under his left ear. . . . My husband's address was calm and mercifully short.

Indeed, Wilson's speech was less than eighteen minutes, but the powerful message he chose to share on MecDec Day in Charlotte reverberated around the globe.

Wilson had been pleading for American neutrality since 1914, when the fighting began in Europe. With the war at a stalemate, Wilson used his MecDec Day speech in 1916 to call for world peace. And to achieve it, Wilson seemed to suggest that all Europe had to do was follow the example and leadership of America and the MecDecers. "For it is an interesting circumstance that the processes of the war stand still," Wilson began. "These hot things that are in contact with each other do not make very much progress against each other. And when you cannot overcome, you must take counsel." In the 141 years since the MecDec, the United States had built itself into a powerful force for liberty and freedom in the world. Now, Wilson wondered, what would we do with all that power: "translate it into force or . . . into peace and the salvation of society?"

The world could be spared from more war, Wilson continued, if only it would follow the prophecy of America, where we had already solved (at least temporarily) the problems Europe was now burning over. "America did not come out of the South, and it did not come out of New England," the president told the 100,000 MecDec supporters standing in rapt silence before him in Charlotte. "The characteristic part of America originated in the middle states . . . because there from the first was that mixture of populations, that mixture of racial stocks, that mixture of antecedents which is the most singular and distinguishing mark of the United States. The most

commander of the allied forces in World War II. For Eisenhower's visit the festivities moved to Freedom Park. Located just a few miles south of Independence Square, the bucolic setting featured a large pond with a band shell built on a small island facing a large grass amphitheater. When the president arrived, he was greeted by an earth-rumbling salute from four howitzers and an introduction by Warren Hull, star of the hit TV show *Strike It Rich*. Ike and the rest of the 30,000 MecDec supporters in attendance then sat down for a good old-fashioned picnic lunch of fried chicken and sweet tea. In a scene straight out of *The Andy Griffith Show*, a handful of kids ate their boxed lunches perched on the edge of the stage, just below the president's podium, with their bare feet dangling in the water.

The president was dressed in a gray, single-breasted suit and matching gray fedora that Ike liked to slap on his thigh while emphasizing a point, or laughing, both of which he did often while visiting with a group of his old West Point classmates who made the trip to Charlotte to surprise the president. Lunch was served by a handful of students from Queen's College sporting picnic table–styled aprons. (Thankfully, the students showed no signs of trauma from the previous night's incident on campus, summed up on the front page of the *Charlotte Observer* as "200 Davidson Students Pull Queens Panty Raid.") Organizers made sure Ike ate at a special table built with wood from the McIntyre Farm cabin, the one MecDecers filled with musket holes during the famous Battle of the Bees, now inscribed with the words of the MecDec.

Outwardly, at least, Ike and the crowd showed no signs of concern over the Supreme Court's ruling that had come down just two days earlier ending school segregation in the South, or the ongoing commie witch hunt hearings of Senator Joseph McCarthy, who was still a few weeks away from having his sense of decency questioned by attorney Joseph Welch. Charlotte Mayor Philip Van Every began the program by proclaiming, "Americans have always fought for their freedoms," and the Mecklenburg Declaration of Independence "was freedom's birth certificate." To which Congressman Charles Jonas added, "No one in North Carolina claims that we have a monopoly on patriotism, but we are entitled to take some natural pride in the fact that our forefathers, right here in this community, were the first Americans to undertake to dissolve the bonds that bound them to the mother country and declare themselves 'a free and independent people.'"

When the president took the podium, he added: "We have met to honor those men of long ago—those men who signed the Mecklenburg Declaration of Independence. Now, the historical record has been disputed by some, particularly those who claim they are descendants of the true authors of all documents of that time. But it matters not exactly how many were gathered in that cabin to sign the document. It matters not that part of the document had to be reconstructed.

"The important thing is that [the MecDec] was an immortal step in our development."

In 1963, Charlotte civil rights pioneer Dr. Reginald Armistice Hawkins chose the anniversary of the MecDec for one of the city's most momentous anti-segregation demonstrations. "The theme of the rally at the courthouse was that Negro citizens had not shared in the freedom demanded by Mecklenburg residents from the British nearly 190 years ago," the *Charlotte Observer* reported. And on the day of the march, an exhausted, exasperated Hawkins made it even more simple. "There is no freedom as long as all of us are not free," he explained.

Born on Armistice Day in 1923 and a US Army captain in World War II, Hawkins graduated from Johnson C. Smith University and earned his dental degree from Howard University in 1948. (Later, he also earned a master's in divinity from JCSU.) Hawkins was a dentist and, later, an ordained Presbyterian minister, but leading the fight for civil rights in Charlotte was his true calling.

In late September 1957, the Little Rock Nine made national news after integrating Central High in Little Rock, Arkansas, with the help of President Eisenhower and the National Guard. Weeks before that, however, in one of the ugliest moments in Charlotte history, on September 4, 1957, when the fifteen-year-old Dorothy Counts enrolled in the all-white Harding High, she endured a seething, threatening mob of students, adults, and teachers as she entered the school. With the Charlotte police nowhere to be found, Hawkins volunteered to escort Counts home from school through the same mob, navigating what he described as "a shower of spittle, pebbles, and sticks." Fearing for her safety, Counts's parents eventually removed her from Harding and enrolled her in an integrated school in Philadelphia. All the while, Charlotte's white leaders advocated for extreme patience regarding integration, an approach that was little more than a veiled form of Jim Crow–styled obstruction. After Harding High in 1957, the esteemed and tenacious Hawkins rose quickly in the civil rights movement, becoming a confidant of Dr. Martin Luther King Jr., a key organizer for King's March on Washington, and the father of the civil rights movement in Charlotte.

Using the MecDec, such a well-known source of public pride in Charlotte, as an instrument to illustrate how many Americans still hadn't obtained the same "freedom and independence" declared in the 1775 document was a biting, yet brilliant, move by Hawkins. To further emphasize that point, on MecDec Day in 1963, Hawkins organized a two-mile march down Trade Street from JSCU to the MecDec obelisk in front of the Charlotte courthouse steps. There he announced in his rapid-fire, thunderous oratory style, "We are not going to cooperate any more with segregation. We shall not be pacified with gradualism; we shall not be satisfied with tokenism.

"We want FREEDOM!" Hawkins declared. "And we want it NOW!"

During the civil rights movement, and after, Charlotte went to great lengths to paint itself as a more progressive Southern city. Oftentimes it was. However, on MecDec Day 1963, the *Observer* reported that the peaceful marchers dressed in suits and church clothes "tramped" across the city and were derided by some citizens as "punks . . . raising hell" who should all be "arrested." At the end of his MecDec Day March, Hawkins implored the demonstrators to stay alert. In the civil rights struggle, he told them, "any day might be D-Day. They can either make this an open and democratic city or there is going to be a long siege. They can choose which way it's going to be."

Afterward, the *Observer* labeled Hawkins a "militant."

Two years later, in 1965, his house was bombed.

In 1966, there was progress.

After a long legal battle Hawkins was finally able to integrate the North Carolina Dental Society. And then, in 1968, Hawkins became the first Black person to run for governor in North Carolina. The campaign was shattered by King's murder in Memphis. (The day King was assassinated he had originally been scheduled to campaign with Hawkins in North Carolina.) Hawkins fell short in his bid for governor, but he exponentially strengthened Black civic engagement in the state and forever changed the political landscape in Charlotte.

As proof, I suppose, on May 20, 1968, then California Governor Ronald Reagan spoke at a hotel in downtown Charlotte. His appearance, and his message about restoring America's greatness, was overshadowed by Lady Bird Johnson who, that same day, drew thousands to a MecDec Day celebration at Hezekiah's Rock House. And while Reagan raced through a stump speech that was so generic, audience members were finishing his punchlines before he could, Lady Bird's MecDec Day comments focused on lifting up the less fortunate in Charlotte to ensure freedom, independence, and happiness for all. "Beyond any doubt what is going on here says a great deal about your heritage," Lady Bird offered between sips of orange punch at the Rock House with the Daughters of the American Revolution. "The legacy of sturdy Scots-Irish settlers who two hundred years ago began to make Mecklenburg County a region of independence, strong religious faith, and educational excellence."

INTERNAL WHITE HOUSE MEMOS IN THE SPRING OF 1975 SHOW THE LOOMing disaster weeks before the massive MecDec Bicentennial Celebration. It was big news in Charlotte when the city was selected by the White House to be the first of President Gerald Ford's many Bicentennial appearances. But it had only been six months since Ford's controversial decision to pardon Richard Nixon for his role in Watergate, and almost right away a skittish (and misinformed) White House staff began debating, and second-guessing, the merits of publicly acknowledging the Mecklenburg Declaration of Independence. The original three-page research memo crafted by Dr. Theodore Marrs was spot-on about the signing of the MecDec, Captain Jack's ride, the critical role of the Hornet's Nest in the Revolutionary War, and the list of presidents who had acknowledged, supported, and visited Charlotte on MecDec Day in the past. Under the heading "PURPOSE," Marrs states that President Ford would be in Charlotte "To celebrate Freedom Day—on May 20th, which is the 200th anniversary of the Mecklenburg Declaration of Independence."

The trouble started on April 28, 1975, when a young researcher on Ford's staff who had recently graduated from the University of North Carolina was persuaded by an assistant professor of history at the school (and the ghost of Old Fatty, I suppose) to "warn" the president and his speechwriters that "all the big names in history in North Carolina do not believe that the Declaration ever existed" and that it would be "terribly embarrassing for the president to take part in an event celebrating the Mecklenburg Declaration."

It was, once again, a strangely malicious load of BS from a school that, frankly, owed a great deal to the MecDec, starting with an apology. UNC was, after all, founded by General William Davie, one of the heroes of the Battle of Charlotte who had been inspired by the MecDec. The school's longest-serving president, former governor and judge David Swain was, perhaps, the biggest MecDec advocate in the state. Right behind him was MecDec witness, war hero, and UNC trustee William Polk. And yet it was UNC scholars who misplaced the critical Davie Copy of the MecDec for more than half a century, allowing their own professor, the notorious Dr. Charles Phillips, to get away with extreme academic fraud in his influential, anti-MecDec magazine hit piece "May, 1775."

Now, far be it from me to question the rigorous research bona fides of an assistant history professor. But in 1975, at the time of this "warning" to President Ford, John McKnitt Alexander's actual MecDec meeting notes from May 1775 and the 1831 NC Governor's Report were easily accessible inside UNC's Wilson Library, which could not have been more than a few hundred feet from the history department's offices. Not to be out-done, apparently, in the buildup to Ford's visit, inexplicably, the MecDec's own hometown newspapers continued to report that there was no proof of the MecDec itself and that none of the previous presidents who had vis-ited Charlotte on MecDec Day throughout the twentieth century had taken sides in the debate, which we all know is 100 percent wrong *and* 100 percent unforgivable.

So, naturally, in keeping with pretty much all of the post–Civil War MecDec discourse, even though it was utterly baseless, the White House "warning" memo worked like a charm.

Because of course it did.

It's all right there in White House documents from the spring of 1975: "The press could really blast us . . . the President would be embarrassed . . . he will need Southern support in 1976." (It was quite a departure from Wil-liam Howard Taft, who, in 1909, basically promised to knock the block off anyone who dared question the MecDec.) For a while Ford's exceptionally paranoid staff even considered canceling the entire trip. Finally, on May 15, Russ Rourke, a special assistant to Ford, concluded: "Totally explored entire headache area [with Charlotte]. Agreed the President's appearance still well advised. . . . Will include language in the speech that will divorce the Pres-ident from the historical dispute itself." Like clockwork, in each subsequent draft of Ford's MecDec Bicentennial speech, the prominence of the decla-ration and the Signers shrinks until, finally, they are left out of the remarks entirely.

Even worse, to preemptively diffuse the situation, the White House press secretary started making light of the MecDec in his briefings with the na-tional media.

MR. NESSEN: All right. Tomorrow, the President, as you know, is going to Charlotte, North Carolina. The purpose of this trip is to take part in a commemorative ceremony on the 200th anniversary of the word reaching Charlotte of the battles of Lexington and Concord. (Laughter)

Now, wait a minute. It gets a little better. (Laughter)

Q: How many days did it take?

MR. NESSEN: On May 19, 1775, which is 200 years ago today, the citizens of Charlotte gathered in what is now the town square of Charlotte, at the court house, and according to local history, drafted the Mecklenburg Declaration of Independence from the British. (Laughter)

It was completed in the early morning hours of May 20th. Now, those documents are said to have been destroyed in a fire of 1800. (Laughter)

I think some of you who have followed this story know that historians frankly disagree as to whether it was the exact date and precisely what the Declaration said, and so forth.

Q: Who has been following this story?

Q: Ron, would you ask a show of hands of those who have followed this story? (Laughter)

MR. NESSEN: It has been in all the papers. Anyhow, I just want you to know that so that you don't get down there and find out that there has been a controversy—not just a controversy, but historians don't agree on the historic facts of the episode.

Q: Are they going to demonstrate, the historians?

Q: Did they get the word of the battles there? Is this the primary bicentennial focus of the celebration?

MR. NESSEN: Yes, it is.

The news of the battles did reach there. Now, what date the Declarations were signed and precisely what they said is in some dispute by historians.

Q: He is going down there to observe the 200th anniversary of the so-called Mecklenburg Declaration of Independence, isn't that right?

MR. NESSEN: He will refer in his remarks tomorrow to his knowledge that there is a dispute about this and he will explain why he thinks it was worth going down there for. (Laughter)

I wish I knew who asked the final question, because they make a great point, one that the White House somehow overlooked after a month of handwringing about the MecDec Bicentennial: just how spineless (and rude) Ford would appear for attending a celebration of brave patriots that he, as the leader of the free world, was too afraid to even mention by name. It was not a good look for a president, especially in a region where in the 1970s, May 20 was so popular that one of the promotional giveaways from the fast-food chain Hardee's was a replica of the MecDec. Ford also missed a golden opportunity to build on the overwhelming support he had in Charlotte in May 1975 for his show of strength in dispatching the Marines to rescue a US merchant ship that had been detained in Cambodia.

Shortly after the president's eighteen-car motorcade arrived at Freedom Park, the first reference to that operation earned Ford a forty-second standing ovation from the record 105,000 North Carolinians who had come to the park for the culmination of a three-day MecDec Bicentennial blowout. The second biggest hit of the day was Ford's teenage daughter, Susan, who tagged along to Charlotte with her dad to shoot photos for a high school project. "Any day I got to spend all day with my dad was a treat," Susan Ford Bales says now. "It was a busy day in Charlotte but a fun day. I do remember the crowds and it being very, very packed at the park."

Even a passing reference to the MecDec by Ford would have brought the house down. Instead, much of the focus that day seemed to be on an unauthorized seventy-six-foot-high royal blue hot air balloon hovering over the park advertising Weiner King hot dogs. The president also enjoyed a picnic lunch that included a large piece of a commemorative MecDec cake. That dessert, however, would be the only time the words "MecDec" passed Ford's lips all day.

Ford's staff was terrified of a misstep with the MecDec, especially in the South and just eighteen months before the election. And they were right. MecDecers never forgot Ford's lackluster appearance at the Bicentennial and his lack of support for the Mecklenburg Declaration of Independence and the country's original Founding Fathers. Now, obviously, there were just a few other minor things going on in the country at the time, but in the 1976 election against Jimmy Carter, Ford somehow managed to lose Mecklenburg County, North Carolina (by a whopping eleven points), and every last inch of the South below Virginia.

But, hey, at least he didn't embarrass himself with the MecDec or that lone assistant history professor in Chapel Hill.

Knowing all this, it seems prophetic that during Ford's visit to Freedom Park, a protestor near the stage held up a sign that read "FORD IS A
TORY." Ford pretended to ignore the signs. Ruth Graham, the wife of Reverend Billy Graham, was having none of it. And when one of the demonstrators got too close to the dais, Ruth, the freakin' rock star, snatched the sign,
stomped on it, and refused to give it back. It wasn't the first time Ford was
shown up by a Graham during the MecDec Bicentennial, though. Before
Ford's milquetoast remarks, Billy Graham took to the podium at Freedom
Park to accept the "Man of the South" award, and he absolutely blew away
the crowd with a roaring oratory on the MecDec and our first Founding
Fathers.

It's long, but it may be the most important and influential statement on
the MecDec over the past fifty years:

> The story of the Mecklenburg Declaration is a high-water mark in American
> history. No less an authority than John Adams said, "The genuine sense of
> America at that moment was never so well-expressed before or since." The
> fact that several presidents have participated in these celebrations, and that
> President Ford is here today, is indicative that America has always taken seri-
> ously the symbol of the Mecklenburg Declaration of Independence, whether
> it was fact or fiction.
>
> When I was a boy we were taught about this declaration to such an extent
> that I must have been in about fifth grade before I heard that a Declaration of
> Independence had (also) been signed in Philadelphia in 1776! Such has been
> the loyalty of the people of this community to Charlotte and Mecklenburg
> County.
>
> As I began to think and to study in later years the character and motives
> of those men who supposedly signed that Declaration, I had a clear definition
> of what kind of men they were. They were, first of all, a tough-minded and
> independent people. . . . They were Scotch-Irish for the most part, down to
> the very marrow of their bones they believed in personal freedom. . . . These
> people were not to be trifled with. As early as twenty years before the Revo-
> lution, a fiery Presbyterian preacher named Alexander Craighead traveled the
> Carolina countryside proclaiming that men should not live under tyranny.

So years before the war officially began, the fever of revolution had gripped the Mecklenburg colony.

As all of us are aware, debate continues to wax hot among scholars as to whether the Mecklenburg Declaration really was signed almost fourteen months in advance of the US Declaration. And respected scholars on both sides of the controversy can present rumors, facts, and fiction to bolster their own opinions.

However, whether there was a genuine Mecklenburg Declaration is of comparative unimportance. Certainly it has been a historic symbol to all America, of American independence. Dr. Chalmers Davidson, the famous Davidson College historian, said, "This day is still worthy of commemoration as the earliest overt act of independence in the thirteen colonies by a legally constituted body."

President Eisenhower, who was here on this date twenty years ago, said, "The important thing is that [the Declaration] was an immortal step in our development."

[The Mecklenburg Declaration of Independence] is the kind of thing this rugged, courageous, self-reliant community of five thousand would have done, for the roots of independence dug deep, caused in part by a belief in God of these freedom-loving Mecklenburgers.

What history shows us, then, is a hardy band of people who played hard and worked hard. They tolerated no foolishness. And they cherished their religious faith and their independence above all earthly things. But what of their leaders, those twenty-seven men who most citizens believed signed a Declaration of Independence on a muggy May morning two hundred years ago today?

What kind of men were those who dared defy the power and the majesty of the greatest nation on earth? Was it sheer arrogance that prompted these men—living in a remote frontier village scarcely the size of Pineville—to go on record as cutting all ties with their mother country? Was it mere bluff and bluster that possessed a bunch of unknowns to declare boldly that "Great Britain cannot be considered hereafter as holding any rights, privileges, or immunities among us"? Obviously, it was neither arrogance nor bluff nor bluster that motivated the signers. A simple study of the composition of this group proves this.

First of all, these were mature men. Men not given to hasty judgments or rash acts. They were Men of poise and presence, Men of conscience and conviction, Men of purpose and high resolve, Men of integrity. These also were well-educated men—five of whom were graduates of Princeton University. And they represented a broad cross-section of their community. Among them were: doctors, surveyors, tailors, ministers, lawyers, constables, military officers, legislators, magistrates, and farmers, men of the soil.

I feel a very real kinship with all the signers of the Mecklenburg Declaration. Perhaps this is because they were courageous, and I admire courage. Perhaps it is because they placed such a premium on freedom and independence, conditions which I also feel are the natural condition of man at a time in history when peoples all over the world are losing their freedom. Perhaps it was because they were resourceful and self-reliant, traits which I, too, believe are essential to an individual and a nation.

But most of all, my affinity with these men stems from the fact that they were—almost without exception—deeply religious. It is significant, I think, that both the signers of the Mecklenburg Declaration and the signers of the US Declaration boldly proclaimed their belief in—and their dependence upon—God.

Their faith was the inner resource that directed their actions and gave meaning and purpose to their lives. It was the most important thing in their lives. The records show that no fewer than fourteen of the signers of the Mecklenburg Declaration were elders in their churches, and two were clergy. In their Declaration, they proclaimed their intentions of becoming "a sovereign and self-governing people under the power of God . . ."

They believed wholeheartedly in the worth and dignity of the individual.

They believed in honor and integrity and their principles.

And they believed that was something worth dying for.

Graham's meticulous and moving sermon on the MecDec brought the 105,000 acolytes at Freedom Park to their feet in praise. It proved to be the highlight of the Bicentennial commemoration in 1975, if not the entire century of MecDec celebrations. Moving forward, this was going to be nearly impossible to top. Sure, the backing from all the presidents was nice, but as the twenty-first century approached, the MecDec now counted among its supporters the most influential Christian leader on the planet.

I guess I knew it all along.

God's a MecDec fan too.

Fourteen

Might As Well Start Practicing the Pronunciation: Semiquincentennial

Charles Jonas III was on the tarmac that day in Charlotte with President Ford in 1975. All of four years old at the time, he had tagged along at the foot of his grandfather, Charles R. Jonas, the renowned Republican congressman from North Carolina, and the sheer size and earth-rumbling roar of Air Force One, set against the clear Carolina blue sky, quickly became one of little Charles's earliest, fondest memories. Even twenty-some years later, when he returned to North Carolina after college in Texas, Jonas could still vividly recall the sight of the president's plane jetting off toward the Charlotte skyline, even though, for the life of him, he couldn't recall a single detail about what President Ford was doing in his hometown that day.

Neither could anyone else.

Ford's fecklessness at the Freedom Park podium on May 20, 1975, and a city-sized hangover after the massive Bicentennial celebration sent the Mec-Dec into a nearly fatal tailspin. A few years later, when the new courthouse was completed, the Signers' marble obelisk was abandoned at the old building, and, pretty soon, once banks and other businesses started to ignore the May 20 holiday, Mecklenburg County officially did away with it in 1982. For some reason the local newspapers continued to support the myth that little evidence existed regarding the MecDec, which is so lazy and blatantly wrong that it almost seems like part of a purposeful campaign to keep the public's focus on Charlotte's evolving image as the banking capitol of the "New South." At the same time, Charlotte's transient population boomed by nearly 40 percent in the '80s and '90s. Charlotte's changing demographics had a lot to do with the MecDec's disappearance. I grew up in a suburb of Detroit, and to this day I will vigorously, and enthusiastically, defend my hometown's honor in any debate about music, sports, history, or chili dogs. Likewise, plenty of historians have poked holes in the legend of Paul Revere over the years, but can you imagine *anyone* from Boston letting outsiders trash talk Revere without defending one of their own? But that's usually what happens with the MecDec in Charlotte. It's bizarre, but it comes down to the fact that most of the people who live in this part of North Carolina aren't actually *from* North Carolina, and without those deep roots there's no pride of ownership with the MecDec and certainly no sense of responsibility to defend it. As more newbies like that flooded in, the town's legacy historical groups got older, more possessive, and insular, and pretty soon, the annual MecDec celebration had deteriorated into little more than a handful of guys with muskets and weird costumes standing on a corner in Charlotte each May 20 while bemused bankers weaved through the ceremony on their way to lunch. When NASCAR blew up in the late 1990s (thanks in large part to that old PR horse-whisperer, Humpy Wheeler), the month of May became "race month" in Charlotte with the annual Coca-Cola 600.

"[The historical groups] had literally become antagonistic to newcomers, like, 'We kept the MecDec alive for forty years, how dare you even talk about it—*it's ours*,'" says Jonas, now fifty-two and a senior leader and head of capital markets at Foundry, an investment and development company. "They meant well, at least I think they did, but they held on to the MecDec so tightly they squeezed it to death and drove it into the gutter." Before anyone knew it, a generation had passed since the last big, meaningful MecDec celebration, and by the early 2000s, says Jonas, "the MecDec was dead—a totally dead piece of history."

So much so that in late 2003 when David Adams, then the COO of the Charlotte Museum of History, shared the MecDec story with Jonas, Syfert, and some of their colleagues (most of them native Charlotteans), the entire group was struck with a severe case of MecDec Face—even Syfert, who grew up here and was a history major at UNC before going to law school. As soon as the group of young professionals recovered, they gave themselves a nickname—the May 20th Society—and a mission: to serve their hometown and honor its rightful place in American history by bringing the MecDec back to life.

"At the time we had all these people coming to Charlotte from different parts of the country," says Jonas, the longtime chairman of the nonprofit May 20th Society. "And what's the first thing you do when you move somewhere new? You search for commonality and connection, oftentimes through the history of your new hometown. But Charlotte really had no anchoring, foundational history. Boston? You know right away what makes it unique. LA? Philly? New York? Chicago? Same thing. But the MecDec was the first time, for all of us, that we had found a unique aspect about *our town* that truly made Charlotte a place unlike any other in the world."

Jonas, Syfert, and Adams, a descendant of a MecDec Signer, then made, perhaps, the most critical decision in May 20th history: in the spring of 2004, they threw their first get-together at an amazing Irish pub in Charlotte called Rí Rá. I'm sure the Jonas and Syfert family names carried a lot of weight. (Scott's mom, Pam, worked for Charlotte for thirty-five years, including more than a decade as the city's top manager.) But the black-and-tans and the amazing Guinness stew with brown bread at Rí Rá certainly couldn't have hurt. Their second-best decision? They didn't ask for permission, and they didn't convene focus groups or hold long organizational meetings—they just jumped right in and invited anyone and everyone to help them rebuild the MecDec plane as they were flying it. "We were still getting a lot of resistance from the old-school MecDec folks," says Jonas. "And then we did something they *really* hated: we just opened the MecDec up and shared it with everybody."

The May 20th Society had stumbled onto an antidote for breaking through the frequently stubborn, historical hierarchy: the infectious, inclusive power of good old-fashioned grassroots and the idea that (with enough beer) relearning history can actually be fun. Just through word of mouth, the May 20th Society's first event drew a who's who list to Rí Rá of nearly three hundred of the city's powerbrokers, politicians, and history nuts. After a quick lesson on the MecDec, the group then proceeded to, let's just say, pay full homage to the Founding Fathers' Scots-Irish heritage. "I'm pretty sure the mayor climbed up on stage and played drums with the band that night," laughs Syfert. "After Rí Rá's it just exploded from there."

Inspired by the event, Charlotte artist Chas Fagan sat down and created the painting of Captain Jack galloping toward Philadelphia with the Mec-Dec. Pretty soon that image was everywhere. The following year, more than a thousand people showed up when the May 20th Society built a full-scale replica of the MecDec courthouse and closed down Trade and Tryon for the festivities, something I'm pretty sure hadn't been done since 1780 when Cornwallis fled Charlotte (the first time . . . or was it the fourth time? He retreated so many times I can't remember). Sold-out guest lectures from high-profile MecDec fans Ken Burns, Cokie Roberts, David McCullough, and others followed, helping to chip away at the false narrative—and apathy—that had calcified over the years with the MecDec. Once they built up a little momentum, Jonas, Syfert, and co. began focusing on ways to institutionalize the Mecklenburg Declaration as a permanent part of American history through murals, plaques, an exhaustively researched, encyclopedic book on the Mec-Dec written by Syfert in 2014, and a Liberty Walk connecting all of Charlotte's historic revolutionary sites downtown.

Right around this time, North Carolina District Court Judge Chase Saunders retired from the bench after twenty-five years. A lifelong advocate for Charlotte and its history (Saunders is the guy who wanted to posthumously censure Old Fatty, the UNC fabulist), the judge became convinced that as Charlotte's population exploded, what the city needed was an iconic symbol for all the natives and the newcomers to unite around. He took the idea to his friend, Dr. Tony Zeiss, the longtime president of Central Piedmont Community College, and, over breakfast one day, the two of them came up with the incredibly ambitious plan for a nineteen-mile Trail of History and greenway renewal project along Little Sugar Creek that would open in 2010 and feature dozens of historical statues.

To really sell it, though, Saunders knew they needed that perfect centerpiece, that moving, iconic bronze figure the entire region (and especially civic and corporate leaders) could relate to and rally around.

It needed to be bigger than life.

It needed to be badass.

It needed to be uniquely Charlotte.

It needed to be . . .

"Captain Jack!" Saunders yelled.

It was the perfect choice: 235 years later, Captain James Jack would ride again.

To fund the statue, Zeiss turned to the May 20th Society for the painstaking task of raising $525,000 through purposefully non-corporate individual donors to give the project a sense of community ownership. Fagan was then selected to create Captain Jack's statue.

A Charlotte transplant who lives next to Freedom Park and first learned of the MecDec story at the Rí Rá party—I mean, meeting—Fagan is a self-taught artist and sculptor who grew up in rural Western Pennsylvania on land that was still bisected by sections of trail once connected to the Great Wagon Road. In the winter the trail and the dense canopy would create a snow tunnel where Fagan loved to play as a kid and daydream about following the path all the way south to its terminus at Trade and Tryon. As a teen Fagan started drawing political cartoons as a hobby but decided to major in Soviet Studies at Yale. And he had fully planned on pursuing that as a career—until he visited Russia. Fagan says he could handle the KGB harassment. He could handle waiting in line every day for food and dropping twenty-five pounds in three and a half months. But it was the dead look in people's eyes, a spark extinguished by the kind of deep, nonstop suffering most of us can only imagine, that made Fagan decide, *hmm, maybe I'll focus on my art when I get home.*

He made the right choice. If you've been to Washington, D.C., any time during the last fifteen years you've probably seen his work. Among Fagan's many prominent pieces are his statue of Ronald Reagan in the rotunda of the US Capitol, his sculpture of Rosa Parks in the Washington National Cathedral, and the official portraits of, among others, Barbara Bush and Mother Teresa.

Fairly early in his career, though, Fagan was drawn to the unique challenges of forging a symbol for a city through the story of Captain Jack. Chief among them, Fagan had actually never sculpted a horse, so the first thing he had to do was take a crash course on equine anatomy. Another big obstacle was how to depict Captain Jack charging north toward Philadelphia for his death-defying 550-mile mission to deliver the MecDec, without, well, "showcasing the horse's backside to people at three different intersections, so they are not all just stopped at a light in Charlotte staring at a large bronze horse's rear end," Fagan laughs.

His solution was to have Jack yanking on the reins while *turning* his steed north. This choice, and Fagan's effortless brilliance as a sculptor, creates the tension, movement, and, yes, emotion in the twelve-foot high, sixteen-foot-long statue. Honestly, when you're standing in front of Fagan's work reading the MecDec Signers' names etched into the base, the second you glance up into Captain Jack's eyes bearing down on you from atop his horse, there's an overwhelming urge to jump out of the way because it feels like Captain Jack is about to run some people over, if need be, to complete his MecDec mission.

"The Spirit of Mecklenburg County" was unveiled in 2010 to rave reviews at a ceremony hosted by Cokie Roberts across the street from a tiny chapel that's become a very popular destination for downtown weddings. Months later, Fagan knew his Captain Jack had begun to connect with his audience when, on Monday mornings, he'd drive by and see Captain Jack adorned with wedding veils, looking like Charlotte's version of Superman.

The energy created by the May 20th Society and Fagan's iconic statue helped convince Olde Mecklenburg Brewery to put out their Captain Jack Pilsner. Jerry Linker even resumed his role as Captain Jack in the annual Thanksgiving Day parade. Then, in 2014 when Charlotte landed a team in the United Soccer League (USL), the franchise decided to name the team the Charlotte Independence with a silhouette of Captain Jack as their logo and "Jack's Militia" as the nickname for their supporters. In 2019, when several area youth soccer clubs merged to form one of the largest soccer programs in the country (with more than twelve thousand members), they also adopted the Independence name and the Captain Jack logo.

So now, two centuries after Charlotte lamented the fact that Captain Jack never got the recognition he deserved for his brave ride, he has his own two-ton bronze statue downtown, and you literally can't drive more than five minutes *anywhere* in this part of North Carolina without seeing a minivan or SUV sporting an Independence Soccer decal emblazoned with Captain Jack's likeness.

Of course, there have been a few misses and setbacks along the way during the MecDec's recent resurgence. A few years ago, a rumor spread like wildfire that the MecDec had been discovered . . . on an episode of *Pawn Stars*. (Nope.) At the 2019 MecDec celebration in Independence Square, one of the large balloon minutemen used as a podium backdrop remained flaccid for most of the program. Plans to work the story of the MecDec into Donald Trump's speech at the 2020 Republican National Convention in Charlotte were derailed by Covid-19. Several subsequent attempts to get George W. Bush to town for MecDec Day have also not panned out, but the May 20th Society is holding out hope of landing W. for 2025 and the big semiquincentennial anniversary of the MecDec.

And America.

ON MY WAY TO MECDEC DAY 2022 IN CHARLOTTE, I FEAR I HAVE FINALLY entered some kind of bizarre time portal, watching in amazement as a Revolutionary War reenactor in full eighteenth-century garb—all the way down to his knee breeches, brass buckle shoes, and long rifle—tries to operate one of the city's new computerized parking meter kiosks. I'm about to offer my assistance, but then I remember sitting in on a planning meeting for this event at the Charles R. Jonas Federal Building just down the street, where an inordinate amount of time was dedicated to managing this regiment of mostly senior-citizen war reenactors who, it turns out, can be quite the collection of divas. At this late stage in my adventure, I don't quite know why, but the idea of gangs of frail silver-haired grampas in soldier costumes beefing hard with each other and, I don't know, possibly throwing down in a Cracker Barrel parking lot just pleases me to no end. From what I could ascertain, the faux infantrymen don't care for the younger, hot-shot cannon corps, and the cannon bros don't particularly like the fancy color guard, and none of these awesome prima donnas like taking commands from event organizers or lowly civilians like me.

So for once, I smartly keep my distance. Eventually my guy figures out the kiosk, in due haste, and then double-times it to join the rest of his Hornet's Nest regiment for the noon MecDec celebration at Independence Square in the center of Charlotte. Infused with the sweet scents emanating from a nearby sidewalk flower stand, this year's event draws a few hundred MecDec fans, including Charlotte Mayor Vi Lyles, Carolina Panthers mascot Sir Purr, and about a dozen or so actual descendants of the original MecDec Signers. The program also features a county-wide proclamation and the usual talk of bringing back the May 20 holiday, hopefully before 2025 and what's sure to be an epic semiquincentennial celebration of the MecDec. An adorable Charlotte middle-schooler then reads an original MecDec poem wherein she manages to beautifully rhyme "plagiarizing" with "independ-i-sizing" and, suddenly, surrounded by a growing sense of communal energy I'm filled with hope that what Syfert and others are saying is true.

After 250 years, the MecDec is making another comeback.

For me, though, the highlight of the program is the brief speech delivered by May 20th Society board member Matt Ridenhour, a former Marine and Mecklenburg County commissioner who occasionally dresses like a colonial soldier sent forward in time to become a Vineyard Vines catalog model. As a primer, Ridenhour fully believes that MecDec Day ranks right up there alongside Christmas. Anyway, Ridenhour tells us that the night before, while doom scrolling on social media like the rest of us, he was overcome, like the rest of us, by a constant sense of dread about America's future. But then (and, sure, it's a little on the nose) Ridenhour thought about the MecDecers and our first Founding Fathers and the historic document they produced in the face of exponentially more terror and uncertainty than we're all dealing with today—and he felt better.

Today, on MecDec Day 2022, at Independence Square across the street from Founders Hall, Ridenhour continues that theme of hope, action, and cooperation while speaking in front of a banner depicting the Charlotte courthouse at the exact moment, 247 years earlier to the day, when Thomas Polk first proclaimed Americans to be "free and independent."

Our first Founding Fathers, Ridenhour says, were "a courageous people living in a sleepy little village who decided they had had enough of tyranny and would stand together for freedom. They knew that this declaration would come at a cost: their homes, their peace, and, perhaps for many of them, their lives. But they deemed this a small price to pay for freedom, a freedom we enjoy and celebrate today. . . . Today we celebrate that history, our history, something that is beautiful about America and the cause of liberty. Liberty is the birthright of all who yearn to be free. And this American story, this American birthright, is our story and our birthright—so claim it. Claim your birthright and fight for it daily. Never let the flame of liberty die. That is our directive from the Founders of our great nation: to improve our country, to work together against oppression and tyranny, to continually strive for a more perfect union. So may we today, on May 20, the date enshrined on our state flag and on the great seal of North Carolina, may we do two things: may we claim our birthright of freedom and liberty, and may we strive this day, and every day, to form a more perfect union. Once again, welcome to your celebration and happy Mecklenburg Declaration of Independence Day—Huzzah!"

The crowd answers back with a raucous "HUZZAH!" And then, Ridenhour's speech is followed by the official reading of the MecDec and a thunderous, slightly terrifying cannon salute by our reenactor friends that violently echoes off the buildings and rattles the windows of a nearby Hooters. Once everyone's hearts restart, the program concludes with an invitation to join the MecDec descendants for a march to Settlers' Cemetery to place a wreath on the grave of Thomas Polk.

Exiting Independence Square one last time, as I head down Trade Street contemplating the end of my MecDec quest, I suddenly find myself right in the middle of the group of MecDecers heading to Polk's grave. It's poetic, at least to me, that from this vantage point it looks like the Mecklenburg militia and all of our original Founding Fathers in Charlotte are about to lay siege to Hooters, now with my help.

"Coming with us?" someone asks.

"Sure, why not," I chuckle. "At this point I'm pretty much official."

"Oh, so you're a MecDec descendant?"

After all this time, the question still catches me off guard.

I laugh, and then, after needing a second or two to think about such an honor, I say:

"Yeah, well, aren't we all?"

ACKNOWLEDGMENTS

To THE SURPRISE OF ABSOLUTELY NO ONE, ON THE FINAL RESEARCH TRIP OF this amazing adventure I got completely turned around on the southwest side of Charlotte while searching for—*what else?*—some obscure, ancient cemetery I had convinced myself was full of MecDec secrets. Once again, though, I wasn't lost at all. I was exactly where I needed to be. I can't tell you how many times this happened while researching and writing this book, but it was often enough that I gave it a cheesy moniker: MecDec Magic. On this day, still miles away from my intended destination and needing to consult (or really swear at) Siri, I pulled into the parking lot of a nondescript housing development where a large, lonesome marble marker caught my eye. The date on top was 1780 and below it read: IN MEMORIAM: *Jane Parks . . . who rode 10 perilous miles to notify American Camp of British evacuation of Charlotte.* MecDec Magic had struck again. Jane Parks, after all, is one of the most incredible MecDecers of them all. And standing in front of her memorial (which until that very moment I had no idea even existed), the thought occurred to me: *She deserves more.* The same can be said for Abigail Adams, Susanna Spratt, Susan Alexander, Adelaide Fries, and countless other amazing, influential, yet underappreciated women at the heart of the MecDec story.

The book you're holding is no different. To attempt something as far out of my comfort zone as *WYFF?* would have been utterly impossible without the extraordinary support, sacrifice, and guidance of my wife, Kim. All of my books (all of my accomplishments in life, really) are by-products of and testaments to Kim's endlessly selfless spirit, tender heart, gifted mind, and iron will. (Not to mention her superhuman patience.) Thanks to Kim, our family is full of extraordinary women just like her. As this tome proves,

I am rarely at a loss for words. But I do struggle to properly express just how much I adore our daughters, Ally and Kate, who seemingly overnight during the course of this project grew from teenagers into remarkable young women. Besides being strong, smart, beautiful, adventurous, and wickedly funny, Ally and Kate (a.k.a. the Queenies) also proved to be excellent (if not somewhat pricey) research assistants on the MecDec. And on the rare occasion when Kim could no longer take one more rant about Thomas Jefferson or Charles Phillips, or one more giddy report on the Freedom Spring or the Monticello gift shop, that duty usually fell to the girls, who always sweetly held back (almost all of) their eye rolls.

After Team Fleming, I am most indebted to Scott Syfert and the rest of the May 20th Society. For decades, Syfert has been the leading historian, author, and advocate on the MecDec, and it is not an exaggeration to say that without his seminal and encyclopedic 2014 work, *The First American Declaration of Independence?*, as a guide, as well as his endless help on everything from the first research call to the final fact check of the manuscript, I would have been completely lost on this project and probably still on my bike circling around downtown Charlotte somewhere searching for the Captain Jack statue. Let me put it this way: if Charlotte named a school after LeGette Blythe, Scott Syfert deserves a library, at least. On behalf of all the history nerds in North Carolina and beyond, I want to thank Syfert, Charles Jonas, Judge Frank Whitney, Judge Chase Saunders, Julie Fogg, Chas Fagan, Dr. Tony Zeiss, and all the other folks associated with the May 20th Society for standing up to centuries of fraudulent historiography in order to resurrect, honor, and expand the MecDec story and the important legacy of our first, true Founding Fathers.

My agent, Jane Dystel, believed in this book when few others did. (How's this for MecDec Magic: Kate and I were standing at Thomas Polk's grave in Charlotte when Jane called to say we had a book deal.) That's when I learned that it would be mine and the MecDec's great fortune to have the project in the hands of Editorial Director Brant Rumble, whose deft literary touch, creativity, humor, and overall passion for the project took *WYFF?* to a whole new level. I have always been extremely fortunate to work with great editors during the last twenty-three years at ESPN, where Vice President

Chris Buckle, Executive Editor Scott Burton, Senior Editor Rebecca Hudson, and so many other colleagues provided yet another crazy idea of mine with unprecedented support. I'm also grateful to my former ESPN editors and friends Gary Belsky and Neil Fine, who now run Elland Road Partners in New York. As he has with all my books (and most of my best work), Gary added his critical and creative touch to the manuscript while Neil inspired the Gonzo-style approach to the book.

My obsession with this story truly kicked in around 2010 with the unveiling of the Captain Jack statue. Along the way, so many people went above and beyond the call to facilitate the oftentimes-bizarre research requirements of this project, and among them I'd especially like to thank Valerie Linker, Ashley Fox, Todd Marlin, and Richard Plumer. As a writer I am also blessed with the most amazing support system of family and friends, starting with my mom, Rosanna Fleming, my brother, Bryan Fleming, as well as Claude Brittingham and all of the Ehlers, Friesens, and Sachs. A few years ago, what finally convinced me to go all-in on this twisted and complicated subject was a touching show of support and an extended roundtable discussion with my beloved Christmas Cove Family, and I remain eternally grateful to all the Waltons, McCartys, and Clauers for decades of love, laughter, adventure, and sweet beans. In Davidson, what often kept me going on the manuscript was the infectious enthusiasm about the MecDec from our friends, especially the Farsons, the O'Briens, the Newells, and the Strodels. Megan and Greg Blackwell also offered up their beautiful mountain cabin for a (desperately needed) writer's retreat that produced the chapter on the transatlantic search for Dispatch 34, one of my favorite parts of the book. I'm also beyond lucky to count among our dearest family friends a PR pro like Sherri Johnson.

I'd also like to thank the following folks for their help: Linda Dalton and Robert Ryals at the Mecklenburg Historical Association; Sara Swanson in the Davidson College Archives and Special Collections (and Davidson student Abbey Blonstein); Matt Turi and Aaron Smithers at the Wilson Special Collections Library at the University of North Carolina; Brandon Lunsford at Johnson C. Smith University; historian Dr. Tom Hanchett from the History South project and the Levine Museum of the New South; as well as the staff members at the Charlotte Museum of History, the Carolina Room at the Charlotte-Mecklenburg Public Library, the Presbyterian Heritage Center, the British National Archives, the Special Collections Research Center at the University of Kentucky, and the History Roundtable group in Charlotte. I think it's safe to say that everyone in this group is with me in hoping for the ultimate bit of MecDec Magic in the buildup to the 250th anniversary: that with all the renewed interest, somewhere, somehow, another original copy, or even the lost edition of the *Cape Fear Mercury*, is finally uncovered.

For now, though, my search is over. After my detour to the Jane Parks memorial, I did eventually locate the Steele Creek Presbyterian Church Cemetery and the final resting place of another MecDec hero, Reverend Humphrey Hunter. The Revolutionary War veteran, noted historian, and MecDec eyewitness is one of many Charlotteans who did their civic duty and helped preserve the record in perpetuity by engraving the details of our original Declaration of Independence onto their tombstones. All the pictures I had seen of Hunter's grave, however, suggested it might be in need of a little TLC. So my idea for the final task of this project was to tidy him up a bit in a small act of service to these great patriots. Ultimately, though, something even better happened. I arrived at Steele Creek with bucket and scrub brush in hand only to find that someone had beaten me to it. Whoever it was, they had done such a good job that below the mention of the MecDec and Hunter's "active part in securing the Independence of his Country," a whole new section had been revealed—one last bit of MecDec Magic, I suppose. Standing there in silence with the setting sun twinkling through the trees, the newly discovered words struck me as the perfect closing line to one of the biggest challenges, and greatest adventures, of my life.

As a parent he was kind & affectionate, as a friend, warm and sincere and as a Minister, persuasive and convincing.

BIBLIOGRAPHY

Adams, John. *The Works of John Adams.* Vol. 10. Boston: Little Brown, 1856.

Alexander, J. B. *The History of Mecklenburg County from 1740 to 1900.* Charlotte: Observer Printing House, 1902.

Arnett, Alex Mathews, and Walter Jackson. *The Story of North Carolina.* Chapel Hill: University of North Carolina Press, 1933.

Arthur, John Preston. *Western North Carolina: A History (From 1730 to 1913).* Asheville: Edward Buncombe Chapter of the Daughters of the American Revolution, 1914.

Ashe, Samuel A'Court. *History of North Carolina from 1584 to 1783.* Vol. 1. Greensboro: Van Noppen, 1908.

Ashe, Samuel A., Stephen B. Weeks, and Charles L. Van Noppen, eds. *Biographical History of North Carolina from Colonial Times to the Present.* Vol. 7. Greensboro: Charles L. Van Noppen, 1908.

Bass, Robert. *The Green Dragon: The Lives of Banastre Tarleton and Mary Robinson.* London: Redman, 1957.

Bingham, Warren L. *George Washington's 1791 Southern Tour.* Charleston, SC: History Press, 2016.

Blythe, LeGette. *Alexandriana.* Harrisburg, PA: Stackpole Sons, 1975.

Blythe, LeGette, and Charles R. Brockman. *Hornets' Nest: The Story of Charlotte and Mecklenburg County.* Charlotte: McNally, 1961.

Boyd, Julian, ed. *The Papers of Thomas Jefferson.* 20 Vols. Princeton: Princeton University Press, 1950–1983.

Bridenbaugh, Carl. *Myths and Realities: Societies of the Colonial South.* New York: Atheneum, 1963.

Bright, John M., Hon. "Oration Delivered at the Centennial Celebration of the Mecklenburg Declaration of Independence, at Charlotte, N.C., May 20, 1875, by Hon. John M. Bright of Tennessee." Nashville: Oration, 1875.

Cappon, Lester J., ed. *The Adams-Jefferson Letters: The Complete Correspondence Between Thomas Jefferson and Abigail and John Adams.* Chapel Hill: University of North Carolina Press, 1988.

Clark, J. C. D. *The Language of Liberty, 1660–1832.* New York: Cambridge University Press, 1994.

Coe, Alexis. *You Never Forget Your First: A Biography of George Washington.* New York: Viking, 2020.

Craighead, Alexander. *Reasons of Receding from Present Judicatures and Constitution.* Philadelphia: B. Franklin, n.d.

––––––. *The Renewal of the Covenants at Middle Octorara in Pennsylvania November 11, 1743 (pamphlet)*. Ben Franklin, 1744, 1748.

Davidson, Chalmers G. "Celebrating May 20 for 200 Years." *The State* 42, no. 11 (April 1975).

Davie, William Richardson, and Blackwell P. Robinson. *The Revolutionary War Sketches of William R. Davie*. Raleigh: North Carolina Dept. of Cultural Resources, Division of Archives and History, 1976.

Davis, Leslie. *History of Independence Hill Baptist Church, Mecklenburg Co., North Carolina*. 1972.

Denman, Jeffrey A., and John F. Walsh. *Greene and Cornwallis in the Carolinas: The Pivotal Struggle in the American Revolution, 1780–1781*. Jefferson, NC: McFarland & Company, 2020.

Dinsmore, John Walker. *The Scotch-Irish in America*. Chicago: Winona, 1906.

Douglas, John. *The History of Steele Creek Presbyterian Church*. Charlotte: Craftsman, 1978.

Draper, Lyman C., and Craig L. Heath, eds. *The Mecklenburg Declaration: Its Origin, History and Actors with a Bibliography of Its Literature, and Explanatory Documents*. Westminster, MD: Heritage Books, 2004.

Edgar, Walter, ed. *The South Carolina Encyclopedia*. Columbia, SC: University of South Carolina, 2006.

Ellis, Joseph J. *American Sphinx: The Character of Thomas Jefferson*. New York: Vintage Books, 1996.

––––––. *Passionate Sage: The Character and Legacy of John Adams*. New York: Norton, 2001.

Fischer, David Hackett. *Albion's Seed: Four British Folkways in America*. New York: Oxford University Press, 2018.

Fleming, Thomas. *The Man from Monticello: An Intimate Life of Thomas Jefferson*. New York: William Morrow & Co., 1969.

Foote, William Henry. *Sketches of North Carolina*. New York: Robert Carter, 1846.

Ford, Paul. *The Writings of Thomas Jefferson*. 10 vols. New York: Putnam, 1892–1899.

Foster, R. F. *Modern Ireland: 1600–1972*. New York: Penguin, 1989.

Fries, Adelaide. *The Mecklenburg Declaration of Independence as Mentioned in the Records of Wachovia*. London: Forgotten Books, 2018.

Garden, Alexander. *Anecdotes of the American Revolution*. Charleston: A. E. Miller, 1828.

Gordon-Reed, Annette. *The Hemingses of Monticello: An American Family*. New York: W. W. Norton, 2009.

––––––. *Thomas Jefferson & Sally Hemings*. Charlottesville, VA: University of Virginia Press, 1998.

Graham, George W., MD. *The Mecklenburg Declaration of Independence, May 20, 1775, and Lives of Its Signers*. New York: Neale, 1905.

Graham, George W., MD, and Alexander Graham, AM. *Why North Carolinians Believe in the Mecklenburg Declaration of Independence of May 20th, 1775*. 2nd ed. Charlotte: Queen City, 1895.

Graham, William Alexander. *General Joseph Graham and His Papers on North Carolina Revolutionary History: With Appendix, an Epitome of North Carolina's Military Services in the Revolutionary War and of the Laws Enacted for Raising Troops*. Raleigh: Edwards & Broughton, 1904.

————. 1804–1875, North Carolina. General Assembly, and 1830–1832 (Montford Stokes) North Carolina. Governor. *The Address of the Hon. Wm. A. Graham On the Mecklenburg Declaration of Independence of the 20th of May, 1775: Delivered At Charlotte, On the 4th Day of Feb'y, 1875, by Request of the Citizens of Mecklenburg County, With Accompanying Documents, Including Those Published by Order of the Legislature of North Carolina In the Year 1831,* New York: E. J. Hale, 1875.

Hanna, Charles A. *The Scotch-Irish: The Scot in North Britain, North Ireland and North America.* New York: G. P. Putnam, 1902.

Harris, William. *Historical Sketch of Poplar Tent Church.* Concord, NC: Times Book and Presses, 1924.

Heckscher, August. *Woodrow Wilson: A Biography.* New York: Scribner, 1991.

Henderson, Archibald. *Cradle of Liberty: Historical Essays Concerning the Mecklenburg Declaration of Independence.* Mecklenburg Historical Association, 1955.

————. *Washington's Southern Tour, 1791.* New York: Houghton Mifflin, 1923.

Hoyt, William Henry, AM. *The Mecklenburg Declaration of Independence: A Study of Evidence Showing That the Alleged Early Declaration of Independence by Mecklenburg County, North Carolina, on May 20th, 1775, Is Spurious.* New York: G. P. Putnam's Sons, 1907.

Hunter, C. L. *Sketches of Western North Carolina.* Raleigh: Raleigh News Stream, 1877.

Jefferson, Thomas. *Notes on the State of Virginia.* New York: Penguin, 1998.

————. *The Works of Thomas Jefferson.* Vol. 11. New York: Cosimo, 2009.

Johnson, Joseph. *Traditions and Reminiscences Chiefly of the American Revolution in the South.* Charleston, SC: Walker & James, 1851.

Jones, H. G. *For History's Sake: The Preservation and Publication of North Carolina History.* Chapel Hill: University of North Carolina Press, 1966.

Jones, Joseph Seawell. *A Defense of the Revolutionary History of the State of North Carolina from the Aspersions of Mr. Jefferson.* Boston: Charles Bowen, 1834.

Jordan, Winthrop. *White Over Black American Attitudes Toward the Negro, 1550–1812.* Chapel Hill: University of North Carolina Press, 2012.

Kars, Marjoleine. *Breaking Loose Together: The Regulator Rebellion in Pre-Revolutionary North Carolina.* Chapel Hill: University of North Carolina Press, 2002.

Keinath, Caroline. *Adams National Historical Park.* The Creative Company, 2008.

Kennedy, John P. *Memoirs of the Life of William Wirt: Attorney-General of the United States.* New York: G. P. Putnam and Sons.

King, Victor. *Lives and Times of the 27 Signers of the Mecklenburg Declaration of Independence.* King/Charlotte, 1956.

Klein, Philip S., and Ari Hoogenboom. *A History of Pennsylvania.* University Park: Penn State Press, 1980.

Kranish, Michael. *Flight From Monticello: Thomas Jefferson at War.* New York: Oxford University Press, 2010.

Kratt, Mary Norton. *Charlotte, North Carolina: A Brief History.* Charleston, SC: History Press, 2009.

————. *Charlotte: Spirit of the New South.* Winston-Salem, NC: John F. Blair, 1992.

Kukla, Jon. *Mr. Jefferson's Women.* New York: Random House, 2007.

Lawson, John, and Hugh Talmage Lefler, eds. *A New Voyage to Carolina.* Chapel Hill: University of North Carolina Press, 1967.

Leyburn, James G. *The Scotch-Irish: A Social History.* Chapel Hill: University of North Carolina Press, 2009.

Looney, J. Jefferson, ed. *The Papers of Thomas Jefferson.* Princeton: Retirement Series. 19 vols. Princeton University Press, 2016.

Maier, Pauline. *American Scripture: Making the Declaration of Independence.* New York: Random House, 1997.

Martin, Francois-Xavier. *The History of North Carolina from the Earliest Period.* Vol. 2. New Orleans: A. T. Penniman, 1829.

McClintock, John, and James Strong. *Cyclopaedia of Biblical, Theological, and Ecclesiastical Literature.* New York: Harper, 1894.

McCulloh, Henry Eustace. *Letter from Henry Eustace McCulloh to Edmund Fanning.* Vol. 7. May 9, 1765. *Colonial and State Records of North Carolina.* Chapel Hill: University of North Carolina, 2004.

McCullough, David. *John Adams.* New York: Simon & Schuster, 2001.

———. *1776.* New York: Simon & Schuster, 2005.

McGeachy, Neill Roderick. *A History of the Sugaw Creek Presbyterian Church.* Rock Hill, SC: Record Printing Co., 1954.

McNitt, V. V. *Chain of Error and the Mecklenburg Declaration of Independence.* Palmer, MA: Hampden Hills Press, 1960.

Meacham, Jon. *American Lion: Andrew Jackson in the White House.* New York: Random House, 2008.

Miller, Charley, and Peter Miller. *Monticello: The Official Guide to Thomas Jefferson's World.* Washington, DC: National Geographic, 2016.

Miller, S. Millington, MD. "The True Cradle of American Liberty; Independence Bell Rang a Year Earlier in Charlotte Than in Philadelphia." *Collier's National Weekly,* July 1, 1905.

Moore, James Hall. *Defense of the Mecklenburg Declaration of Independence: An Exhaustive Review of and Answer to All Attacks on the Declaration.* Raleigh: Edwards Broughton, 1908.

Morrill, Dan L. *Historic Charlotte: An Illustrated History of Charlotte and Mecklenburg County.* San Antonio: Historical Publishing Network, 2009.

Niles, Hezekiah, 1777–1839, and Sidney Edward Bouverie Pusey. *Principles And Acts of the Revolution In America: Or, An Attempt to Collect And Preserve Some of the Speeches, Orations, & Proceedings, With Sketches And Remarks Belonging to the Men of the Revolutionary Period in the United States.* Baltimore: W. O. Niles, 1822.

North Carolina Historical Commission. *Records of the Moravians in North Carolina (1752–1775).* Vol. 2. Raleigh: Edwards & Broughton, 1925.

Owen, Benjamin F., Richard Locke, and George Craig. "Letters of Rev. Richard Locke and Rev. George Craig." *Pennsylvania Magazine of History and Biography,* Vol. 24, No. 4 (1900): 467–478.

Patterson, Daniel. *The True Image: Gravestone Art and the Culture of Scotch-Irish Settlers in the Pennsylvania and Carolina Backcountry.* Chapel Hill: University of North Carolina Press, 2012.

Pepe, William and Elaine. *Quincy.* Charleston, SC: Arcadia, 2008.

Philbrick, Nathaniel. *Travels with George: In Search of Washington and His Legacy.* New York: Viking, 2021.

Plumer, Richard P. *Charlotte and the American Revolution: Reverend Alexander Craighead, the Mecklenburg Declaration, and the Foothills Fight for Independence.* Charleston, SC: History Press, 2014.

Polk, William. *Autobiography of Colonel William Polk (manuscript).* Library of Congress.

———. *Polk Family and Kinsmen.* London: Forgotten Books, 2018.

Powell, William S., ed. *Dictionary of North Carolina Biography.* 6 vols. Chapel Hill: University of North Carolina Press, 2016.

———. *Encyclopedia of North Carolina.* Chapel Hill: University of North Carolina Press, 2006.

Preyer, Norris W. *Hezekiah Alexander and the Revolution in the Backcountry.* Charlotte: Heritage, 1987.

Ramsay, David. *The History of the American Revolution.* 2 vols. Indianapolis: Liberty Fund, 1990.

Ramsey, Dr. J. G. M., and William B. Hesseltine, eds. *Dr. J.G.M. Ramsey Autobiography and Letters.* Knoxville: University of Tennessee Press, 2002.

Ray, Lila McGeachy. *Alexander Craighead: With Drawn Sword.* Master's thesis, Pittsburgh Theological Seminary, 2001.

Rayner, B. L. *Sketches of Thomas Jefferson.* New York: Boardman, 1832.

Saberton, Ian. *The Cornwallis Papers, Volume 1, The Campaigns of 1780 and 1781 in the Southern Theatre of the American Revolutionary War.* Ukfield, England: Naval and Military Press, 2010.

Salley, A. S., Jr., and Worthington Ford. "S. Millington Miller and the Mecklenburg Declaration." *American Historical Review* 11, no. 3 (1906): 548–558.

———. "The Mecklenburg Declaration: The Present Status of the Question." *American Historical Review* 13, no. 1 (1908): 16–43.

Smylie, James H. *A Brief History of the Presbyterians.* Louisville, KY: Geneva Press, 1996.

Sommerville, Charles William. *The History of Hopewell Presbyterian Church: For 175 Years from the Assigned Date of Its Organization, 1762.* Charlotte: Hopewell Presbyterian Church, 1939.

Spence, Thomas Hugh. *The Presbyterian Congregation on Rocky River.* Concord, NC: Rocky River Presbyterian Church, 1954.

Spratt, Thomas Dryden. *Recollections of His Family (manuscript).* Rock Hill, SC: Winthrop University Special Collections, 1875.

Stedman, C. *The History of the Origin, Progress, and Termination of the American War.* Gale ECCO, 2010.

Stumpf, Vernon. *Josiah Martin: The Last Royal Governor of North Carolina.* Durham, NC: Carolina Academic Press, 1986.

Syfert, Scott. *Eminent Charlotteans: Twelve Historical Profiles from North Carolina's Queen City.* Jefferson, NC: McFarland & Company, 2018.

———. *The First American Declaration of Independence? The Disputed History of the Mecklenburg Declaration of May 20, 1775.* Jefferson, NC: McFarland & Company, 2014.

Tarleton, Banastre. *A History of the Campaigns of 1780 and 1781 in the Southern Provinces of North America.* North Stratford, NH: Ayer, 2007.

Thompson, Ernest Trice. *Presbyterians in the South.* Richmond, VA: John Knox Press, 1963.

Tompkins, D. A. *History of Mecklenburg County and the City of Charlotte.* Vol. 1. Charlotte: Observer Printing House, 1903.

Trinterud, Leonard J. *The Forming of an American Tradition: Colonial Presbyterianism.* Philadelphia: Westminster Press, 1949.

Tucker, George. *The Life and Philosophy of George Tucker (manuscript).* Bristol: Thoemmes Press, 2004.

———. *The Life of Thomas Jefferson, Parts I and II.* London: Charles Knight, 1837.

Tyerman, Luke. *The Life of the Rev. George Whitefield.* London: Watson and Viney, 1876.

Vos, Johannes G. *The Scottish Covenanteers.* Blue Banner, 1998.

Wayland, Francis Fry. *Andrew Stevenson.* Philadelphia: University of Pennsylvania Press, 1949.

Webb, James. *Born Fighting: How the Scots-Irish Shaped America.* Broadway Books, 2011.

Weeks, Stephen Beauregard. *Truth and Justice for the History of North Carolina: The Mecklenburg Resolves of May 31, 1775, vs. "The Mecklenburg Declaration of May 20, 1775."* Greensboro: Charles L. Van Noppen, 1908.

Wheeler, John Hill. *Historical Sketches of North Carolina.* Vol. 1. Elibron Classics, 2007.

———. *Reminiscences and Memoirs of North Carolina and Eminent North Carolinians.* Washington: Henkle, 1885.

Wiencek, Henry. *Master of the Mountain: Thomas Jefferson and His Slaves.* New York: Farrar, Straus, and Giroux, 2012.

Wilson, Edith. *My Memoir.* Indianapolis: Bobbs-Merrill, 1939.

Wirt, William. *Sketches of the Life and Character of Patrick Henry.* Philadelphia: James Webster, 1817.

Wood, Gordon. *Friends Divided: John Adams and Thomas Jefferson.* New York: Penguin, 2018.

Woodmason, Charles. *The Carolina Backcountry on the Eve of the Revolution: The Journal and Other Writings of Charles Woodmason, Anglican Itinerant.* Edited by Richard J. Hooker. Chapel Hill: University of North Carolina Press, 1953.

Source Notes

Guide

CSR: Colonial and State Records of North Carolina

BNA: British National Archives

SHC: Southern Historical Collection

MDP: Mecklenburg Declaration Papers (at the SHC)

DCA: Davidson College Archives

VHS: Virginia Historical Society

MHA: Mecklenburg Historical Association

NCGR: North Carolina Governor's Report

CML: Charlotte Mecklenburg Library (Carolina Room)

CMH: Charlotte Museum of History

Chapter One

Ripley's: Pepe, *Quincy*, 31.

Bill Rosenberg: Details on Rosenberg and Dunkin' Donuts are from the University of New Hampshire's Rosenberg International Franchise Center "Pioneers" information website; "Obit for Rosenberg," *Associated Press*, September 23, 2002; and "Dunkin's Run: A Love Story," *Boston Magazine*, August 30, 2010.

classic New England–style country home: Author visit, May 2022. See also: Keinath, *Adams*, 11.

the mold Abigail Adams used: Ibid., 9.

the Bible: Ibid., 33.

"remember the ladies": Ibid., 9.

next to the legal notices and ads for crockery: DCA, *Register*, June 5, 1819.

Scots-Irish: See Chapter 2 source notes.

whiskey-loving Princeton intellectuals: See Chapter 5 source notes.

firebrand preacher: See Chapter 3 source notes.

Composed during: See Chapter 6 source notes.

Captain James Jack: See Chapter 7 source notes.

Jefferson . . . plagiarized: See Chapter 8 source notes.

Adams refused to attend: McCullough, *Adams*, 564.

"total incapacity": Ellis, *Passionate Sage*, 115.

New Year's Day 1812 . . . reconciliation: Cappon, *Adams-Jefferson Letters*, 286.

158 letters: Keinath, / *Adams*, 20.

folding desk: Ibid.

"May I enclose to you . . .": Cappon, *Adams-Jefferson Letters*, 542. (These letters, and others, have been edited to reflect contemporary spelling and punctuation unless doing so would change the meaning or context.)

"spurious": Ibid., 543.

"A few weeks ago . . .": Adams, *Works of John Adams*, 220.

"Either these resolutions . . .": Ibid., 221.

eleven US presidents: Details on the presidents, Taft, and Graham, are in Chapter 13 source notes.

"There is no question . . .": Syfert, *First American Declaration*, 214–215.

"All my instincts . . .": Ibid.

"I think it's true": Ibid.

George Will: Ibid; see also: George F. Will. "Independence Days." *Washington Post*, July 3, 2008.

"should be . . . investigated": Adams, *Works of John Adams*, 221.

"made known to . . . future generation": Ibid., 220.

"Jefferson survives": McCullough, *Adams*, 646.

"This is the Fourth": Ibid.

"Divine favor": Ibid., 647.

Adams' crypt: Author visit, May 2022.

CHAPTER TWO

starting in 1819: *Charlotte Observer*, January 31, 1974.

one-eyed surgeon: Sommerville, *History of Hopewell Presbyterian Church*, 249–252.

A Princeton lawyer who nearly killed: Draper, *Mecklenburg Declaration*, 208–218.

the South's Paul Revere: Syfert, *Eminent Charlotteans*, 66.

powerful, ruthless family: Graham, *MecDec and Lives of Its Signers*, 100–117.

revolutionary preacher: Ray, *With Drawn Sword*, 1.

"high-souled cavalier": Graham, *MecDec and Lives of Its Signers*, 98.

"backbone": Leyburn, *Scotch-Irish*, 308.

saved the Liberty Bell: Syfert, *Eminent Charlotteans*, 60; see also: Polk, *Polk Family and Kinsmen*, 1912.

close confidant to Nathanael Greene: Draper, *Mecklenburg Declaration*, 157–172.

outnumbered fifteen to one: Denman and Walsh, *Greene and Cornwallis*, 43–49.

the annotated legend: Draper, *Mecklenburg Declaration*, 157–172.

closer to barbarism: Leyburn, *Scotch-Irish*, xv.

radicals of the . . . highest order: Details on the history of the lowland Scots, unless otherwise noted, are from Leyburn's *Scotch-Irish*, Webb's *Born Fighting*, Dinsmore's *Scotch-Irish in America*; and the Ulster-Scots Society of America, Ulster-Scots Agency (Belfast), and discoverulsterscots.com.

nearly half a million: Webb, *Born Fighting*, 132.

twenty-seven million: Webb, *Born Fighting*, back cover.

Barack Obama: Frances Stead Sellers, and Aaron Blake. "Our First Black President Plays Up His Scots-Irish Heritage—and It Has Everything to Do with Trump," *Washington Post*, July 28, 2016.

Queen Elizabeth had tried in vain: Leyburn, *Scotch-Irish*, 83.

a single solution: Ibid., 83–119.

enthusiastic colonizer: Ibid., 89.

four million acres: Dinsmore, *Scotch-Irish in America*, 38.

nearly ten thousand: Leyburn, *Scotch-Irish*, 88.

more than four hundred thousand: Webb, *Born Fighting*, 116.

Thomas Polk's ancestors . . . Lifford: Draper, *Mecklenburg Declaration*, 159.

oppressive mismanagement: Leyburn, *Scotch-Irish*, 157–170.

Anglican bishop: Webb, *Born Fighting*, 153.

James Anthony Froude: Ibid.

40 percent of the Revolutionary Army: Webb, *Born Fighting*, 10.

"the most God-provoking democrats . . .": Ibid., 162; see also: Foster, *Modern Ireland*.

Hessian captain: Ibid.

Polk was born: Draper, *Mecklenburg Declaration*, 157–172.

He fell madly in love: Kratt, *Charlotte: Spirit of the New South*, 20; see also: Draper, *Mecklenburg Declaration*, CML Special Collections, and King, *Lives and Times*, 39.

James Logan: Klein, *History of Pennsylvania*, 44.

encouraged to migrate south: Webb, *Born Fighting*, 135–140.

Mesopotamia: Syfert, *First American Declaration*, 23.

"Delicious country": Lawson, *Voyage to Carolina*.

first white settlers to cross: Kratt, *Charlotte: Spirit of the New South*, 20.

"only the knapsack upon his back": Draper, *Mecklenburg Declaration*, 160.

ten thousand years: Details on the Catawba, the trails, and topography relating to pre-Charlotte are from CML and CMH (guides and website), Kratt's *Charlotte: Spirit of the New South*, and Syfert's *First American Declaration*.

Queen Charlotte: Kratt, *Charlotte: Spirit of the New South*, 24.

"most outstanding": King, *Lives and Times*, 39.

town's founder and treasurer: Details on the life of Thomas Polk are from NCpedia.org /polk-thomas; see also: Ashe, *Biographical History of North Carolina, Volume II*.

"a very trifling place": VHS, *Diaries of George Washington*, Saturday, May 28, 1791.

dirt-floor log cabins: Descriptions of early Charlotte are from the CML and CMH (guides, displays and website), Kratt's *Charlotte: Spirit of the New South* and Syfert's *First American Declaration*.

manure, and hogs: Syfert, *First American Declaration*, 7.

forty years: Ibid., 26.

a royal decree was needed: CSR, "Acts of NC General Assembly," March 1774.

Long Bullets: Syfert, *Eminent Charlotteans*, 34.

"drunkenness": Saberton, *The Cornwallis Papers Volume I*, 34.

five shillings . . . six pence: Syfert, *Eminent Charlotteans*, 34.

right ear was bit off: Patterson, *True Image*, 298.

seventy-six gallons: *Charlotte Observer*, May 18, 1975.

one legendary bender: Spratt, *Recollections*, 49.

Charles Woodmason: Woodmason, *Carolina Backcountry*, 50–60.

to get back at the . . . outsider: Syfert, *First American Declaration*, 37.

Augean Stable: Merriam-webster.com.

CHAPTER THREE

Alexander Craighead: Details on Craighead are from Lila McGeachy Ray's 130-page 2001 Master's Thesis at the Pittsburgh Theological Seminary titled *Alexander Craighead: With Drawn Sword*; McGeachy, *History of Sugaw Creek*, 13–50; Syfert's *Eminent Charlotteans* and *First American Declaration*.

"Son of Thunder": Spence, *Rocky River*, 6–20.

"foremost American": Hanna, *Scotch-Irish*, 40.

"possibly insane": Syfert, *First American Declaration*, 29; see also: Ray, *With Drawn Sword*, 2.

Covenanters: Ibid., 28.

70 percent . . . as much as 25 percent: Plumer, *Charlotte*, 120.

"None of this happens": Ray interview, June 2021.

highest crime rates: CMPD, "Report to Charlotte City Council," January 6, 2020.

Charlotte native DaBaby: WCNC, "DaBaby," June 15, 2022.

"without a gun": Lee interview, June 2021.

half a dozen generations: Details on Lee, his family, and his career are from multiple interviews in June 2021.

Colonel Tom Black: Ibid.

"Craghead" or "Creaghead": Ray, *With Drawn Sword*, 4–5.

"off-in" stone blocks: Lee interview, June 2021.

brick schoolhouse . . . in 1837: Charlotte-Mecklenburg Historic Landmarks Commission report on "Sugaw Creek School House."

Sugaw Creek Burying Ground: Author visit, June 2021.

the Campbell family plot: McGeachy, *History of Sugaw Creek*, 31.

sassafras saplings: Ibid.

gavel and the current pulpit: Ibid.

He was born in March 1707 in Donegal: Ray, *With Drawn Sword*, 6.

"like wild beasts": Ibid., 11.

head and his hands . . . torn off: Vos, *Scottish Covenanters*, 94–125.

The Killing Time: Ibid.

"chasing and killing . . .": Ibid.

1723 . . . joined the mass exodus: Ray, *With Drawn Sword*, 17.

"Brewed in Scotland . . .": Ibid.

Lancaster County: Ibid., 21.

"unhappy gift of discord . . .": Ibid., 28.

barred his poor wife . . . from communion: Ibid., 24.

"so excoriating and unconscionable . . .": Ibid., 25.

"problem person": Ibid., 28.

"Farewell!": Ibid.

Duke . . . 1974: Duke 2022 Men's Basketball Media Guide, 151.

kin to Craighead: Ray interview, June 2021.

Benjamin Franklin: Ibid.

George Whitefield: Ray, *With Drawn Sword*, 52–56; see also: Tyerman, *The Life of the Rev. George Whitefield*, 386.

crowds of . . . five thousand: Syfert, *First American Declaration*, 30.

riding through the woods with Craighead: Ray, *With Drawn Sword*, 52–56; see also: Tyerman, *The Life of the Rev. George Whitefield*, 38.

"incidents of weeping . . .": Smylie, *History of the Presbyterians*, 49.

"their Sacrament with a gun . . .": Owen, *Philadelphia Magazine of History and Biography*.

"foremost in propagating": Ibid., 30.

"mad fellow": Ray, *With Drawn Sword*, 70.

the entire spectacle: Details of the trial are from Ray, *With Drawn Sword*, 57–60; see also: Trinterud, *Colonial Presbyterianism*, 108; and Spence, *Rocky River*, 6–20.

He called George II: Ray, *With Drawn Sword*, 67; see also: Craighead pamphlet *The Renewal of the Covenants* (printed by Ben Franklin), Nov. 11, 1743.

he would no longer abide: Craighead, *The Renewal of the Covenants*, Nov. 11, 1743.

asked them . . . to draw their swords: Ray, *With Drawn Sword*, 67.

"The Declaration, Protestation, and Testimony": Spence, *Rocky River*, 10.

"Our drawing the sword . . .": Craighead, *The Renewal of the Covenants*, Nov. 11, 1743; see also: truecovenanter.com, and Clark, *Language*, 264.

1758 . . . Rocky River Church: Spence, *Rocky River*, 6–20.

"The individual traits . . .": Bridenbaugh, *Myths and Realities*, 120.

the only spiritual authority . . . between the Catawba and Yadkin: Ray, *With Drawn Sword*, 86.

Foote: Foote, *Sketches*, 185.

At Sugaw Creek . . . in the afternoon: McGeachy, *History of Sugaw Creek*, 14.

he'd ride deep into the woods: Ray, *With Drawn Sword*, 87.

"disposed to melancholy": Ibid., 93.

chief shepherd . . . of seven churches: Ibid., 89.

Marriage and Vestry Acts: Details on these Acts are from Syfert, *First American Declaration*, 34–35; see also: Hanna, *Scotch-Irish*, 15 and CSR, 1769, p. 1016.

CHAPTER FOUR

1761 . . . 1810: Powell, *Dictionary of North Carolina Biography*.

"pack of brutal sons-of-bitches": CSR, "Minutes of the NC Governor's Council," May 1765, 10–31.

"the very stereotype . . .": Syfert, *First American Declaration*, 39.

"young in life . . .": Details of the McCulloh family and the Sugar Creek War, unless otherwise noted, are from CSR, "Minutes of the NC Governor's Council," May 1765, 10–31 (this includes the extensive letters written on the events by McCulloh); Powell's *Encyclopedia of North Carolina*; Kars's *Breaking Loose Together*, 36–54; a paper written by the MHA's Jim Williams, "The Sugar Creek War," 2017; and Syfert's *First American Declaration*, 36–45.

1.2 million acres: Powell, *Encyclopedia of North Carolina*, 49.

four shillings per one hundred acres: Williams, "Sugar Creek War," 1.

"Now I doubt . . .": Kars, *Breaking Loose*, 36.

Craighead resigned: McGeachy, *History of Sugaw Creek*, 15.

baptismal spring: Ibid., 30.

missing . . . eight full pages: CSR, "Minutes of the NC Governor's Council," May 9, 1765, 25.

"infested": Woodmason, *Carolina Backcountry*, 50–60, and 80–81.

twelve pounds per one hundred acres: Kars, *Breaking Loose*, 43.

on March 4: Details of the Sugar Creek War, unless otherwise noted, are from CSR, "Minutes of the NC Governor's Council," May 1765, 10–31 (this includes the extensive letters written on the events by McCulloh); Powell's *Encyclopedia of North Carolina*; Kars's *Breaking Loose Together*, 36–54; Williams, "The Sugar Creek War"; and Syfert's *First American Declaration*, 36–45.

"the long agrarian tradition . . .": Kars, *Breaking Loose*, 45.

money-back guarantee: Williams, "Sugar Creek War," 7.

30 percent less: Ibid.

"parcel of blockheads": Ibid.

Polk . . . announced: Ibid.

"more like wolves . . . carried over the Yadkin": CSR, "Minutes of the NC Governor's Council," May 1765, 24–25.

at nine the very next morning: Ibid.

Polk himself then snatched: Ibid.

fifteen Proc per one hundred acres: Williams, "Sugar Creek War," 7.

"Damn thee Tom Polk": Kars, *Breaking Loose*, 47.

one thousand pounds: Ibid., 46.

English Black Act: Ibid., 45.

six farmers were hanged: Powell's *Encyclopedia of North Carolina*, 958.

Emboldened: Kars, *Breaking Loose*, 45.

draw up his will: Ibid.

May 7, 1765: CSR, "Minutes of the NC Governor's Council," May 1765, 10–31.

John Frohock: Kars, *Breaking Loose*, 45.

skull . . . cracked open: CSR, "Minutes of the NC Governor's Council," May 1765, McCulloh letter, 32–34.

Tryon formally charged: Kars, *Breaking Loose*, 46.

full pardons . . . none of the Charlotteans came forward: Ibid.

Stamp Act . . . backlog of one thousand cases: Williams, "Sugar Creek War," 9.

thirteen pounds Proc: Ibid.

360 acres . . . ninety pounds (Proc): Syfert, *First American Declaration*, 45.

the assembly appointed: Kratt, *Charlotte: Spirit of the New South*, 21.

"beginning at a white oak . . .": Ibid.

built a courthouse: Ibid., 24.

C'est Bon . . . boobie barrier: Long, *Charlotte Observer*, Oct. 15, 2019.

bankrupt . . . in a British asylum: Powell, *Dictionary of North Carolina Biography*, 134.

Charlotte Country Club: Details on CCC, its history, and its dress code are from charlottecountryclub.org.

$85,000 . . . $12,480: Crane, Williams, *Axios*, Sept. 2, 2019.

CHAPTER FIVE

originally named Craighead: Huntersville.org.

150-year-old: Davis, *Independence Hill*, 1.

average farm . . . one hundred acres: CMH tour, October 2021.

own ten square miles: McNitt, *Error*, 133.

thirty-five land purchases: Ibid.

1,500 acres: Ibid., 67.

noted on area maps: Syfert, *First American Declaration*, 63.

to the Baptists in 1868: Independence Hill historian Leslie Davis, via Marlin interview, October 2021.

dedicated as Oak Grove: Davis, *Independence Hill*, 4.

agreed to rename their church: Ibid.

Abraham Alexander, the committee chairman: SHC, "Mecklenburg Declaration of Independence Papers: Rough Notes," 1775.

1954 newspaper article: Gary, *Charlotte Observer*, May 17, 1954.

1960 textbook: McNitt, *Error*, 26.

McKnitt would frequently host . . . shaded natural alcove: Ibid.

"hot enough to strangle": Ibid.

"The famous 'Declaration Spring'": King, *Lives and Times*, 71.

black-and-white photo from 1941: Author visit, October 25, 2021.

five-thousand-square-foot: Details on the 1774 Alexander Rock House, the CMH grounds, displays, and tour are from the CMH website and guides, and author visit, October 2021.

last remaining structure: Ibid.

1779 trial: Syfert, *First American Declaration*, 66.

Queen's College: Ibid.

six . . . MecDec Signers were Alexanders: McNitt, *Error*, 132–133.

more than ten thousand acres: Ibid.

half a million in cash: King, *Lives and Times*, 67.

20 percent of the town's population: Syfert, *First American Declaration*, 66.

audience with George Washington: Henderson, *Washington's Southern Tour*, 287–292.

written by . . . an Alexander: Alexander, *The History of Mecklenburg County from 1740 to 1900*, 1902.

seventeen enslaved persons: CMH website.

Many of the Alexanders . . . owned slaves: 1790 Mecklenburg County Census Information via Ancestry.com.

Polks . . . owned slaves: Powell, *Dictionary of North Carolina Biography*.

several other MecDec Signers: Ibid. See also: 1790 Census.

so did Reverend Craighead: Ray, *With Drawn Sword*, 111.

1,608 enslaved . . . more than 10 percent: 1790 Mecklenburg County Census Information via CMH display.

in 1679 . . . on the ship *Welcome*: Syfert, *First American Declaration*, 61.

Maryland . . . real estate holdings: Ibid., 62.

In 1754: Ibid.

acorn-hard: Ibid., 60.

"Three Day" rule: Powell, *Charlotte Observer*, May 21, 1997.

field trip: Herran interview, Sept. 28, 2021.

Ramsey . . . lifelong supporter of the Confederacy: Ramsey, *Autobiography*, xxvi. Editor's footnote 31: "Ramsey's views concerning black inferiority did not fade after emancipation. In a letter (from 1871) Ramsey said: 'None of them aspire to equality. They are savages and barbarians, know it and submit to the inferiority it implies.'"

Ramsey describes McKnitt: Ramsey, *Autobiography*, 5.

nine-button mohair coats: Syfert, *First American Declaration*, 62, via Alexander family historian Mary Boyer.

side hustle: Ibid.

sales receipts: Ibid.

seventy-five years ago . . . baptismal font: Davis, *Independence Hill*, 3.

most influential leaders: King, *Lives and Times*, 63.

"princely": Ibid., 64.

finest furnishings: Syfert, *First American Declaration*, *63*.

all the rage at Princeton: Ibid., 66.

Craighead's son, Thomas: McGeachy, *History of Sugaw Creek*, 43.

At Princeton, Balch: McNitt, *Error*, 27. McNitt's information on all the MecDec Princeton grads comes from a document provided by the university's office of the secretary in 1959; see also: James McLachlan's *Princetonians, 1748–1768*, via the DCA.

censure: Spence, *Rocky River*, 21.

Reese . . . doctorate in divinity from Princeton: McNitt, *Error*, 28. See above.

All eight Brevard brothers: Sommerville, *Hopewell*, 250.

roaring flames: Ibid.

blinded him in one eye: Ibid.

Princeton in 1768: McNitt, *Error*, 28; See above.

Dr. David Ramsay: W. Curtis Worthington, in Edgar, ed., *South Carolina Encyclopedia*.

A Latin Salutatorian at Princeton: McNitt, *Error*, 27. See above.

roomed with Oliver Ellsworth: Ibid.

North Carolina's first attorney general: Powell, *Dictionary of North Carolina Biography*.

"natural and inalienable rights": McNitt, *Error*, 30.

twelve pounds: SHC, *North Carolina University Magazine*, August 1855, 242–264.

"I soon perceived the neighbor drunk . . .": Ibid.

"more sarcastic . . .": Draper, *Mecklenburg Declaration*, 208–218.

"refer to Bacon": Details of the Avery-Jackson duel are from the *Daily Alta California*, November 5, 1886; Draper, *Mecklenburg Declaration*, 208–218; and the North Carolina Museum of History.

Sir: When a man's feelings: Ibid.

granddaughter's version: Draper, *Mecklenburg Declaration*, 208–218.

Riot Act: Kars, *Breaking Loose*, 187.

several droughts: Syfert, *First American Declaration*, 51.

fees: Ibid.

twenty shillings a gallon: CMH guided tour.

three thousand men . . . threatening to attack the courthouse: Syfert, *First American Declaration*, 53.

Mecklenburg militia: Ibid.

two conditions: Ibid.

Tryon approved: NCpedia, "Queen's College"; see also: CSR, "Acts of the NC General Assembly," 1770–1771.

Weddings . . . gander pulling: Leyburn, *Scotch-Irish*, 265.

all named college trustees: NCpedia, "Queen's College."

Alexander and Brevard . . . professors: Ibid.

thirty-five volumes of books: Ibid.

erected by Polk: Ibid.

Battle of Alamance: Powell, *Encyclopedia of North Carolina*, 23–24.

In a 1769 petition, Avery: McNitt, *Error*, 29.

black soot: Kars, *Breaking Loose*, 126.

the plantation of John Phifer: Spence, *Rocky River*, 23.

fourteen prisoners: Kars, *Breaking Loose*, 206–207.

twelve Regulators were found guilty and six . . . hanged: Ibid.

Fanning . . . gave the order: Ibid.

"good seed sown . . .": Ibid.

Thumbs down. On all counts: CSR, "Order of the Privy Council of Great Britain Concerning Acts of NCGA," April 22, 1772; CSR, "Proclamation of Josiah Martin Concerning . . . Queen's College," June 28, 1773.

"state of general frenzy": CSR, "Letter from (William Legge) Earl of Dartmouth to Josiah Martin," May 3, 1775.

"open and avowed rebellion": King George III, "Proclamation of Rebellion," August, 1775.

April 7, 1775: Howard, NCpedia, 2010.

CHAPTER SIX

just after sunrise: Syfert, *First American Declaration*, 3.

"tolerable": McNitt, *Error*, 23.

the commercial and governmental center: Syfert, *First American Declaration*, 48–49.

buzzing with excitement: NCGR, "Graham Testimony," 19.

the rest . . . were all Scots-Irish Presbyterians: McNitt, *Errors*, 132–138.

Billy Graham: Gerald R. Ford Presidential Library and Museum, Digital Collections, May 20, 1975.

"that illustrious hero": Ray, *With Drawn Sword*, 100–101.

"Craighead should have been": *Charlotte Observer*, May 20, 1975.

"half the men in the [area]": NCGR, "Graham Testimony," 18.

Wilson Library: Author visit, November 2021.

sworn testimony: NCGR, 1831.

a governor, a judge . . .: Ibid.

Humphrey Hunter: Douglas, *Steele Creek*, 40–42.

"clothed with ample powers": SHC, Alexander, *Rough Notes*.

authenticated . . . by . . . Henderson: Henderson, "News of Battle of Lexington Reaches Charlotte, May 19, 1775. A Scientific Demonstration," *Charlotte Observer*, May 20, 1916.

bayoneted old . . . colonists: *South Carolina and American General Gazette* via Syfert, *First American Declaration*, 69.

one hundred head of cattle: SHC, Alexander, *Rough Notes.*

"The cause . . . of Boston": CSR, "Resolutions by Inhabitants of Rowan County," August 8, 1774.

committee chair: *Raleigh Register*, April 30, 1819; see also: NCGR, 13–15.

Abraham Alexander: Details on Alexander are from McNitt, *Errors*, 132.

"give relief": SHC, Alexander, *Rough Notes.*

"the question was taken": NCGR, "Graham Testimony," 18–20.

"Every delegate felt": *Raleigh Register*, April 30, 1819; see also: NCGR, 13.

a subcommittee was formed: NCGR, see also: SHC, Alexander, *Rough Notes.*

a family member found: *Southern Home*, July 5, 1875, via Draper, *Mecklenburg Declaration*, 367.

"He was distinguished": Spence, *Rocky River*, 22.

inside the library of Queen's College: Syfert, *First American Declaration*, 71.

Graham's written testimony: NCGR, "Graham Testimony," 18–20.

early morning of May 20: NCGR, see also: SHC, Alexander, *Rough Notes*, and *Raleigh Register*, April 30, 1819.

The first and second ones: Details of the MecDec Resolves are from NCGR; see also: SHC, Alexander, *Rough Notes*, and *Raleigh Register*, April 30, 1819.

Robert Henry: Arthur, *Western North Carolina*, 381; see also: Sondley, *Asheville Citizen*, March 4, 1928.

"*solemn* and *awful* vote": SHC, Alexander, *Rough Notes.*

"Nem-Con": Ibid.

"not a dissenting voice": NCGR, "Humphrey Testimony," 20–22.

"a more correct and formal draft": Ibid.

an eyewitness: NCGR, "Governor's Stokes statement," vi.

William Polk: Details of Polk are from Powell (McFarland), *Dictionary of North Carolina Biography*, 1994.

blackout drunk: DCA, Dryden Spratt, *Recollections*, 45–50.

"Devil Charley": Graham, *Mecklenburg Declaration Signers*, 98.

Thomas Spratt: Details on Spratt are from Syfert, *Eminent Charlotteans*, 25–30.

"under the shouts and huzzas": NCGR, 24.

"unanimously adopted": NCGR, 20–25.

Polk unfurled the Mecklenburg Declaration of Independence: NCGR, "Humphrey Testimony," 20–22; see also: SHC, Alexander, *Rough Notes*, NCGR testimony of James Jack, Graham. For an exhaustively researched recreation of the MecDec's creation, see Syfert's *First American Declaration*, 68–75.

RESOLVED!: MecDec text is from *Raleigh Register*, April 30, 1819; NCGR; SHC, Alexander, *Rough Notes*; and SHC, *Davie Copy.*

"every demonstration of joy": NCGR, "Jack Testimony," 16.

". . . and the hats thrown": NCGR, "Graham Testimony," 18–20; see also: Dryden Spratt, *Recollections*, 45–50.

CHAPTER SEVEN

West Trade Street: Powell, *Dictionary of North Carolina Biography*, 262.

1772: Ibid.

forty-four: Syfert, *Eminent Charlotteans*, 69.

"crack many an Irish joke . . .": Hunter, *Sketches*, 61–80.

1661, the Reverend William Jack: Details of Captain Jack's ancestry are from Hunter's chapter on the Jack family in *Sketches*; Syfert's *Eminent Charlotteans* and *First American Declaration*; and the James Jack entry in Powell's *Dictionary of North Carolina Biography*.

Ballykelly: Ibid.

Lancaster County: Ibid.

1760 the Jacks also moved south: Hunter, *Sketches*, 61–80.

"the favorite place of resort": Ibid.

"for some time previous": NCGR, "Captain Jack's Certificate," 16; witnessed Dec. 7, 1819, by Job Weston and attorney James Oliver.

Mecklenburg Resolves: (Discovered by Peter Force) *South Carolina Gazette and Country Journal,* June 13, 1775; see also: Syfert, *First American Declaration*, 150–158.

Bancroft and Grigsby: Draper, *Mecklenburg Declaration*, 176–177.

"to go express . . .": SHC, Alexander, *Rough Notes*.

A conscription: Syfert, *First American Declaration*, 86.

"solicited to be . . .": NCGR, "Captain Jack's Certificate," 16; witnessed Dec. 7, 1819, by Job Weston and attorney James Oliver.

fifty miles a day: Syfert, *First American Declaration*, 86.

Moravians . . . journaling: Ibid.

covered more than forty miles: Hunter, *Sketches*, 61–80.

Cheerwine soda: Cheerwine.com/about; see also: myhome.unctv.org/cheerwine/.

William Kennon: McNitt, *Error*, 136.

called upon him: NCGR, "Captain Jack's Certificate," 16; witnessed Dec. 7, 1819, by Job Weston and attorney James Oliver.

"He drew his pistols": Graham, *General Joseph Graham*, 25–26.

three-shilling: William Alexander, Diary, 1776–1778; see also: Kratt, *Charlotte: Spirit of the New South*, 28.

"Captain Jack resumed his journey": Hunter, *Sketches*, 61–80.

four young children: Ibid. According to Hunter, the Jack's fifth child, Archibald, "died young."

Paul Revere: Details on Revere's ride come from David Hackett Fischer's deconstruction of Revere's ride in 1996, Beck, *Journal of the American Revolution*, April 9, 2014, and the National Parks website paulreverehouse.org.

"It's understandable why . . .": Dyer, *Charlotte Observer*, May 17, 2007.

Martin . . . wrote several letters: CSR, "Letter from Gov. Martin to the Earl of Dartmouth," August 28, 1775.

the Spin Doctors: Cheerwinefest.com.

"Humpy" Wheeler: North Carolina Sports Hall of Fame biography.

40-2 as a Golden Gloves boxer: Ibid.

Grenada: David Newton, ESPN, May 6, 2008.

vice chairman: Calhoun, *Charlotte Observer*, May 30, 1975.

seven-year-old blood-red Arabian: Ibid., May 7, 1975.

twenty-five miles . . . tungsten carbide: Linker interview, Georgetown, Kentucky, February 10, 2022.

RV . . . 4-H groups: Ibid.

seventy-two applicants: Schumer, *Charlotte Observer*, March 6, 1975.

a third-generation farrier: Details on Linker, his family, background, audition, and ride to Philadelphia are from an interview with Jerry Linker in Georgetown, Kentucky, on February 10, 2022, and an interview with Valerie Linker (Jerry's daughter) and Karen Linker (Jerry's wife) on August 7, 2021.

backflip: Ibid.

eighth (and final) wife: Ibid.

scar tissue from a fire: Ibid.

bull fell on him . . . shrunk . . . two inches: Ibid.

jail . . . asylum: Ibid.

father decked him: Ibid.

two years . . . two weeks: Ibid.

In preparation: Calhoun, *Charlotte Observer*, May 30, 1975.

fifty-fifty chance: Calhoun, *Charlotte Observer*, May 30, 1975.

full-scale re-creation: Schumer, *Charlotte Observer*, March 6, 1975.

Two hundred years and eleven days: Details of Linker's departure are from Lisenby, *Charlotte News*, May 31, 1975.

following what's I-81 today: Map, *Charlotte Observer*, 2010.

fifteen hours a day in the saddle: Linker interview, Georgetown, Kentucky, February 10, 2022.

tripping in a pothole: Ibid.

Monticello: Details on the problems at Monticello and the ceremony at Michie Tavern are from Linker; *Charlotte Observer*, June 14, 1975; and *Charlotte News,* June 11, 1975.

Michie Tavern: Michietavern.com/the-tavern-history.

taken into custody: Details on the arrest and situation in Culpepper are from Linker and *Charlotte News,* June 17, 1975; *Charlotte Observer,* June 20, 1975; and the *Associated Press* (via *Cumberland News*), June 20, 1975.

$1,000 fine: Ibid.

district court judge: Ibid.

good physical condition: Ibid.

charges were then dropped: Ibid.

front page news across the country: Valerie and Karen Linker interview August 7, 2021.

Bags of fan mail: Ibid.

Colonel Patrick Jack: Lanser, *Chambersburg Public Opinion*, June 23, 1975.

***Sports Illustrated*:** Ottum, *Scorecard*, June 30, 1975.

***Mike Douglas Show*:** Linker interview, Georgetown, Kentucky, February 10, 2022.

President Gerald Ford: Ibid.

***Hollywood Squares*:** Lanser, *Chambersburg Public Opinion*, June 23, 1975.

crowd of 1,500: Calhoun, *Charlotte Observer*, June 30, 1975.

2nd Pennsylvania Regiment: Thompson, *Philadelphia Inquirer,* June 30, 1975.

". . . really far out": Calhoun, *Charlotte Observer*, June 30, 1975.

replica of the Liberty Bell: Linker interview, Georgetown, Kentucky, February 10, 2022.

"knighted": *Charlotte News*, June 28, 1975.

Sharek's horseshoes . . . in City Hall: Ibid., July 3, 1975.

gained ten pounds: Linker interview, Georgetown, Kentucky, February 10, 2022.

"GET OUTTA . . .": Calhoun, *Charlotte Observer*, June 30, 1975. (Although the paper left "damn" out of the published quote, Linker remembers it distinctly.)

bumped into Captain Jack: NCGR, "Testimony from Alphonso, Amos and John Alexander Nov. 29, 1830," 17.

"grand entrance": Ellis, *Sphinx*, 27.

"Olive Branch Petition": Journals of the Continental Congress, "Petition to the King, July 8, 1775."

"Upon his arrival": Hunter, *Sketches*, 68–69.

"Congress never had": SHC, Alexander, *Rough Notes*.

"timidity of the delegates": Adams, *Works of John Adams*, 221.

"not a greater Tory in Congress": Cappon, *Adams-Jefferson Letters*, 543.

Hooper's biography: Powell (Marie Claire Engstrom), *Dictionary of North Carolina Biography*, 200–202.

"the orators of the congress": Ibid.

dragged through the streets: Ibid.

"Cruel suggestion!": North Carolina Provincial Congress Records (extracted: NIU digital library), Hooper, "Address to the Inhabitants of the British Empire," Sept. 8, 1775.

August 2, 1776: Powell (Marie Claire Engstrom), *Dictionary of North Carolina Biography*, 200–202.

died at forty-eight . . . before his daughter's wedding: Ibid.

1813 letter: Adams, *Works of John Adams*, 19–20.

"would have been squelched": Dyer, *Charlotte Observer*, May 17, 2007.

"a long, full, complacent letter": SHC, Alexander, *Rough Notes*.

Johann Michael Graff . . . "addresses": North Carolina Historical Commission (later: NC Office of Archives and History), *Records of the Moravians*, 874–877. See also: Fries, *Moravian Archives: Volume 1–7*, 1922–1947 (accessed via Moravianarchives.org).

"a man from Mecklenburg": Ibid.

"Undoubtedly Captain Jack": Ibid.

"commencement to close": Powell (Norris Preyer), *Dictionary of North Carolina Biography*.

so beloved: Ibid.

obituary: *Raleigh Register*, January 17, 1823.

7,646 pounds: Powell (Norris Preyer), *Dictionary of North Carolina Biography*.

perished before reaching Captain Jack: Ibid.

Texas Supreme Court: Texasdar.org/chapters/CaptainJamesJack/History.html; see also: University of Texas Tarlton Law Library, "Justice of Texas" (accessed via tarltonapps.law.utexas.edu/justices/profile/view/57).

Daughters of the American Revolution: Ibid.

CHAPTER EIGHT

at the foot of the Rotunda: Author visit, July 7–10, 2021.

ninety-five pages: Dr. Maurie McInnis (via C-Span), Lecture: "Slave Labor in 19th Century Virginia."

streaking: Details on the UVA streaking ritual come from the UVA tour guide, UVA graduates, and Whitelaw Reid, *Virginia Magazine*, "Streak Show," July 27, 2021.

"Architecture is my delight": Rayner, *Sketches of Thomas Jefferson*, 524.

"father of our national architecture": Fiske Kimball via Monticello.org.

energy left for an illicit affair: Ellis, *Sphinx*, via Wiencek, *Master of the Mountain*, 193.

serpentine brick walls: Miller, *Monticello*, 128.

conceal the school's expansive slave quarters: Dr. Maurie McInnis (via C-Span), Lecture: "Slave Labor in 19th Century Virginia."

owned 607 slaves: Miller, *Monticello*, 105.

did free two: Monticello.org/slavery.

completely out of sight: Wiencek, *Master of the Mountain*, 16.

DNA testing concluded: Eric Lander and Joseph Ellis, "Founding Father," *Nature* 396 (1998): 13–14.

at least six children: Monticello.org/sallyhemings.

copulated with "Oranootans": Jefferson, *Notes* (electronic), 1062.

"most profligate liars": Wiencek, *Master of the Mountain*, 269.

"virtually ceased": Historian David Brion Davis via Henry Wiencek, "The Dark Side of Thomas Jefferson," *Smithsonian Magazine*, October 2012.

"more fame for what he did not do": Wiencek, *Master of the Mountain*, 7.

Monster of Monticello: Paul Finkelman, "The Monster of Monticello," *New York Times*, November 30, 2012.

"TJ is a racist and rapist": Williamson, WSLS-10, Sept. 12, 2017.

New York's city hall: Jeffrey Mays and Zachary Small, "Thomas Jefferson Statue Evicted from City Hall Will Go to Museum," *New York Times*, November 15, 2021.

"communicated to Dr. Ben Franklin": Draper, *Mecklenburg Declaration*, 191.

confided to William Bentley: Adams, *Adams*, 220.

on May 23, 1776: Ellis, *Sphinx*, 53.

horseflies . . . tavern: Fleming, *Man from Monticello*, 37–38.

eighty-six edits: National Park Service website: nps.gov/education.

28 percent: Jefferson's rough draft (Boyd, *The Papers of Thomas Jefferson*) is 1,690 words; Harvard's Declaration Resources Project says the final draft is approximately 1,320 words long.

"extremely sensitive": Ellis, *Sphinx*, 50.

story of the hatmaker: Looney, *Papers of Thomas Jefferson*, 462–465.

"workaday" . . . all but forgotten: Maier, *American Scripture*, (e-text), 93; details on the creation and context of the JeffDec, unless otherwise noted, are from Maier's *American Scripture* and Ellis's *Sphinx*, chapter 1.

"all the Glory of it": Wood, *Friends Divided*, 401.

"utterly useless": Ellis, *Sphinx*, 35.

the top choices for the assignment: Ibid., 58.

"all genuine wisdom": Ibid., 54.

"cut-and-paste job": Ibid., 65.

published in the *Pennsylvania Gazette*: Ibid.

"For they are identical": Tucker, *Jefferson*, 471–473.

"neither aiming at originality": Ford, *Writings of Jefferson*, "Jefferson letter to Richard Henry Lee," May 8, 1825.

$40,000: Ellis, *Sphinx*, 326.

"If the name McKnitt . . .": Cappon, *Adams-Jefferson Letters*, 545.

PRIVY VENT: Author visit, July 7–10, 2021.

concealed under a bathroom: Thompson, *Washington Post*, February 19, 2017.

The Thigh Men of Dad History: Coe, *You Never Forget*, (e-text), 108.

"Jefferson specialists": Gordon-Reed, *Jefferson-Hemings*, 5.

"a clear consensus": Ellis, *Sphinx*, 366.

sexually harassing . . . Walker's wife *for years*: Details of Jefferson's behavior are from Wiencek, *Master of the Mountain*, 193–194; see also: Jon Kukla, *Mr. Jefferson's Women*, 189–198.

"All this time": Ibid.

"Most Americans": Gordon-Reed, *Jefferson-Hemings*, 230–231.

"uniquely unpleasant": Coe, *You Never Forget*, (e-text), 1019–1021.

". . . the most detestable": Ibid.

Bill Barker: C-Span.org/BillBarker.com.

Christianity: Monticello.org; see also: Cappon, *Adams-Jefferson*, 359.

"not a word more": Miller, *Monticello*, 121.

CHAPTER NINE

"this was *the* pivotal battle": Author visit, Sept. 4–5, 2021.

led to . . . Cornwallis's ultimate surrender: Denman and Walsh, *Greene and Cornwallis*, 2.

"the deciding theatre of battle": Ibid., 136.

fence-sitting colonists would join his ranks: Ibid., 2.

General George Graham: NCGR, "Graham Testimony," 24.

Raised as an orphan: McNitt, *Error*, 36.

graduate from Princeton: Powell, *Dictionary of North Carolina Biography*.

Seriously wounded: Ibid.

"Father" of the University of North Carolina: Ibid.

special envoy to France: Ibid.

Rural Hill: Details of Rural Hill, John Davidson, and the connections to Davidson College are from Ruralhill.net/a-brief-history-of-rural-hill; see also: *The Rural Hill Farm Journals of Adam Brevard Davidson* edited by Jim and Ann Williams.

provided the lumber: Ibid.

"A Signer of the Mecklenburg Declaration": Author visit, Sept. 4–5, 2021.

burned down in 1886: Ruralhill.net/a-brief-history-of-rural-hill.

Cannon King: Author visit, Sept. 4–5, 2021.

Sting: Graham, *Joseph Graham*, viii.

four years old and living in Berks County: Details of Joseph Graham are from Draper's *Mecklenburg Declaration*, 251–255; Graham's *Joseph Graham*; Powell's *Dictionary of North Carolina Biography* (by Max Williams 1986); and Syfert, *Eminent Charlotteans*, 93–112.

"distinguished among his fellow students": Graham, *Joseph Graham*, 32–45.

peach brandy: Syfert, *Eminent Charlotteans*, 111.

witnessing, firsthand: NCGR, "Graham Testimony," 19–20.

4th North Carolina Regiment: Graham, *Joseph Graham*, 53.

three-year exemption: Ibid., 48.

plowing his mother's fields: Syfert, *Eminent Charlotteans*, 97–99.

college . . . turned into a field hospital: Ibid.

England's Southern strategy: John Ferling, "Myths of the American Revolution," *Smithsonian Magazine*, January 2010.

Colonel Banastre Tarleton: Details of Tarleton are from Bass, *The Green Dragon*; world historyproject.org/battle-of-waxhaws; and *Journal of the American Revolution*, August 18, 2016.

Buford raised the white flag: Ibid.

"indiscriminate carnage . . .": Ibid; see also: 1821 letter from Brownfield to William James.

credited with winning . . . Saratoga: Denman and Walsh, *Greene and Cornwallis*, 41–50.

worst defeats in the history of the American military: Ibid.

forgot to take any prisoners: worldhistoryproject.org/battle-of-hanging-rock.

half-starved troops: Denman and Walsh, *Greene and Cornwallis*, 41–50.

twenty-two miles to the north: Ibid.

Gates took off on his horse: Ibid.

two thousand dead or wounded: Ibid; see also: battlefields.org and *Cornwallis Papers*, August 21, 1780.

"We hope for relief": CSR, "Letter from Polk to Gates," Sept. 10–11, 1780.

wouldn't hold off Cornwallis: Denman and Walsh, *Greene and Cornwallis*, 41–50.

"put to death": Ibid.

John Dunn and Benjamin Booth mouthing off: Graham, *Joseph Graham*, 25.

dog was named Tory: Syfert, *First American Declaration*, 79.

banished to Florida: Graham, *Joseph Graham*, 35.

Jefferson utterly failed: Michael Kranish, "Jefferson Fled Monticello to Avoid Being Captured," *Washington Post*, June 2, 2017; see also: Kranish, *Flight from Monticello*.

leaving Virginia leaderless: Ibid.

"Fire away, then": Ibid.

sat down and continued writing: Wiencek, *Master of the Mountain*, 42.

Jane Parks McDowell: Jane Parks McDowell marker, Daughters of the American Revolution.

". . . the British run like sheep": Graham, *Joseph Graham*, 281.

"respectful distance": Ibid., 250.

predawn hours of September 26, 1780 . . . two miles south of town: Ibid.

"cut him down in his tracks": Ibid., 62.

Tarleton . . . yellow fever: Syfert, *Eminent Charlotteans*, 102.

George Hanger: Ibid.

150 soldiers: Denman and Walsh, *Greene and Cornwallis*, 41–50; see also: Davie, *Sketches*, 24.

25 percent of the colony's troops: Plumer, *Charlotte and the Revolution*, 120.

The young ladies . . .: Kratt, *Charlotte: Spirit of the New South*, 35; see also: *South Carolina and American General Gazette*.

three stacked lines: Details on the Battle of Charlotte, unless otherwise noted, are from Graham's *Joseph Graham*; CMH detailed displays of the battle sequences created by Robert Ryals; Syfert's *Eminent*; Denman and Walsh's *Greene and Cornwallis*; and Davie's *Sketches*.

to within fifty yards: Graham, *Joseph Graham*, 252.

"in the utmost confusion": Davie, *Sketches*, 24.

repulsed for a third time: CMH/Ryals displays.

"Legion": Syfert, *Eminent Charlotteans*, 104.

"The whole of the British Army": Stedman, *American War*, 216.

"literally cut to pieces": Graham, *Joseph Graham*, 255.

losing a portion of his brains: Ibid., 60–66.

"Put up your pistol": Ibid.

nine wounds: Ibid.

Susan Alexander: Ibid.

caked in dry blood: Ibid.

convalesced for almost three months: Ibid.

the buckle that saved his life: Ibid., 66.

in place of a cravat: Ibid.

Aunt Susie: Ibid.

war pension: Ibid.

snatching Polk's home: Kratt, *Charlotte: Spirit of the New South*, 38.

Cornwallis ordered his troops: Powell (Preyer), *Dictionary of North Carolina Biography*, 1988.

Waightstill: Draper, *Mecklenburg Declaration*, 212.

Ochiltree "turned coat": McNitt, *Error*, 138. (McNitt spelled his name "Ogiltree.")

stricken from the MecDec: Ibid.

signaling system: Graham, *Joseph Graham*, 29.

exceptional snipers: CMH guide, October 2021.

"This is murder": Graham, *Joseph Graham*, 270; see also Tarleton, *History*, 160–161.

"with unwearied perseverance": Tarleton, *History*, 160–161.

"Mecklenburg is the most rebellious": Cornwallis, *Papers*, October 1780.

McIntyre Farm: Details on the skirmish are from Norris, *Encyclopedia of North Carolina*, 2006; Graham, *Joseph Graham*, 258–263; and Hunter, *Sketches*.

Captain James Thompson: Ibid.

eight redcoats: Ibid.

patriot bullets lodged: Norris, *Encyclopedia of North Carolina*, 2006.

first came from Tarleton: Graham, *Joseph Graham*, 84.

"A glorious affair": CSR, "Letter from Polk to NCBOW," Oct. 11, 1780,

named Nathanael Greene: founders.archives.gov, "Letter from Washington to Greene," October 14, 1780, founders.archives.gov/documents/Washington/03-18-02-0389.

"accompanied Greene as a pilot": Draper, *Mecklenburg Declaration*, 192.

Camp McKnitt Alexander: Ibid.

fifteen skirmishes: Powell's *Dictionary of North Carolina Biography* (by Max Williams 1986).

war pension hearing: Graham, *Joseph Graham*, 45.

North Carolina state senate: Powell's *Dictionary of North Carolina Biography* (by Max Williams 1986).

Vesuvius: Details on Graham's life after the war are from Graham, *Joseph Graham*, 160–162.

"would challenge . . . the young men": Ibid.

spring of 1781: Details on Cornwallis and Greene are from Denman and Walsh, *Greene and Cornwallis*, 93–106.

Davidson was shot: Sommerville, *Hopewell*, 221; (nipple) see also: Graham, *Joseph Graham*, 336.

a quarter of his men: history.com/topics/american-revolution/battle-of-guilford-courthouse.

"Another such victory": Charles James Fox via Ibid.

CHAPTER TEN

famed Southern Tour: The primary source for Washington's Southern Tour is Volume Six of *The Diaries of George Washington*, an extensive, daily tour diary kept by the president, edited by the University of Virginia, and maintained by the Virginia Historical Society and the Library of Congress.

inauspicious start: Philbrick, *Travels*, 193–196.

the menu: Ibid.

amazing tennis player: Bingham, *Southern Tour*, 30.

Betsy Brandon: Henderson, *Washington's Southern Tour*, 296.

Dr. Charles Caldwell: Ibid., 278–287.

"where independence was declared about a year before . . .": Ibid.

"very trifling place": VHS, *Diaries of George Washington*, Saturday, May 28, 1791.

Revolutionary War pension applications: References to the MecDec in pension applications are from the MHA (via Syfert) and were originally uncovered by researcher Rebecca Fried.

the streets of Charlotte: Henderson, *Washington's Southern Tour*, 287–292.

box of wig powder: Ibid.

"powdering the heads . . .": Graham lecture, *Charlotte Observer*, Dec. 25, 1893.

Conrad Reed: Powell, *Encyclopedia of North Carolina*, 954.

$3.50: Kratt, *Charlotte: A Brief History*, 59.

earliest authenticated discovery of gold: Ibid.

twenty-eight pounds: Ibid.

fifty gold mining companies: Powell, *Encyclopedia of North Carolina*, 512.

US Mint: Ibid.

only state producing gold: Ibid.

"To the citizens of Mecklenburg": Syfert, *First American Declaration*, 147.

The fire . . . April 6, 1800: Ibid., 102.

fire destroyed Thomas Jefferson's childhood home: Ellis, *Sphinx*, 165.

Rough Notes: McNitt, *Chain of Error*, 32–38. (The Rough Notes originals are in the SHC at UNC.)

"proverbial for his scrupulous accuracy": SHC, letter from Israel Pickens to General Lenoir, March 23, 1823.

Copy in an Unknown Hand: McNitt, *Error*, 32–38.

Raleigh's Most Illustrious Citizen: Ashe, *Biographical History of North Carolina, Volume II*, 360–370.

"oral history can sometimes be more visceral and honest than written history": Excerpt of speech given by Roberts in Charlotte on May 19, 2011, via Syfert, *First American Declaration*, 214.

a 1775 letter . . . Josiah Martin: CSR, "Letter from Gov. Martin to the Earl of Dartmouth," June 30, 1775.

a copy was sent to . . . Johnson: Wheeler, *Historical Sketches of North Carolina*, 70. See also: Summary Chart of MecDec Originals and Copies by Syfert.

Graham and Hunter were also . . . given copies: Ibid. (Syfert) and Alexander, *History of Mecklenburg County*, 40.

Brevard's brother said: Draper, *Mecklenburg Declaration*, 122–123.

Stokes . . . testify: *North Carolina Governor's 1831 Report on The Declaration of Independence by the Citizens of Mecklenburg County*, 5.

William Polk: Details on Polk's life are from Ashe, *Biographical History of North Carolina, Volume II*, 360–370; Wheeler, *Memoirs of North Carolina*; William Polk's declaration of his military service at the CSR; and Polk, *Autobiography of Colonel William Polk (manuscript)*.

copies to . . . William Davidson and . . . A. D. Murphy: McNitt, *Error*, 33–34.

wasn't lost to time: McNitt, *Error*, 73.

in 1787: Ibid.

"true copy": Ibid., 39–40.

"The entire sheet . . .": SHC via Syfert, *First American Declaration*, 108.

General William Davie: NCpedia.org/davie-william-richardson; see also: Ashe, *Biographical History of North Carolina, Volume II*.

"certainly correct": Draper, *Mecklenburg Declaration*, 355.

William Wirt: Details on Wirt are from Kennedy, *Memoirs of the Life of William Wirt*, Justice .gov/ag/bio/wirt-william, and UVA's Miller Center; as well as *Appletons' Cyclopedia of American Biography* (which does not have bylines for most entries and has been found to contain many fake and/or suspicious entries).

"knew nothing of Henry": Wirt, *Patrick Henry*, v–x.

"clearing away difficulties of fact": Ibid.

authentic history: Wirt, *Patrick Henry*, 1.

"too remote . . . for vulgar apprehension": Wirt, *Patrick Henry* (digital), 416.

"Had it depended . . .": Ibid.

"than that of Virginia": Wirt, *Patrick Henry* (digital), 80.

inspired William Davidson: Syfert, *First American Declaration*, 105. See also: MDP.

a Princeton grad and renaissance man: Sommerville, *Hopewell*, 106; see also: Syfert, *First American Declaration*, 229.

"indications of . . . genius": Ibid:

"The foregoing is a true copy": NCGR, 15.

Raleigh Register: NCGR (reprinted), *Register*, April 30, 1819.

"spurious": Cappon, *Adams-Jefferson Letters*, July 9, 1819.

"subject to the inspection": Syfert, *First American Declaration*, 136.

"apocryphal gospel": Cappon, *Adams-Jefferson Letters*, July 9, 1819.

volcano erupting: Ibid.

"liars and slanderers": Wallis, *National Intelligencer*, August 13, 1857.

"our birthright": Alexander, *Yadkin and Catawba Journal*, Nov. 9, 1830.

Winslow Alexander: SHC, *Catawba Journal*, Oct. 19, 1824.

legendary North Carolinian bon vivant Joseph Seawell Jones: Details and tales of Shocco Jones, unless otherwise noted, are from Jones (Seawell), *A Defense of the Revolutionary History of the State of North Carolina*; Jones, *North Carolina History*, 157–165; Edwin A. Miles, "Joseph Seawell Jones of Shocco—Historian and Humbug, *North Carolina Historical Review* 34, no. 4 (1957): 483–506; Thomas Cherry, "The Future of Our Past," North Carolina Libraries, 2003: 62–66.

Justice Joseph Story: Miles, "Shocco—Historian and Humbug," *NC Historical Review*, 490.

"the Sage of Monticello": Jones (Seawell), *A Defense of the Revolutionary History of the State of North Carolina* (digital), 8.

fifteen-thousand-word report: NCGR (courtesy of the Presbyterian Heritage Center, Montreat, North Carolina).

he had seen the Williamson Copy: Ibid., 5.

"More satisfactory evidence . . .": Ibid.

confirmed Freemason: Worldhistory.us, "The Candidacy of William Wirt: The Ironic Candidate of the Free Mason Party in 1832," April 12, 2018.

severe cold: Ibid.

stolen his skull: Peter Carlson, "Tale from the Crypt," *Washington Post,* October 20, 2005.

"his mother's basement": Ibid.

"For they are identical": Tucker, *Jefferson,* 464.

solicited help: Wayland, *Stevenson,* 166.

CHAPTER ELEVEN

London: Author visit, March 12–19, 2022.

British Archives: Ibid.

Tryon . . . "promoted": Powell, *Dictionary of North Carolina Biography.*

"death was preferable": Details of Martin and his life are from Stumpf, *Josiah Martin.*

delivering the double-cross decree: CSR, "Proclamation by Josiah Martin . . ." June 28, 1773, 665.

dissolving the North Carolina General Assembly: Syfert, *First American Declaration*, 81.

so many panicky letters: CSR, "Documents by Martin, Josiah, 1737–1786."

his father's hopes: Stumpf, *Martin.*

in a letter to Dartmouth: CSR, "Letter from Gov. Martin to the Earl of Dartmouth," June 30, 1775.

Five weeks later, Martin would repeat his request: CSR, "Letter from Gov. Martin to the Earl of Dartmouth," August 28, 1775.

Later in life, Tucker developed: Details of Tucker and his life are from *The Life and Philosophy of George Tucker, Vol. 1 (2004),* which is largely based on Tucker's own unpublished autobiography.

gambling addiction: Ibid., viii.

until 1824: Ibid.

"livelier ambition": Ibid.

science-fiction novelist: Ibid.

His first lame argument: Tucker, *Jefferson,* 471.

because Charlotte . . . close to the frontier: Ibid.

Tucker . . . in writing: Wayland, *Stevenson,* 166.

a letter to Stevenson: Ibid.

"Richmond Junto": Wayland, *Stevenson,* 247.

burst into laughter: Ibid., 242.

quid pro quo: Ibid.

almost say slavery: Ibid., 158.

slave *breeding*: Details and quotes of the Stevenson-O'Connell incident are from Wayland's *Stevenson,* 183–189, and are based, in part, on Stevenson's diary and correspondence, which is archived in the Library of Congress.

British Foreign Minister's reply: Wayland, *Stevenson*, 166–167.

Stevenson . . . replied: Ibid.

the final page of Dispatch 34: Viewed at BNA, Colonial America Collections, "Letter from Gov. Martin to the Earl of Dartmouth," June 30, 1775.

"What Stevenson did . . . remains an enigma": Wayland, *Stevenson*, 167.

"the copy had once been in his possession": Graham and Graham, *Why North Carolinians Believe*, 41.

"His reply to Tucker's inquiry": Ibid.

President James Polk . . . still writing: SHC, Massachusetts Historical Society, *Proceedings (Letters from President Polk to George Bancroft)*, 102–114.

***Herald . . .* transcript:** DCA, *Herald*, May 17, 1875.

In the bombshell story: Details on the Cape Fear Hoax and Dr. S. Millington Miller, unless otherwise noted, are from *Collier's*, July 1, 1905; *Charlotte Observer*, August 27, 1905, October 13, 1905, and January 1, 1906; and *Raleigh News and Charlotte Observer*, September 25, 1966, a story based largely on the 1906 investigation by Salley and Ford, "S. Millington Miller," 548–558.

"hysterical rubbish": Ibid.

$50,000: Ibid.

$5,000 just to stay put: Ibid.

Louis R. Wilson . . . "blood and bruises": *Raleigh News and Charlotte Observer*, Sept. 25, 1966.

"swung his mighty left": Ibid.

CHAPTER TWELVE

advocating for posthumous disciplinary action: Saunders interview, May 9, 2022.

nineteenth-century remembrance: For all details on the life of Phillips, unless otherwise noted, see: Richard Battle, "Memoir of Rev. Charles Phillips," *North Carolina University Magazine*, No. 1.

"inclined to be overbearing": McNitt, *Error*, 111.

sickly, obese: Battle, "Memoir," see note above.

still in his grasp: Ibid.

"the Puritan notion . . .": Battle, "Memoir."

Swain . . . coauthored: McNitt, *Error*, 77.

"critical examination": Ibid., 90.

"journals and records": All details on the contents of the Davie Copy come from the document which is archived at the University of North Carolina, Wilson Library, SHC (Southern Historical Collection), Mecklenburg Declaration of Independence Papers, Davie Copy.

"no true gentlemen": McNitt, *Error*, 89.

"Jefferson brought that stuff from Paris": State Historical Society of Wisconsin, Phillips letter to Dr. Draper, May 25, 1875.

there is no mention: Phillips, "May, 1775," *North Carolina University Magazine* (1853), 168.

Phillips's entire argument: Ibid.

the Davie Copy itself states: SHC/MDP. See above.

"journals and records . . .": Ibid.

Phillips wrote: State Historical Society of Wisconsin, Phillips letter to Dr. Draper, 1875.

Phillips also reinserted deleted words: This discovery was first made in 1960 by McNitt and published in *Error* and was advanced in 2016 by Syfert in *The First American Declaration.*

Davie Copy . . . went missing: McNitt, *Error,* 97.

celebrate May 20 instead of July 4: DCA, *Charlotte Observer,* May 26, 1940.

Marshal Michel Ney: Details on the Ney legend are from NCpedia.org and LeGette Bly-the *Marshal Ney: A Dual Life,* New York: Stackpole, 1937.

a series of letters: McNitt, *Error,* 104.

told Draper: Ibid., 108–109.

Special Verdict: Ibid.

without ever revealing: *New York Evening Post,* May 19, 1875.

despicable behind-the-scenes campaign: State Historical Society of Wisconsin, Phillips letters to Dr. Draper, 1875.

invalid: Battle, "Memoir," 1889.

to the state flag: NCpedia.org/Stateflag.

became a holiday: NC Digital Collections, Laws and Resolutions of the State of North Carolina, passed by the General Assembly (1881), 516.

marble obelisk: McNitt, *Error,* 122.

CHAPTER THIRTEEN

Taft loved possums: Adrienne LaFrance, "President Taft Ate a Lot of Possums," *Atlantic,* November 26, 2015.

at a banquet in Atlanta: *Mental Floss,* June 10, 2013.

steak for breakfast: Michael Rosenwald, "The Nation's Fattest President," *Washington Post,* December 29, 2018.

Biddle University . . . faculty pooled its resources: *Souvenir of the President's Visit,* 1909, Johnson C. Smith Archives.

rendition of the fight song: *Charlotte Observer,* May 21, 1909.

Roosevelt: Ibid.

Beilage: Details of the Moravian *Beilage* are from Fries, *Records of Wachovia,* 1–11; see also: Syfert, *First American Declaration,* 202–204.

Salley: Ibid.

Leland: Ibid.

Bruce: Ibid.

In a 1916 letter: Syfert, *First American Declaration,* 203–204; see also: Adelaide L. Fries Papers, Special Collections, UNC-Charlotte.

festooned with American flags . . . : Details, names, statistics, quotes, anecdotes, and excerpts from Taft's 1909 MecDec Day visit to Charlotte from 242–247, unless otherwise noted, are from accounts published by the *Charlotte Observer,* the *Charlotte Evening Chronicle,* the *Charlotte News,* the *New York Herald,* and the official *Souvenir of the President's Visit.*

Jackson was Charlotte royalty: Powell, *Dictionary of North Carolina Biography.*

largest wake ever held: Dr. Tony Zeiss, May 20, 2022.

"Billy Possum": *Stone and Webster Public Service Journal,* 1909.

Wilson standing outside . . . : James Morton, *The Davidsonian,* 1976.

in his pajamas: Ibid.

assaulted in Charlotte: DCA, *Charlotte Observer*, May 1976. (This lengthy, in-depth article on the history of MecDec celebrations was likely authored by renowned Davidson professor and MecDec scholar Chalmers G. Davidson.)

MecDec Day 1916 . . .: Details, names, statistics, quotes, anecdotes, and excerpts from Wilson's 1916 MecDec Day visit to Charlotte, unless otherwise noted, are from accounts published by the *Charlotte Observer* on May 21–25, 1916, the *Charlotte News* (1916 & 1966), and research compiled by Chalmers G. Davidson via DCA.

Edith was still throwing . . . shade: Edith Wilson, *My Memoir*, 1939, 98–99.

Shout Freedom!: *Charlotte Observer* and *News*, May 15–21, 1948.

budget: Ibid.

Set in a foggy, dreamlike state: Ibid.

Alexandriana: Ibid.

Eisenhower: Frank Whitney (son) interview, May 20, 2022.

Eisenhower's visit . . .: Details, names, statistics, quotes, anecdotes, and excerpts from Ike's 1954 MecDec Day visit to Charlotte, unless otherwise noted, are from accounts published by the *Charlotte Observer* and the *Charlotte News*, May 19–21, 1954.

volunteered to escort Counts: NCpedia.org, 2018.

a confidant of Dr. Martin Luther King Jr.: *Charlotte Observer*, Sept. 11, 2007.

Hawkins organized a two-mile march: *Charlotte Observer*, May 21, 1963.

"militant": *Charlotte Observer*, Sept. 11, 2007.

bombed: Ibid.

first Black person: Ibid.

scheduled to campaign with Hawkins: Ibid.

Ronald Reagan spoke: *News*, May 21, 1968.

Lady Bird: *News, Charlotte Observer*, May 21, 1968.

crafted by Dr. Theodore Marrs: Gerald R. Ford Presidential Library and Museum, Digital Collections, 1975.

The trouble started: Ibid.

Davie: Powell, *Encyclopedia of North Carolina*, 1,151.

Swain: NCpedia.org.

White House documents: Gerald R. Ford Presidential Library and Museum, Digital Collections, April 28, 1975.

Ford's MecDec Bicentennial speech: Ibid.

briefings with the national media: Gerald R. Ford Presidential Library and Museum, Digital Collection (Press Briefing #223).

Hardee's: May 20th Society post Sept. 5, 2022.

second biggest hit: Ford interview, June 21, 2022.

Weiner King: *Charlotte Observer*, May 21, 1975.

MecDec cake: Ibid.

1976 election: Uselectionatlas.org.

"FORD IS A TORY": *Charlotte Observer*, May 21, 1975.

Ruth, the freakin' rock star: Ibid.

Billy Graham took to the podium: Gerald R. Ford Presidential Library and Museum, Digital Collections, 1975.

on the tarmac: Jonas interview, June 9, 2022.

May 20 holiday: *Charlotte Observer*, February 3, 1982.

population boomed: macrotrends.net.

Rí Rá: Jonas interview, June 9, 2022; *Charlotte Observer*, March 2004.

a thousand people: Ibid.

took the idea to his friend, Dr. Tony Zeiss: Saunders interview, May 9, 2022.

$525,000 through . . . individual donors: *Charlotte Observer*, May 2010; Jonas interview, June 9, 2022.

A Charlotte transplant . . .: Fagan interview, August 2021.

he visited Russia: Ibid.

wedding veils: Ibid.

Charlotte Independence: Charlotteindependence.com.

Pawn Stars: Richard P. Plumer interview, October 2021

Donald Trump's speech . . . George W. Bush: Jonas, Syfert interview, June 9, 2022.

MecDec Day 2022: Author visit, May 20, 2022.

Index

302

304